Scenes from
a Highland Life

By the same author

THE NET AND THE QUEST
LEISURE – PENALTY OR PRIZE?
THE NEW HIGH PRIESTHOOD

Scenes from a Highland Life

Ralph Glasser

HODDER AND STOUGHTON
LONDON SYDNEY AUCKLAND TORONTO

to

Roland Saul
and Miranda Rachel

British Library Cataloguing in Publication Data

Glasser, Ralph
  Scenes from a highland life.
  1. Highlands of Scotland – Social life
  and customs
  I. Title
  941.1'5   DA880.H7
  ISBN 0-340-25564-1

Phototypeset in Linotron 202 Plantin by
Western Printing Services Ltd, Bristol.
Printed in Great Britain for Hodder and Stoughton Limited,
Mill Road, Dunton Green, Sevenoaks, Kent, by
St. Edmundsbury Press, Bury St. Edmunds.
Hodder and Stoughton Editorial Office: 47 Bedford Square, London
WC1B 3DP.

Preface

You will not find my glen, for I have brought together its features and attributes from many parts of the Scottish Highlands. But the people's thoughts and sentiments and perplexities are universal.

RALPH GLASSER

Acknowledgments

It is impossible to list all those who helped me, but in particular I gratefully acknowledge the important help I received from the City of London Polytechnic and Shell UK and, among individuals, Archie Paterson, the London Director of the Scottish Council – Development and Industry; involved and enthusiastic from the very beginning, always ready to talk at large and to offer valuable practical advice, he was of crucial assistance.

And my debt to 'J' – beyond estimation or speech – is written on every page.

Contents

One

Ne'erday

For three days I had gone to George Macfarlane's door. No sound came from the house. No light was visible. There was no sign of the little children, Daniel and Hamish. The glen and its scattered houses crouched subdued in the twilit aftermath of Ne'erday.

Ne'erday, the passing of the old year into the new, stretches far beyond New Year's Day. But it is more than a period of time. It is a state of the mind, of the heart, a drawing together, listening to the dark forces turning the world.

Ne'erday, the void between past and future, between the old year and the new, between the old life and what might come.

Might come.

For the people of the glen – the true inheritors that is, not the incomers – Ne'erday carries portents, fears, strange shapes and powers, to be treated with respect, placated. They must be faced, contemplated steadily. For that one needs courage and help.

Though cynics crack their worn jokes about the bottle, Ne'erday here is not the simple Saturnalia that many outsiders imagine. People seek hope and reassurance from each other in a free flow of feeling and sympathy while the earth is stilled and hovers in a terrifying equipoise of northern darkness between life and death, when time itself has run down – Ne'erday.

Paradoxically they prolong that empty time. Joined together they stare it out. Mutual comfort must be full, without end. It is not enough to meet, drink, pass on. One needs time to absorb strength from each other.

So, in the glen, Ne'erday is a slow experience. It takes about a week. Each day is really only half a day. The dim morning – it is not truly daylight till after eight-thirty – is lost in sleep, digesting the sentiment and flights of fancy of the night. In the afternoon there is the silent, meditative tidying up and the subdued preparation for another night.

The glen lies deep in an isolated peninsula, surrounded by mountains except for the Sound that divides it from the Islands. General Wade's military road, more than two hundred and fifty years old, is the only way in. When that is blocked by snow the district is cut off except, weather permitting, by boat. Its single track climbs steeply to 1,200 feet, where, at a clearing, you can contemplate a tumbled sea of massive mountain crests. They lean towards you almost near enough to touch, especially when, as now, the snow lies deep and the gullies glint steel blue in the distant winter sun and you feel the awesome magnetism drawing all the world close upon your shoulders.

The road then drops gently through the pass between Beinn Dhu and Beinn à Shellach, and you look down on to a narrow strip of good pasture on the glen floor. It meanders on downwards to where the land opens out on to the long flat approach to the foreshore. Then it winds south to Muirton's dispersed houses that stand like a straggle of spectators shrinking away from the once busy stage of the foreshore. A limbo-like quiet prevails even as the few people you see about – those not at work up in the forest plantations or on their pieces of land – move imperceptibly, enclosed, preoccupied, figures in a still-life landscape.

In the middle of the only street, a little limewashed granite house contains the general store and sub-post office. The road wanders among the low dwellings past a piece of open yard where the Inn, burnt down a few years ago, had stood, now replaced by what looks like an old army hut.

The road branches round the walls of the graveyard within which stands the Church of Scotland, then becomes one again. Here the main group of houses ends. A hundred yards further on, lonely on a promontory, is the 1914–18 War Memorial, a dark, dramatic group of statuary. A great winged figure holds a laurel wreath above the head of a kilted soldier who stands with head bent over his rifle. With its other hand the figure seems to reject the plea of a naked woman who kneels beseechingly at its feet. On the plinth are carved the dark names. It is hard to believe that so many could have come from these hamlets and the scatter of houses along the shore.

On this crisp day the silence rings in the mind like steel on stone. The sun sparkles on clean snow on the towering mountains and turns the lower slopes a duller white as surface layers melt. The sullen sea whispers on the shingle. The houses stand stiff and separate. The glen seems fixed in a mute defence, holding the line; but only just.

And what was I doing here, the stranger? No, not altogether a stranger; a returned wanderer, renewing visions. I had come to listen, to draw close, discover how this traditional community had survived for so long with so much of its beliefs, identity, faith in itself intact when all over the world the metropolitan influences sucked the life out of such places. And then, drawing on my study of traditional communities in other lands – the universal truths repeating themselves – I would show how we can make 'progress' less of a destroyer of the soul, and how such a community, if it would reach down to its own emotional tap roots, could quicken itself from within.

Although the glen clings to more of its identity than most other communities in the Highlands, its life blood is thinned and draining away fast. In official language it suffers from rural deprivation. Crofting does not pay enough; and apart from some isolated work on the big estates, virtually the only major source of supplementary employment is on the Forestry Commission plantations. But this is limited and likely to shrink.

George Macfarlane is tall and wiry, with a short black beard and piercing dark eyes, a manner slow and precise, a flickering smile. His wife Margaret is slim and straight too, and a thoughtful smile hovers on her sensitive lips. Their grey granite house, its walls three feet thick, with a pointed wooden portico, leans against a wall of General Wade's barracks whose massive granite shell stands solid on the shore, where once was a thriving port. Roofless, the great structure stubbornly awaits another life.

George is a special person in the glen. Young as he is they speak of him as a man of stature. A serious but not a solemn young man.

He was born in the main hamlet of Muirton about thirty years ago, of a family that has lived there for generations. He has made his home here and intends to live out his life on this shore. If he succeeds he will be one of the lucky ones. Out of forty or so schoolfellows only three remain, and of these only one lives and works in the district. The other two work away from home for most of the year. George 'has a trade in his hands', as they say; he is a plumber and serves the whole glen and much of the surrounding district. He wants to see his children in their turn make their homes and earn their living in the locality. That, he knows, is going to be a fight against heavy odds.

I had kept clear of the glen since Christmas, staying at the little hotel by the sea loch beyond the great pass. I had brought small presents for Daniel and Hamish.

Calum Johnson of the village shop, white haired, ruddy, lantern jawed, seemed to bear the moment lightly, unlike the few customers who went about hushed, monosyllabic, with the distant gaze of sleep-walkers, then faded away.

"Och George and Margaret were around yesterday," he said. "They're most likely asleep the now, after last night's *ceilidh*."

"You're up and about now, though?"

It was well after lunch-time.

"Och I'm always up early! I have tae be – or folk wouldna' get their milk or bread or papers!"

Even when the pass is drifted over with snow, he always gets through.

Slightly built, erect and boyish looking, he looks at one intently: "Someone has tae do it," he said.

As I turned to go, he said, "Aye, ye'll probably find George later on up at the Village Hall doing some clearing up."

"I'll go up."

He wanted to say something else. He weighed the matter. Then with the air of someone opening his door an inch wider to the stranger; "Folk here need at least a week to get over Ne'erday. Apart from anything else, ye need that time to get around everyone and spend some time with each one. Aye, ye go in wi' a bottle and sit down and talk, and before ye know it a couple of hours have gone. Others come in while ye're there. Ye go to another hoose and so it goes on. Another night people come to your house. And so the nights are full. And time means nothing. We need this. The rest of the year things don't come to a stop like this. We're all far too busy."

Too busy with the present! Ne'erday puts the present far away; it is the past that dominates the mind. They renew their links with it and, through it, with one another.

In that backward perspective one great shadow stalks the glen, General Wade the efficient pacifier of the Highlands after the Jacobite Risings. They speak of him familiarly as if his power had been here only yesterday, an overlord who was not in his heart an enemy. They speak with respect. Proconsul of the occupying power, he is remembered in local folk history as much more than the tough soldier, as a tactful and a caring man. He imposed strong and predictable authority. He gave people roads and bridges and tamed the wildness of their land a little. True, these things served a superior purpose, but the economic gains, and the social ones too, are quietly recognised.

By contrast, present authority is regarded as unsympathetic, capricious. Margaret is a fast and clever hand knitter. She makes a little extra money selling original designs in jumpers, cardigans and so forth. She applied to the Highlands and Islands Development Board for a grant of a few hundred pounds to buy a home knitting machine.

"They turned me down." She smiled sadly.

George put in, "Aye, an' the incomers get money from the Board wi' nae bother at a'! Doon the road, John Logan is putting up a fine new extension to his hotel with £200,000 from the Board. £200,000! And only a wee bit in the way of a few occasional domestic jobs comes with that. And John Logan isn't even from Scotland, never mind from the Highlands."

I have spoken to John Logan. He *is* from Scotland though not from the Highlands or Islands. In essence he confirmed what George told me.

"I tried for ten years to get money from the Board," John Logan said, and I know that that . . . neighbour of mine – he's an Austrian – got plenty

12

and many others round here as well. A few months ago I decided to get it off my chest. I would give myself the satisfaction of telling them what I thought of them. I rang up the Board and demanded an appointment with the chairman. Lo and behold I got one! I was so fed up I didn't mince my words one little bit. I must have talked solidly for half an hour, telling him what I thought of them. And then . . ." he paused and the sharp little eyes in the broad face studied me, "you'll never guess what happened?"

"He promised you something?"

He waved a hand. "Some such words, I thought no more of it. I went away with just one thought in my mind 'to hell with the lot of them'. Anyway, the next day I got a phone call from one of his minions. Would I come up to see them? I said, 'If you've got something constructive to say, you come here! If not, I'm too busy.' They were here the next day."

"You got your money?"

"Every penny I asked for. £200,000. I'm wishing now I'd asked for more."

His tone carried the businessman's contempt for the bureaucrat.

"I don't mind telling you," he added, "in five years' time I'll sell out and move on."

"How do you explain it?"

"It's an unfair world," he said heavily. "And these people are not businessmen. They're paper pushers thinking about their jobs. If you make a great fuss, if you sound as though you can make trouble for them, their instinct is to get rid of you smoothly. But if you are a little fellow, in the sense that they think you can't make trouble for them, well . . ." he spread his hands, "you're unlucky."

One hears these stories all over the Highlands.

"Och it seems to be the pattern," George Macfarlane mused, "for the incomers to do better than us in getting money and help. Ye have tae be an incomer for them to listen to you."

'Incomers'. 'Them'.

Incomers. The word is revealing. 'We,' George seemed to say, 'are inside, where we were born and where we *belong*, inside these mountain walls, our life. *They* are from beyond, from that other world.'

Certainly the glen gives one the feeling of being separate from that world.

Later in the afternoon I found George in the little Village Hall next to the school. He was slowly sweeping the floor, lost in contemplation, his red windcheater swinging open with each rhythmic stroke, a solitary dance. The marked out badminton court was strewn with bits of coloured paper, corks, cake casings, cigarette ends, bits of ribbon. Rows of smeared glasses occupied the window-sills.

Awakened by my voice he turned like a slow automaton, a bearded Petrouchka, and blinked. We clasped hands in New Year greeting.

"Aye, Margaret's still in bed," he said. "The children are up with my parents. Och come on up. I'll take ye up in the car."

He planted the broom in a corner.

His parents live in a cottage near a group of Forestry Commission houses, high-pitched, faced with boards of a blackened chestnut colour, across a meadow from the Village Hall. He insisted on driving me there. His own position, and mine, seemingly required him to convey me there with as much style as possible.

He talked about a proposal, before the Community Council, for a Job Creation project.

I said, "Will it be a short-term effort, giving someone work for a few months? Or will it be something permanent?"

"Oh no," he answered. "Temporary."

"Won't that be discouraging? A shot in the arm and then – nothing?"

"Aye, I agree with ye. But it's hard to get people to shift their ideas."

"You yourself – you would like to see a permanent scheme?"

"Aye, I would. And some of the other younger folk too."

"For instance, what about a bakery? You import bread every day from nearly a hundred miles away. Surely there's room for a modest bakery – perhaps even a part-time affair, an adjunct to someone's other occupation – to serve the district? The bread would probably be better than this factory-made stuff."

"Aye – it's funny ye should mention that! It's an idea that's come up now an' again. It's a guid idea but . . ."

He shrugged. I was to see a shrug like that – so often – up and down the glen.

"Ye'll get a different view," he added, "if you ask Calum Johnson at the shop."

Later in the day I did go into the shop to buy, among other things, some bread. The open-necked shirt, tight-fitting tweed jacket, the open air face, somehow emphasise Calum Johnson's seriousness, the impression he gives of solemnly following, line by line with pointed finger, the book of life.

"I was wondering," I observed to him, "about the fact that there's not a single bakery in this huge area of the Highlands?"

His face darkened and the ramrod back stiffened even more.

"We get regular supplies. No one complains."

I decided to ignore the stonewalling. "George Macfarlane tells me that the Community Council are to consider a Job Creation project, and that a bakery could be a serious proposal?"

"Aye – well, if anyone wants to do it they can apply for permission. And then – ye see – it would depend on whether folk here objected."

"How could they possibly object?" I said in surprise. "Surely it would be in people's interests to have bread made locally? And since on this small scale it would be virtually hand made, it would be far better!"

"The smell, you see."

"But it's rather a pleasant and wholesome smell!"

"Aye – maybe – but some folk wouldna' like it."

There was no doubt of that; some folk meant himself. He would lose his monopoly.

A short-sighted view certainly. The bakery would not serve the glen alone but the whole district. Even if the enterprise were no more than a part-time one at the outset, perhaps an adjunct to a crofter's work, it would be a regular addition to the income of the glen, and must benefit Calum's business too. Later, when the bake-shop employed a full-time baker with a helper, a common pattern for a small craft bakery, there would be two full incomes more, a step towards rebuilding the glen's weak economy. Everyone, including Calum, must gain.

Bread! What powerful symbolism – what encouragement that could bring!

"It so happens," I said, "that I need some bread today. Where is it?"

Irritably he pointed to a doorway a few feet across the tiny room, that led into what had been the bedroom of the cottage. There in a corner lay a little pile of wrapped and sliced spongy material passing for bread.

Sullenly he took my money.

He knows the truth of the matter, and knows that I know. But his drawbridge is up. He keeps his powder dry.

People affirm that he works hard, is conscientious, reliable. But behind these tributes, even in the fact that they are made at all, there lurks the pervading uneasiness; a sense that the Furies are hovering. His is a strong voice in the Community Council. They know that his leadership is narrow. Although they follow, they hope for something more wholesome.

They long for a *deus ex machina* to work magic for them. Far away, in Inverness, in Edinburgh, in Whitehall, surely someone will one day think of us – at last? The hope dies over and over again like a failing candle.

Old and young express the hope in automatic fashion, as if learnt by rote. Mrs. Macduff and her daughter talked in this way over a cup of tea at the Bring and Buy Sale, before Christmas, held in the school hall for the Kampuchea children. Mary, a bright, ginger-haired girl, was eagerly waiting to leave for her first nursing post at the Inverness hospital. Her mother, a sprightly widow in early middle age, was no doubt prompted by thoughts of Mary leaving home. Why couldn't the glen give young people a future?

"Why," I wondered aloud, "couldn't the people of the glen initiate change themselves? These things are possible."

Significantly, sadly, it was Mary who replied, in words I had already heard so many times. "Och we're not pushy enough! Aye – that's why the incomers do well and we don't. They get everything, houses for instance, while young folk can't. They even try to stop progress, like bringing the electricity into the glen. They wanted the pylons kept out. We beat them that time! Och maybe it was luck. Maybe it was because we did make a special effort. But generally we don't. We're just not pushy enough!"

Pushy. What a world of excuse is there, of self-justification and twisted pride. Can it be, since General Wade lives on so clearly in memory, that they also remember that time, long ago, when they *were* 'pushy' and were crushed?

'We are not pushy enough' also makes an affirmation of virtue. We are good people. We are not grasping. We go quietly about our demure, prudent lives. We stand aside and let others, the greedy, the shameless ones from beyond the mountains, come in and profit from our purity and forbearance.

In their hearts they must know this for pretence. In an interesting way, Calum Johnson implicitly acknowledges it. His monopoly might be seen to bear particularly heavily upon the elderly. Every few weeks he organises a coach-load for a shopping expedition beyond the mountains.

In one respect, however, his conscience does rule his business instinct, but the loss must be small.

One day I asked him for a copy of the *West Highland Free Press*. His creaky voice became shrill. "I willna' keep it! Not since they published an article demanding the abolition of the monarchy. I will not have that paper here."

Seeing my astonishment, he galloped on. "Aye – I willna' give countenance or support to such behaviour. I wrote tae the editor and asked him tae publish an apology tae the Queen. I havena' had the politeness of a reply. So I willna' keep it in my shop."

He alone would hold the pass against the corrupting world.

"Strange," I murmured, "I could have sworn I got a copy here."

"You didna' get it in *my* shop!"

"Well, somewhere in the village. I am sure I couldn't have got it anywhere else."

He thought about it. "Aye – well, ye might have got it at George Macfarlane's hoose. He often has it."

His calculation was clear. George Macfarlane is a coming man in the glen. His father is influential still. Conciliate them a trifle.

They step carefully. The net of relationships enforces that.

To reach Murdo Macfarlane's house we drove along an avenue of oaks that sweeps magnificently from Wade's barracks to where the military road begins the long climb to the pass. The sun, slanting low now over the sea, sent gleams of reddish yellow between the trunks on to the mountain-side. In the fields, clumps of brown stubble stood forlorn in pools left by recent rains now topped with ice. Here and there, where the ice had cracked, the edges sparkled with diamond light.

In the row of forestry houses, standing in the lee of the mountain facing the sea, the windows burned in the sun like sheets of copper. But for a moment only. As we turned towards them the radiance faded, and the silvery blue of dusk began to darken the glen.

The sea had a stored up inner brightness that dimmed slowly. Sleeping now, it would retain its mysterious sheen into the night.

Was that why the people of the glen looked more to the sea than to the land? They talk of 'the mainland', meaning the world beyond the pass, as if they were islanders. Their backs were turned to that mountain wall and to the dark world beyond it. The sea brought light, movement, renewal.

Long ago the hardy inhabitants sailed the rough waters among the islands in the slender boats they built here. With them they swam cattle from island to island to the old port here, to be herded for the great drove road to the south. Lower jaw lashed to the tail in front, the beasts thrashed through the waves, driven by blows and fear. The ancient slipway survives, its great stones worn smooth as glass by those hooves churning the shallows to gain the land.

Nowadays the hardiness is declining, not because of the rigours of life but because of technology and drink. Few people walk, for example. Old Colonel Marriott, a local landowner, talked about that one day in tones of acidity and sadness. "When I came back from Hitler's war and started farming here, there were only two cars, mine and the chap at the Inn. Now? Just look at the blighters! They'll get on their tractor to fetch a pail of water. Cars, trucks, you name it they've got it. Talk about soft!"

We stood in his smoky little study looking through leaded panes down a gently sloping lawn to the river. On the left, just visible in a barn, stood a thirty-year-old Bentley. He motioned towards it with his cigarette. "Funny, isn't it? In a little while I fancy we'll be the only one-car family in the glen!"

Few women walk anywhere. Even in the main village where no house is more than three hundred yards from the shop, the car is used to pick up a loaf of bread or a packet of washing powder. Washing machines and vacuum cleaners and the new cleaning materials have abolished most of the old need for elbow grease.

By chance or not, with this slackening of physical muscle tone has come a spiritual weakening. The old sureness of identity has gone.

Insecurity is nourished by emotional isolation.

The disappearance of the old crafts has deprived people of places where they could meet in the course of their ordinary comings and goings and be sure of meeting, or at least sighting, nearly everyone else as they walked to and fro. There was the smithy, the bakery, the joiner's shop . . . In this way you were kept aware of one another's changes of mood and circumstance, noted the news and gossip, the ebb and flow of the amorous tides, kept track of events that might affect you and your family or the locality.

Again, fishing along this coast has declined and much of what remains has been industrialised and has become personally remote, and for many communities the excitement and movement and coming together at the fish quay have gone for ever. Here there is one boat left, its owner a part-time fisherman.

And in the locality as a whole movement is too fast, too enclosed and solitary in car or truck, to allow the survival of the old conversational progress with neighbours along roads and byways, or the natural stop at cross-roads to exchange news while beasts cropped at the grass verges. With such channels for the transmission of knowledge and self-expression destroyed, the communal net – the web of responsibility and obligation – is less and less able to maintain codes of behaviour and sustain identity.

Lack of knowledge of one another makes people feel insecure. We need people as landmarks to steer by. If their movements, their changes of attitude, become difficult to track, it is as if they disappeared from one's personal radar screen and one's navigation becomes less sure, increasingly charged with anxiety and self-doubt.

It is chronicled that the men of the glen often imported their wives from the outside; and then, after the wedding feast, drove away the bride's visiting relatives with sticks and stones. A desperate affirmation of their new possession. Perhaps this marrying 'out', for husbands as well as brides, came from their natural linkage with the restless sea, commerce with the Islands, movement.

Certainly it continues. The bringing in of new blood having been so deeply rooted, how was local identity and loyalty, still strong even in its present decline, maintained at all?

Murdo Macfarlane is a retired gamekeeper. He still has a strong-looking figure, only a little rounded at the waist; and the keen eyes of his trade. His sparse hair is white, but the bristling little moustache, Lloyd George style, still with a good deal of black, underlines the look of vigour. On the wall above the sofa where he sat, a plaque honours his forty-five years of service to the community. He speaks in the rounded, shrewd, quizzical manner of the politician, the manipulator.

As if to remind me that he still had influence, perhaps even as a warning, he said, with characteristic obliqueness, "Aye – ye see I've got a' the local papers here. I take time tae read them a'."

I looked at the newspapers strewn about him. The word 'local' included *The Scotsman* from Edinburgh, *The Press and Journal* from Aberdeen, *The Oban Times* and *The Stornoway Gazette*. I noticed the *West Highland Free Press*, and recalled how Calum Johnson had ranted away about it.

Murdo added, 'Och ye see I never know when someone's goin' tae come here tae ask for an opinion or some advice."

What had he said, I wondered, to those who must have sought his opinion on my comings and goings in the glen?

He could have been listening to my thoughts. "Sometimes I have to reserve judgment," he said quietly. "I wait tae see how things shape up."

George stood by, thumbs hooked in trouser pockets, noting the performance, refining himself on the model. One day before Christmas he had given me a sample of his developing sense of political balance. "Ye know there's a petition being got up about Bill Walsh's application for a Sunday licence for the Inn? Och it's not a petition exactly – people are tae put their names down for or against."

The 'petition' was to be a prelude to the hearing of Bill Walsh's application before the District Licensing Board.

He talked on, deploying the arguments. I saw that he was less concerned with principle than with calculating the odds. He said, "A lot o' folk will be opposed on religious grounds."

"You sound as though you think the application will be granted."

"Aye – it might. Bill applied two years ago and was turned down."

"Also because of the religious opposition?"

"I think so."

"Then what is different this time?"

"Aye – well, ye see there have been changes. Some o' the older folk have died. The younger folk?" he tugged at his beard, "Och no' so many are hard-line church folk anyway. The place is dead on Sunday. So there should be more support shown in the petition."

How many of the younger set, I wondered, would put their names down in support of the application, in open defiance of the elders?

"Where do you stand?"

He regarded me with the steady calculation of his father. "Och I dinna' care which way it goes! So I'm no' going tae put ma' name doon one way or the other."

Paradoxically, many people do mourn the disappearance of the Inn, an elegant white building in Regency style set in a pleasant garden on a knoll above the incurving foreshore. Since the mysterious fire, the makeshift bar that stands there has had no Sunday licence. The glen has been dry on the Sabbath.

19

The strong religious attachment were happy about that result and still are, a satisfaction that has provoked mutterings in the younger set. The fire could have been started deliberately.

"Ah wouldna put it past some o' them holy folk," said young Matthew Maclellan in the bar one evening. He is not a heavy drinker as yet, but likes to have a pint of dark beer at hand while he plays at the bar pool table.

His cousin Andrew, tall, lean, black-bearded, two years older, looked quickly to the other end of the long narrow bar, stone-floored with bare limewashed walls, where a group of crofters sat. "Wheesht! Ye'd better no let the older folk hear ye."

Matthew doubled a ball smartly into the middle pocket. "Och ah've said as much to their face before!"

"What did they say tae ye?"

"Something about God working his will in strange ways! Ye can make of that wha' ye like, but ah know what ah make of it."

Andrew chalked his cue thoughtfully. "Ah suppose if *we* felt like the holy folk, that going to the Inn on the Sabbath was devil's work and must be stopped, *we* wouldna' mind how it was done."

A classic act of purgation by fire? Such things have happened.

It could have been a drunken accident. Hard drinking, of hard liquor, is prevalent – always has been. Melancholy, obsessional, it expresses atavistic fantasies of masculinity, libido, local pride, lost glory. Above all – hatred! Hatred of 'them' – the standard scapegoats – government, officialdom, foreigners, city people, incomers.

Whatever its cause the fire has left an irremovable stain. They cannot forget it. Hardly a day passes but I hear it mentioned. Is it guilt? Or is it the old guard continuing, unconsciously, to drive home their point, holding the line? Could it be the younger folk striking at the older set for denying them a livelier Sunday? Or is it no more than a sign of general disquiet, as the people of the glen compare themselves with those emissaries of another view of life, the tourists and the incomers?

The old Inn certainly brought more money to the community. The present bar and its adjoining refreshment room – open in summer only – employ a girl and a middle-aged woman, part-time in winter, full-time in the season.

The people of the glen take the outsiders' money eagerly enough but try to forget how they earn it. They feel outnumbered, deposed to the hated status of quaintness, backwardness, the naïve and ingratiating peasant. They know that these assumed attributes are a necessary part of the 'atmosphere', seemingly static and uncomplicated, that attracts the visitors and the incomers, and that they themselves, their homes and way of life, are thus put on sale. They must play out a piece of theatre.

Murdo Macfarlane's family, and all the other bed-and-breakfast people, understand that they must do this so that their urban customers can indulge a fantasy of the full and simple life. They feel that there is condescension here and in their hearts they hate the visitors for that.

Hate is not too strong a word.

They hate the visitors, too, for their volition. *They* can come and go as they like, but we are stuck here. And *they* corrupt the place with their evil example, late night and noisy orgies on the foreshore after the Inn closes, lascivious behaviour in public even in daytime. They bring the contagion of the city.

They hate the incomers the more. Murdo Macfarlane's sardonic, pithy name for them, 'the new white settlers', is especially apt for the craftsmen, jewellers, potters, weavers, workers in metal, wood and stone, who flee the metropolitan life to set up house and business in these localities. It asserts that they do so precisely because there exists here a 'backward' population that gives the place the atmosphere they find congenial – and secretly feel separate from – and provides the local supplies and services they need in order to live and do business here. Thus the locals see them as new style colonialists, sustaining their superior life on the backs of the 'natives'.

What label, I wondered, did they have for me? They were still stepping carefully round me, reserving judgment. None of their stock prejudices fit me. I am not simply a visitor; I am to stay for the year. I am not a 'new white settler' for I have not bought my cottage nor do I propose to set up a business here like Duncan and Flora Burke with their boatyard or Adrian and Nellie Templer with their arts and crafts workshop. I am renting my cottage on the land of Robert Morton the crofter and walking the glen, as I did long ago as a student, trying to understand.

"Understand what?" asked Murdo quickly.

"Where is the heart in the onion!" I answered, thinking of Peer Gynt.

He fidgeted with the edge of one of the papers on his knee. "Aye – well, ye're takin' a lot on," he said drily. "I hear ye're a psychologist *and* an economist! And a writer into the bargain! That's a frightening combination. Still, George here thinks your heart's in the right place. Aye – an' I've been getting reports about you from others. Folk come and tell me things. Ye don't seem to have an axe to grind – hard to believe, I must say. But if it's true I'm very pleased to hear it. We don't want interference. But I'll tell you this much," he had talked himself out of the shock, "if ye succeed we'll never forgive you for it!"

In the tiny parlour were about a dozen people, sons, nephews, a daughter-in-law, George's two little boys, Murdo's wife. Every grown-up was intent on some interest of the moment, reading, knitting, playing with the children, Mrs. Macfarlane moving to and from the adjoining kitchen –

and at the same time each kept a place in the intermittent conversation, or rather an endlessly episodic one, entering it to say a word, add a comment, ask a question, then retreating into the interest of the moment for a little while, to emerge again into the main stream.

A powerful quietude flowed beneath the animation. There was none of the contrived intimacy one finds when some families come together, and there is not enough of true emotional sympathy to feed upon and all is forced.

George's mother, a stocky little woman with round, lively features, wearing large modish spectacles, and dressed in an old-fashioned wrap-over apron, bustled about with cups of tea. Like most wives in the glen she is much younger than her husband. Men marry late here, when they have 'built up a livelihood', have a house, and so are eligible. There is almost no scope for a young woman to become a fully independent wage earner, able to contribute to a joint income that could support an earlier marriage. In any case people in the glen still feel that it is a man's duty to support his wife from the start.

Nowadays girls get out as soon as they can, but a few cannot; and their wistfulness consumes them. But those who do go become embittered too, discovering that they cannot take the glen's ambience, its relationships and well-understood responses, away with them, except in a fantasy that becomes too painful to sustain.

Morag Mackinnon, the young girl who helps in the shop sometimes, may not get away. In her, and in others among the young folk, we shall see the working out of conflicts – between the allure of flight, an imprecise vision of fulfilment outside, and the pull of home, of familiar emotions, inherited ideals, loyalties.

Mrs. Macfarlane brought out a dish of biscuits; no ordinary dish, but one that showed the persistence of old attitudes even in its name. A display dish; a series of decorated plates arranged in tiers on a vertical shaft with an ornate handle at the top. It has a cherished place in the house lucky enough to possess one.

The phone rang in the little lobby. Mrs. Macfarlane came back smiling happily. "Aye – that's another booking," she told her husband. "Nearly all the times are taken now."

He looked at me, head tilted to the side, pretending self-pity. "That's the way it goes. Another bed and breakfast season's upon us while we're still getting over the last one!" He sighed. "The money's good but your life's not your own any more."

Two

Echoes in the mist

January is nearly over but the day still fades early, about four. Snow lies heavily on the higher slopes and on the far mountains visible beyond the bealach – the great pass – and on the island peaks across the water. Here in the glen's milder climate it seldom lies long on the lower slopes. A heavy fall can come, as it did this morning, and in an hour the glen's entire ground is covered, the trees in feathery white tracery, the stubble bending under large blobs of it like soap bubbles, the taller clumps of brown pushing through. Then, after lunch came a heavy shower of rain; and just as suddenly the lower covering is gone; and soon the hillsides glisten as the swollen burns snake down frothing silvery white, bursting out of their gullies and spreading the foam over the hill as they try to carry away the onrush of new water from the melted snow.

The glen is always quiet. Narrow and sinuous between the steep mountain-sides, its shape seems to damp down noise. Only sounds close at hand intrude upon one's thoughts. In the night air they flow perhaps more freely, and I hear the rustle of cattle shifting position in the meadow between my cottage and the river. In the daytime the occasional vehicle is almost upon you before you hear it. On some days the silence hangs so heavily you feel the weight of it, especially when the clouds sink down low and wisps of grey vapour float down the scree slope that stands like a wall before my sitting-room window. They steal down further still, and long feathery fingers touch the boulders in the cascading burn that feeds my water tank. Then they creep along the dry stone wall that maintains the downhill edge of the military road as it traverses the mountain-side.

Parts of the wall are broken, the more recent are jagged like grey stone teeth, the older are covered with creeping grass. They will not be repaired, for the art of dry stone building is as good as dead.

Sometimes the bottom of the cloud, seemingly heavier than the layers above, breaks away and drops on to the fields, leaving an expanse of clear air above it, a long twilit cavity roofed over by the main body of greyness. The layers shift position from minute to minute. Today the restless grey shapes slide down the wall on to the road itself. My footsteps are muffled.

Rounded bundles, vaguely seen, move around me, ghostly sheep disconsolate in the obscurity, turning towards me, seeking comfort. Somewhere behind me I hear steady footsteps. I look back and see nothing. They come nearer. At last they seem nearly upon me and I step carefully to the road's edge to be out of the way. A broad-shouldered man materialises, of medium height and fine ruddy features, clad in heather mixture tweed jacket and knee breeches with thick green stockings and a cream shirt open at the neck. It is old Jamie Macleod, whose croft lies four miles back up the glen, beyond that of Robert Morton, my landlord.

His vigorous step and bearing suggest a man in the prime of middle life. I am amazed to discover his real age – eighty-two. He has lived in the glen all his life, except for the 1914–18 War. "I walk to the croft and back every day," he said. "I always have done. It gives me time to think."

"So you still work the croft?"

"Och well, aye – I do a bit. But ma son's taken it over now."

He turned to look back. The grey mass that had enveloped us had parted horizontally. The bottom layer covered the glen floor. Through it a black cow waded as in a steam bath. In the clear space between it and the main cloud hanging low over our heads I could just discern, far away towards the upper glen on a flat knoll above the river, a white-ended cottage. "Aye – I was born there," he observed, "and ma' faether afore me. Now ma son's got the hoose."

He himself lives in a trim new bungalow a couple of miles down the glen nearer the sea. I pass it every day, and see a new-looking car in the garage adjoining it; new-looking, perhaps, because he so seldom uses it. He is one of the few locals I ever see walking.

We had halted beside an old demesne wall, not a dry stone one, but a thick masonry wall of granite blocks topped with smooth slabs sloping outwards and covered with bright green moss. It was a wall that spoke of substance and status, a place cared for, sophisticated, for people above the common clay. Behind the wall a copse covered the sloping ground, and a beech drive led down to a sheltered paddock. On its edge, facing the west, stood a substantial mansion, with large conservatory and a wide stone terrace.

"That's the old Church of Scotland manse," he said with a wry turn of the lip, studying me.

"A big place, that house must have about twenty rooms."

"Aye, all of that. All this is glebe land, ye know. The minister lived in a bit o' style in the auld days! Och when ah was a lad ye got a lassie in service for a few shillin' a month! Ye didn' have tae be a rich man tae have a skivvy in yer hoose – like ye have tae be today. Everything's changed now. Religion's gone doon – an' the minister's position with it!"

He stared at the wall, and spoke to me out of the past. "Aye – an' he *had*

24

a position – as was his due. Nowadays! Folk dinna' expect the minister tae live in the auld style – like a wee laird, wi' a cook maybe, an' a serving maid. Look at the minister the noo! The Church o' Scotland one I mean, we havena' got a Free Kirk one – och well, the puir wee man lives in a bungalow. A wee bungalow if ye please – it's nae bigger than the but' an'ben ah've got!"

We stood looking down at the big house. Though the gates appeared newly painted, and the house itself well-cared for, there was no sign of occupation.

"Those were spacious days," I said.

"Aye," he sighed, "I remember all that as a boy. We walked past a house like that with respect. Mind you, the great folk hereabouts used tae take an interest. With money I mean. Aye – and in other ways as well. They owed it to themselves to keep up the position o' the minister and through him the influence o' religion. That's all gone now."

He thought about it. "Och I'm no' sayin' anythin' against their minister. I wouldna' do that. The puir auld soul's a guid man. Still they dinna' get ministers – of the one church or the ither if it comes tae the bit – like they used tae. Aye – they were right big men in the auld days. An' they left their mark! Ah'll tell ye this. There was a minister here, Dr. McGregor, he was here a hundred an' fifty year ago! An' his name is remembered still! That's all over."

He clicked his tongue and looked down the slope to the big white house. "Aye – well, there it is – it's standin' empty nearly all the year."

"Who does live there?"

"The owner doesna' live there. He's a businessman from down South. The place stood empty for – och for many years. He bought it a few years ago and spent a mint o' money on it. He lets it to summer visitors."

"He never lives there himself?"

"Oh no. Never. He bought it as an investment you see."

"Like so many others."

He looked up. "What? Aye that's right enough. There's plenty of that. Too much."

"What do you mean 'too much'?"

He kicked the ground, and shivered a little. We turned together and walked on towards the sea.

"Ye see, a lot o' the folk here are either sellin' oot or changin' intae – I mean changin' from gettin' their livin' oot o' the land intae . . ." He sighed again. "It's difficult to put a word tae it without soundin' insulting to them, which I wouldna' want to be – shall I say turnin' tae exploitin' the commercial side of things? Take Robert Morton, that you're renting your cottage from. He occupies a croft right enough but he isnae any longer a true crofter. Crofting is no longer his principal enterprise. Och anyway that's how it seems tae me. Robert's a guid man. But he doesnae cultivate his land any more. Aye – well – he runs some sheep, an' a cow' an' a few chickens for his hoose. But he's really gone over to the tourist business – with his caravans and so on. A few more like him and the glen willnae be worth livin' in."

He went on, "Aye – for many folk the crofting is now a part-time affair. That is what's wrong with the Highlands. What was once good enough as a livelihood is so no longer! Folk want so many things that are unnecessary; and that a croft alone cannot give them. My son – well for the moment he and his wife are reasonably content with what the croft can bring. And he works it thoroughly as he should. But how long will they be content? He and some o' the others in the glen?"

"What would you like to see happen?"

"What would I *like*?" He puckered his brow and pondered the matter reluctantly.

"Let me put it dramatically! If you had complete authority in the glen, what would you try to bring about here?"

He stopped and faced me for a long stare, then turned and gestured with a wide sweep of the arm, taking in the low lying land before us. We stood near the old graveyard. It occupies a bluff, jutting out into the river which here rushed round it in an angry arc over great stones. Here the glen floor, where it showed through gaps in the ground mist, was a lush green even at this dim season. The growth, however, was rough and mixed, showing no sign of care.

"Aye – well I'd make them cultivate every inch of the land possible, and do it thoroughly and with care! All the land here needs to be thoroughly attended to, technically I mean – all the heart's gone out of it. Och it's a shame to see it in this state."

"Why do they abandon it?"

"Och that's putting it too strongly." He scratched his head. "Years – generations – of what I call half-hearted farming or crofting have weakened the land, drawn the heart out of it and put nothing back. An' the heavy rainfall in these parts has washed away a lot of its strength. You may think I'm speakin' against ma ain folk but I say as much to their faces. We dream too much. Aye – dream! Dream o' the past – and make do with the present. Another thing – folk forget that the Highlander was never a fully committed cultivator; ours was principally a grazing economy, with cultivation secondary. Och ye must know that the clan system didna' encourage men to tie themselves to the long-drawn oot demands o' cultivation! Your fighting man could leave his little herd or flock to his womenfolk while he went on a foray. Aye! It goes far back, ye see? In a way we've inherited something o' that dislike o' the commitment tae cultivation. So now they turn to easier things – the forestry or the bed and breakfast, odd jobs here and there."

"Anything but working the land?"

He grunted assent, shoved his hands deep in his trouser pockets and turned to resume his march.

"Aye – they say I'm embittered," he went on. "But what I say is no more than the truth, and they know it in their heart of hearts. If ye lose touch with the land, where all things come from, where we ourselves come from, then ye lose touch wi' the heart o' life. Ye lose whatever ye started with, I mean as a person. Ye've then got nothin', no bearings, no sense of purpose, nothin' to guide ye as to who you are, where ye should be aimin' at as a person – what anythin' means."

The carpet of mist rose up again from the land and we were walking once more through the bottom of the cloud.

He broke the silence. "Aye – an' I'd do something else. I would clear out the deer and put sheep on that land instead." He gestured back the way we had come, to the great deer forest covering the slopes at the head of the glen.

"Even lookin' at it from the business point o' view, comparin' the price of venison with what ye get for the mutton and wool there's nae comparison'. Apart from that there's so much poaching of the deer! Too expensive to protect, you see? No, sheep would be a better investment up there every time. Given good management, of course."

"If you did that to the estates here, how many head of sheep could you put on what is now deer forest?"

Evidently the matter had occupied his thoughts for many a long day, for he took no time to think. "About six thousand."

"They say, don't they, that you need about four hundred ewes to support a family?"

"About that – say four to six hundred."

"So you'd get about ten to twelve additional families on to the land that way?"

"There's more to it than that. It's not only this little glen. Think of the great mass of the Highlands. Think of the other crafts and occupations and enterprises ye could encourage. Think of the wool economy. Why don't we Highlanders wake up to what technology can do tae help us for a change? We could process oor ain wool clip in this district instead o' sendin' it tae Evanton and then tae Bradford an' then buyin' it back again. High technology, micro chip processors – all these things have made mass-production a thing of the past. For many things nowadays you don't need to think only of big factories and big investment."

He grew eloquent, his eyes gleamed. I listened to the inner echoes of his hours and days of solitary thought over the years.

"Have you thought," I said after a while, "of getting some of your ideas put into practice? At any rate some of the more modest changes that lie within people's own power here, more intensive cultivation, more club farming perhaps, new small enterprises to create more employment in the glen? Even the more ambitious things, such as putting sheep on to the higher ground in place of the deer, are not all that unthinkable! Times are changing. Attitudes among estate owners might change too?"

Chin lowered, he answered roughly, railing at the world, "I'm too old – *now*!"

I said, "It is your vision the folk here need. And your leadership. Especially to the younger people. Your son, for instance. And the others."

"My son?" He shook his head. "He's not exactly a young man, and besides . . ."

He lapsed into meditative silence.

I should not have mentioned his son, Charles. About forty-five, he is hard-working and conscientious, but dour, not an initiator. Perhaps, as often happens with the son of a dominant and long-lived father, Charles had long ago stopped trying to assert himself and push new ideas.

"Still, there are others," I said. "George Macfarlane, for example, and Robert Wallace, perhaps a few more, who want to do something constructive. They might follow you?"

He stopped again and turned to me. He looked at me hard. "I've heard about their talks with you! Let me ask ye something. What is your interest here? Are ye looking for something to put your money in? Do ye want these folk to work for ye? Ye don't mind me putting it tae ye straight?"

"No. None of these things."

"Ye don't strike me as the missionary type."

A grin shone forth.

I talked as I had to Murdo Macfarlane.

"The heart in the onion!" he repeated. "Och that's gone for sure! And ye want to restore it? Ye're asking a lot.

"Tell me something else," he continued in the same tight-lipped fashion. "Would ye put *your* money into, say, the bakery? Or some such business?"

The same question put differently, containing a trap.

"You mean, am I deliberately seeking to do that? Or would I show my confidence by risking my own money in it?"

"I suppose I mean the second, to show your confidence."

"Let me be equally blunt. These ideas will only be realised if you people want them to. If the business, be it bakery or anything else, is not going to wash its face then it won't do *anybody* any good."

"But *would* you?"

"If I did I would be simply yet another incomer taking profit from the glen! No, let's be practical. I see myself as at the most a catalyst, perhaps an *active* catalyst if that isn't a contradiction, but that's all."

We had reached his gate.

"A catalyst, eh." He sighed and shook his head slowly, not unkindly, "I wish you luck. But our folk need more than that. They need hope – and push. Yes, push."

We are not pushy enough. That cry constantly returning, containing so much counterpoint and pathos, sad sweetness, exculpation, fading hope, bitterness, entreaty.

I walked on towards the old port. There the mist swirled over pools and channels that marked out old boundaries, roadways, tracks, where once had been the buildings, dwellings, cattle pens. The whole area resembled a flooded archaeological dig from which the seekers and their marking posts had long since departed.

My thoughts were interrupted by a voice that seemed to come from almost above my head but behind me. I had halted in front of a partly built house that I had often noticed and wondered about. It was no more than a shell, with the windows in and glazed, but roofed as yet only by a layer of tarred felting over which down-sloping wooden slats were fixed; they would take the framework for the slates that I could see stacked ready on the ground beside it. The cloud had descended so low that I had not observed the man perched on the roof, on a slatted plank hooked on the roof tree. It was Robert Wallace, a burly young man with deep-set blue eyes and a bristling Van Dyck beard.

"Hello," I called back. "I didn't know this was your house. How long have you been building it?"

"Och about a year now." He turned carefully so that he could straighten himself to face me with both heels on the same slat on the plank. "That's better. It's a bit solitary up here." He laughed. "Aye – it'll be another year or so by the time I finish. It's – well – it depends on how the money comes in, ye see?"

I nodded. "How do you manage?"

"You mean with money or with time to do it?"

"I didn't mean to be so personal. I was really thinking how wonderful to see a man building his house with his own two hands."

"Aye, not many can do that – I mean *have* the chance to do it. I could never have done it in Fort William if I'd stayed on there."

He had returned to the glen seven years ago with his wife and child to take over his father's croft.

As with Jamie Macleod, his solitary thinking spilled over, but with more immediate concerns – his inner tug-of-war, still continuing between the pros and cons of life in the town and in the glen.

"Do you think you'll ever change your mind and leave the glen?"

He took time to reply. He surveyed the waterlogged land on whose edge, a bare hundred yards away, the sleepy sea lapped with a loud whisper. A grey curtain of mist drifted down on the water, dulling its sheen. The sea birds were silent. From across the glen there came the buzz of a power saw, overlaid suddenly by the quick jangle of the school bell near at hand, finishing the day; and then came the chatter of children's clear voices, and the scamper of their feet in the school yard.

"Och when I'm oot here," he said at last, "I think I could never leave. This is all mine! *My* land, I have come back to this life. One of the few. Och it's a good life. Maybe it isn't materially. But we manage."

The question remained on the table.

He said, "I just wish there were one or two small industries here, something more interesting. I do a bit at the forestry. That's dull, heavy work. Drudgery. I'm glad to have it but – it's no' very interesting."

"How do you get the time off to look after your croft? And to work on your house?"

He responded with that knowing half-smile with which country folk the world over confront questioners who seek to understand how they evade the constraints of authority or system – the conjuring tricks of survival, their precious secrets.

"Och it's no' that difficult! It's a case of fitting things together at the right time."

I was not going to press the point, but to forestall me if I did, he switched quickly. "Have you heard the outcome of Bill Walsh's Sunday licence hearing?"

"No."

"They turned it doon! That surprises ye?"

"I must say it does. George Macfarlane thought he would get it this time."

"George abstained, didn't he? That didn't help."

The anti-Walsh campaign was planned with care. A mini-bus was hired to take a dozen 'witnesses' to oppose the unsuspecting Bill Walsh. Bill had no local person with him, only a meek young solicitor from Oban; though in the event he had done most of the talking himself. I could fancy that his blustery manner would not have endeared him to the Licensing Board.

Jenny Cairns, a brisk little woman whose house is close to the old Inn site, had said in evidence – in the context of the 'disturbance' caused – that her little row of houses was so close that "I can watch them playing bar pool from my window". At this point a bearded man in a kilt, sitting in front of her, had laughed out loud. Later she had asked him why. "Och I was thinking of the chief objector in our village. He rants away aboot the disturbance from oot pub and he lives five miles away!"

"Did you win your objection?" she asked him.

30

"Aye, of course we did," he answered in surprise. "The Free Kirk is strong in oor village as well!"

Robert said, "I hear Bill's going to appeal. In a way I'm sorry for him. He is not liked and he canna' see why. As an incomer he carries a handicap anyway. But as well as that he seems to have no sensitivity at all! He will insist on butting into folk's talk at the bar. He will contradict about local things he knows nothing about. He will insist on havin' the last word. He will not go out of his way to understand."

I thought of George Macfarlane. He had played his cards wisely. His day would come.

I said, "What do you think of Bill's chances in the appeal?"

"Aye, I was thinkin' about that when you came along just now." He turned again, shifting his left foot a slat higher on the plank, his right wedged sideways on the one below, and slopped some liquid on to the wooden framework with a broad paper-hanger's brush.

He said, "The trouble is that Bill's strongest argument goes to the heart of what worries folk most – the visitor trade – the fact that he needs the Sunday licence for the visitors. The local folk will not face the reality, the implications, of that – the visitor trade, I mean. Do they want the visitors' money or not?"

"You refer to the people here as 'the local folk' and 'they' as if you were different. I'm pulling your leg."

He laughed, "Och aye – you're right in a way. I'm a different generation. I'm impatient. No, that's not the whole of it. I haven't got George's finesse."

"You are in a stronger position, Robert. You've got your own croft. You have a stake in the land. Broadly speaking your livelihood does not depend on people's opinion. Not at any rate to the extent that his does. George is in commerce. He can't afford to ruffle the feelings of his clients or potential clients. He must impress them always as a sound man, someone who will not take up a position in local life that they disapprove of."

"Aye," he said, "there's something in that. I'm not beholden to anyone to earn my living."

He added, "I suppose I would have to be like George if I were to start some kind of business. Havin' tae mind what I say, watch my step, never be on the losing or unpopular side!"

"Have you thought seriously about a business?"

"Och no, nothing specific. Ideas go through your head. The business o' the glen should not be in the hands o' one person. In my father's time there were three shops. Aye an' there was a joiner's shop, a bakery, and a couple of smiddies."

The cloud was beginning to drip with rain. Dusk was upon us. Even at this small distance his features were becoming indistinct. He turned away from the roof again, replaced the lid tightly on his paint pot, and moved carefully on his heels down the plank to the gutter edge, then stepped on to the planks laid on the portable tubular scaffolding ranged against the wall.

He put his materials away, and prepared to replace the nailed up frame that served as a plug to the empty doorway.

I wondered if this was a good moment to mention my talk with old Jamie Macleod. Perhaps it would do no harm.

"Your name came up when I was talking to Jamie Macleod a while ago."

"Aye."

We walked back along the muddy surface of what had been the main supply road from the port for Wade's fortified barracks.

He said, "Och ye must be especially favoured! Old Jamie seldom talks to anyone these days."

"He thinks no one wants to listen."

He pondered this. "He wants tae turn the clock back, tae go back tae the good old days when we lived on oats and potatoes and a bit of fish. And when folk sometimes shared a roof with their beasts."

"Do you really think so?" I said carefully, "He talks in a very up-to-date fashion, of using modern methods to restore the economy of the glen, and for that matter of the locality as a whole, and bringing back local industry. If something like that does *not* happen here, what will become of the way of life that you, for instance, left Fort William to come back to?"

"Aye, I know. That thought worries me as well. But who's going tae do all that? Who's going tae start all those new businesses, apart from all those bigger schemes of his? Does he really think that *we* can – the younger folk?"

"In a small way perhaps."

Our ways lay together till the earthen road ended at the great rounded archway, the principal entrance to the barracks, surmounted by two square gunports and flanked by musket loopholes in a zigzag line along the corbelled perimeter wall. Here the road joined another; one branch led off to the right into the avenue of oaks, the other wound away round the hummocky shore to the ferry. His ancestral cottage, where he was living until he could move into the new house, lay a quarter of a mile along this track.

We arrived at the barracks in silence.

He said, making an effort to be casual, "Which way do you want to go?"

The words were appropriate. They no doubt echoed his thoughts.

Not 'which way do you want to go?' but 'which way is it easiest to go?'

For him, coming here from the life of the town, that question was harder. The young exiles to the town found that they could not take the glen with them; neither could you bring the town with you to the glen.

I said, "You're asking *yourself* that question, aren't you?"

32

"What? Och I see what you mean."

He said his farewell 'Aye' a shade abruptly and turned away, but [...] and faced me. "Och I'm sorry! I shouldn't have been thrown off b[...] by this talk but I was. You really think we can do something?"

"Jamie Macleod thinks so."

"Aye, but do *you*?"

"Take things bit by bit. Start small. The bakery? The market is th[...] There isn't a baker in the whole area from Oban to Inverness! It sh[...] work if it's run well. And if you can overcome the opposition here[...]

"Opposition?" he repeated wonderingly. "You mean Calum Johnso[...] He waved a hand in dismissal. "That's not so important. He's only [...] man in the end."

His brow furrowed. Squaring up to the question he was half-surpris[...] that he could. Youth propelled him. Ancient caution, fatalism, tugge[...] him back. The inner contest stirred unhappiness.

I said: "Let's talk again; when you've thought a bit more – about wher[...] you want to go?"

"Where I want to . . .? Aye, I see." He laughed shortly. "All right then, we'll do that."

He turned to go, with the local gesture of farewell, the arm held straight out nearly horizontal and the open palm facing you.

He needed to be away from me.

Which is the true way forward? Which inner voice is to be trusted? To which vision of himself should he be faithful?

Echo of Peer Gynt again: 'Which is the Gyntian self?'

Do these Northern twilights always breed self-doubt? Here, always on the edge of the thrusting world, neither truly a part of it nor ever wholly free of it, did they always welcome the winter darkness – and the mist that comes in magically from the sea, helping them to dream? Sweeping the doubt away?

I thought again of Morag Mackinnon, the slim, thoughtful girl of eighteen who seems so rich in the luminous certainty of her years, alas so misleading. Dark hair falling round her shoulders, cheeks ruddy, lips long and full, her large brown eyes contemplate the world steadily through gold spectacles. She floats rather than walks.

"What do you do in the winter?" I once asked her.

"Nothing." She smiled faintly.

"It is very difficult to do nothing."

She looked at me seriously. The thought came to her as a shock. At last she said, "Och you see we've got cows and so . . ." Her voice trailed away.

They have three cows. She helps with them and with other tasks on the croft. In saying she did nothing she expressed her longing for a role so well defined that she would need to exercise no judgment, make no

difficult choices, a utopian vision of an outside world where everything was clearly labelled and all perspectives unambiguous; where there was none of that interfusing of relationships, full of challenge, demanding constant flexibility of response, that her grandmother's generation had never questioned.

In her grandmother's time an unmarried girl stayed at home as an integral part of it, sharing in its varied tasks, without any feeling of playing an allotted role. She was part of a collective life, working as one of its limbs on the land and in the household, sharing in its view of itself as a unity, until she assumed a wife's responsibilities under a roof of her own, when the slow nurture of the new collective unit would start all over again. For Morag that state of affairs retains its atavistic attraction. But, listening to new voices speaking of a simplistic world beyond the mountains, she dreams of floating away to a single, cell-like identity. Compared with it the many-stranded life of home, seemingly so simple, is disturbing in its constant emotional demands. It promises so much and yet, superficially at least, offers so little.

Yet she is not sure about that facile fulfilment in the world outside. In her heart she feels that she will not leave until she is married. But marriageable men here are so few.

"Will you go away?" I asked, meaning 'like all the others'.

"Oh yes!" A great smile shone forth, shadowed immediately by a little frown of disquiet, "One day, I hope."

"You would really like to?"

She passed her tongue between her lips.

"Och yes, there's more going on. You feel you're doing something."

Inverness is the metropolitan outpost for this region. Like everyone else hereabouts, Morag had to live away from home from about the age of twelve to get her secondary schooling. So the authorities decree. She went to Inverness. It is a sensitive age at which to cut a child's moorings, when great damage can be done.

In the city, isolated in the hostel or in the 'boarding-out' house, a child is conditioned to a wintry and insecure speculation about life, a bitter fatalism that leaves little warmth of spirit behind; and confirms, during weekend visits home, that the timeless certainty of childhood is no longer to be found there, or anywhere.

Can this attack on the spirit be defended? Legislators and bureaucrats muster economic facts to suit the narrow view of the moment. There is not enough money coming in from local rates to run a secondary school in every scattered village or even within daily travelling distance. George Macfarlane and Morag, and many others, ask uncomfortable questions.

"What does this education fit young folk for?"

"Do we want schooling that prepares us only for alienation and exile?"

"Isn't the emotional damage too high a price to pay for what schooling *may* give us?"

Certainly the schooling they are now getting does not fit them to make a life in localities such as the glen. Almost the only jobs are 'in the forestry' – as work for the Forestry Commission is referred to – but these do not call for much more than elementary schooling. And thoughts of making a life in these localities, and the aptitudes and skills needed, are not encouraged – either emotionally or practically – by the present slant of schooling. The ruling ethos still persuades young people to turn away from such 'humbler' occupations – an outdated expression, still current hereabouts, that conveys the derogatory valuation – and from the skills, and more particularly the way of life, associated with them.

There is a peculiar irony here. Such skills and occupations – spinning and weaving, candle-making, wood and metal working and many other old crafts – now aim themselves at a market quite other than the local, subsistence life whence they sprang. Paradoxically their main attraction is not that they produce the old necessities of life but that their products enable the urban sophisticate to assert an individuality and strike a blow at the mass-production world; the world into which present schooling propels the rising generation.

For George Macfarlane and his generation to scout the value of education is emotionally traumatic. It shows disdain for the optimism of their elders, devalues their faith, their spiritual trial, their self-denial.

Scottish tradition, going back to Knox and beyond, holds education in high regard. Plain living and high thinking. The plain living hardly needed emphasis. High thinking in its virtuoso form was respected if not always followed. Often, however, its pure gold is alloyed, and in its baser form recent tradition has proclaimed a faith in well-drilled schooling as a means of attaining high position, influence, riches.

'Follow the shining example of Andrew Carnegie!' was a credo dinned into the minds of Scottish children in the schools until fairly recent years. In that spirit of dedication and hope it was thought perfectly normal, in the Thirties, for a little boy to walk five miles to school carrying with him, for his day's food, a slice of cold porridge and two pieces of dry bread.

To question and diminish all that is to deny the gospel of the enlightenment.

On a grey afternoon in the shop, there had been some talk about young people going away. Morag was tidying up, a little less smoothly than usual and something possessed me to ask her, "Tell me, Morag, you'll be nineteen soon. What is to stop you going?"

I wished I had not spoken.

She straightened slowly from stowing some matches under the counter. Her eyes brimmed with tears and she half-turned away, took off her

35

spectacles and lifted the hem of her apron to wipe the smeared lenses.

She spoke unsteadily. "How can I? I havena' got any training. I didna' get enough Highers tae go tae college. So I couldna' go for a teacher. The only other way out for me would have been tae go for nursing training. Most of the girls here do that. But . . ." she gulped and wiped her eyes with the back of her hand, "I couldn't – I just *couldn't* pretend to like being a nurse!"

Pretend.

"You got friends in Inverness, haven't you?"

"I have." She sounded surprised. "Girls I knew at school there."

"If you really want so much to go, what would your parents say if you said you would like to go and stay with the family of one of these girls and simply get a job – in a shop or a factory where you wouldn't need special qualifications?"

She faced me, shocked. "I could *never* even think of doing that! My parents would be horrified. It would be like – like . . ." she blushed and looked away from me, "like running away from home!"

"Yet leaving home to go nursing would be all right?"

"Of course. That's a *profession*!"

An acceptable cover for escape. Without it the glen would think of her departure into unmarried independence as little better than going on the streets. 'Running away from home' was the nearest she could bring herself to saying it.

Three

Belonging

The winter has not been severe, they say, already speaking of it in the past. No great drifts have closed the bealach. No sheep have been trapped up on the mountain. Still, the road has been covered with ice on most nights; and on one very cold day there were long icicles hanging from the edge of my roof guttering. Now the days are at last noticeably longer. On recent nights, under a crystal clear sky, the glen has seemed to stretch itself in sleep, preparing to awake. But not yet.

In this mid-way season tempers are delicate. Passion is near the surface. Fights at the Inn seldom happen in the summer. That, no doubt, would be bad for the visitor trade. Or is it that the fights are private, local matters? They work out local emotions, express identity. They must happen, therefore, when the world is away.

Sometimes a boastful poacher from 'the mainland' – the country beyond the bealach – will be taught a sharp lesson by the locals. Sometimes the 'Garroch men' – the habitués of John Falconer's bar in the village on the great sea loch beyond the bealach – will come over and throw their weight about, and go back over the bealach with sore heads.

There is some worry about recent Garroch forays. There are theories that the traditional rivalry between Garroch and the glen is being manipulated by John Falconer and his partners in order to discredit the Inn here, thwart Bill Walsh's licensing appeal, and at the same time turn opinion against his other plans to develop the Inn site, and the nearby waters of the bay, into a 'leisure complex'. If that can be achieved by frequent disturbances here, then the holiday complex proposed at Garroch would be completed first and establish itself in a clear field.

Perhaps the present feelings of the glen folk towards the Garroch men reflect their bitterness about John Falconer's attitudes, his rough treatment of Highland sensibility. Falconer belongs to that wave of middle-class people who in the years after the last war, set up as hoteliers in former country houses. Like some of these, Falconer succumbed to the temptation to assume the manners, as he interpreted them, of the country gentleman.

Flamboyantly and with total seriousness he acted the part of the ex-army, tweedy Highland laird, or rather an unconscious caricature of that stock character, oblivious of local responses, a compound of careful politeness, incredulity, and subtle contempt.

The latter sentiment, I imagine, would not trouble him even if he sensed it. One day I happened to mention to him that I had had an interesting conversation with Lachlan Graham, a lean and sensitive man of charm and learning, who lives on a small croft some five miles from Garroch. He walks to the bar most evenings and trudges all the way back, staggering a little, after it closes.

"Lachlan!" roared Falconer, slapping his thigh. "A good for nothing! Inherited a good farm and drank it all away. These people are like 'blacks', you know? They really are." He paused for emphasis; Lachlan, with that description, was for him beyond consideration, "When Lachlan gets opinionated I simply throw him out – just like that. Oh yes, I've done it many times."

Hearing of these battles – they are always retailed to me in detail, and in differing versions – it never seems that there was any pre-planning. But by some common empathy, at the one proper moment, the local men close ranks and the enemy rues the day.

'No bugles sound but still the warriors gather . . .'

Not that all fights are of this type, with local interest or honour at stake. Many brawls flare up and are quickly, efficiently contained. Yet, when a fight of 'the glen against the ithers' is imminent, there is always a feeling about it in the air beforehand. The wind whispers with a quickened heartbeat, like a lover's anticipation of passion. They know . . .

For this one, strangely, they wanted to show me something. Why? I am still not certain. Some special pride was to be displayed. No, more than that, a new stiffening of resolve. A small sign that they think of themselves as a community with a soul?

February is running out. Each day the sun is a little higher and probes deeper into the glen. It will be some time before it throws its light on the north-facing slopes of Beinn à Shellach that have been lost in shadow since November. Each day the line that marks that sunless land, running the length of the glen, moves a trifle south as during the night the gods move their footrule of the turning year and the Eumenides rearrange their shadow.

With the lengthening days people's chemistry is in subtle change too. They begin to look outwards.

Big Donald Macallum stopped me in the street one afternoon. He is six foot three and seems nearly as broad. His lean, sallow face has laughter lines at the mouth. His dark eyes are sparkling and shrewd and unfailingly good-humoured, though ever watchful. He is one of the few serious drinkers I have known whom I have never seen in a black mood. He lives out his days in his working rig of gum boots, denims and great donkey jacket strengthened with leather across the mighty shoulders, yet is invariably fresh and well-groomed; his black hair, thinning a bit, is brushed neatly straight back.

"I am glad I met you," he spoke a little thickly. "I think you ought to come to the pub tomorrow night."

Our meeting, I felt, had not been by chance. Like most of the glen I too have evolved a pattern of going about. So it is known that I come down to the shop and for a wander on foot along the shore and through the hamlets between two-thirty and three o'clock. My Land-Rover, distinguishable from all the others in canary yellow and white, is recognisable a mile off. I know from the hints of casual conversation that they keep my movements carefully logged, reporting them to one another, puzzling over them, divining significances.

I said, "You know I hardly ever go to the Inn in the evening."

He laughed and took my shoulder in a huge hand, partly to steady himself. Seeing me wince, he loosened his grip a fraction.

"Come all the same! You should be there. Murdo told me what you said about 'the heart in the onion'. Those were your words, weren't they? I think you should be there."

He blinked at me.

I said, "What is going to . . .?"

"Wait!" He shook his head, searching for a thought. "Aye, I've got it." He frowned and looked at me with concern. "This is important. You must promise me something. Stay next tae me all the time. I mean *this* close!" He pulled on my shoulder till I stood close beside him. "This close *every single moment*. And there's something else." He paused for emphasis. "If I say: 'Go!' don't ask why! Just go. At once."

"You mean 'when' not 'if'?"

"When?" He shook his head slowly, "Och I see what ye mean! Och we're no' sure. I'm no' takin' any chances wi' yer safety that's a'. Ye must get oot at once! Even if I have tae carry ye oot mysel'!"

He easily could. I once saw him walking down the street carrying Matthew Maclellan under his arm like a parcel. Matthew is a rangy six-footer. Donald had come out of the Inn and found him fast asleep in his car, with the engine running and the hand brake off. Matthew had presumably lurched out, made to start off and, leaning back for a moment to close his eyes, fallen instantly asleep. Had he had time to put the car into gear it could have surged forward the few yards to the edge of the knoll and tumbled some forty feet into the sea. The tide was high.

Donald could well have confined himself to leaning into the car to switch off the ignition, leaving Matthew to wake up in his own good time.

39

"Och it's a cold day," he had observed. "He might catch his death. Aye – I'd better take him along to Mary and let her look after him."

Off he had strolled down the street to the Maclellan cottage, Matthew's arms and legs hanging down straight and swinging gently.

I said, "What is supposed to happen tomorrow night? As opposed to what you think might happen?"

"The Garroch men are comin' over for a pool match." He grimaced. "Och we don't know! We just have a feelin'. Somethin's in the air."

He avoided my eye.

"Donald," I said carefully. "If there's a fight, will you be able to stay out of it?"

The air of the calm afternoon froze. He stared at the ground. I noticed George Macfarlane at the door of his house. He looked up and down the street, sauntered to his car a few feet away and back again aimlessly.

Donald met my eye at last. "When I was in the army – I was only a youngster, not knowing my strength then – I was in a boxing match and my opponent caught me in a clinch and butted me with his head and broke my nose. The pain drove me mad. As I broke out o' the clinch I connected with his jaw, throwing all my weight into the blow." He shook his head sadly and looked away. "I've regretted that blow for over twenty years. It did something to his brain, made him feeble minded. A whole life of a man wasted! I go and see him sometimes. His father has a croft across the Loch." He sighed again. "I have *never* hit a man since. I spend a lot of time pulling men away from each other, stopping fights. Folk say there are fewer scraps when I am around."

That is not to be wondered at. His size alone, to say nothing of his renowned strength, would make any sensible man think twice about running into trouble with him.

Donald stood meditating. George Macfarlane continued to hover at his door. Further off, not far from where a track led down to his land, Robert Wallace stood and contemplated the pile of hay packed into the back seat of his little car.

Why did they want me to see how they behaved tomorrow? Why so eager to show me something about themselves? Something, presumably, that would present them in a different aspect, a better one, than they felt they had shown me hitherto. Better? What would they mean by that?

Was it the season, the year turning again, the sea mists clearing – completion of the long mystical journey from that inner communion of Ne'erday? Were they facing outwards at last?

Donald spoke reflectively. "The Garroch men have been *used* – we don't know who by. That doesna' matter. Och we've nae brief fer Walsh. But the holy folk've let things go too far. An' now a man's got killed on the bealach after goin' over tae get a dram on the Sabbath. We knew somethin'

40

like that'd happen sooner or later. They took no notice of us, neither them nor the incomers. Aye – well, we've got tae make up *oor* minds frae now on – how *we* want things tae be."

A few weeks ago Robert Clunie crashed to his death at a bridge on a tortuous stretch of the old military road on his way back from a middle of the day session at the Garroch bar. He was a taciturn but charming old shepherd who lived alone in a picturesque granite cottage in the village street. It was a Sunday. No other vehicle was involved. Big Donald, following a short distance behind, saw the car go over the side into the ravine. The old bridge had long ago lost its stone parapet. Donald accelerated the hundred yards or so that had divided them and leapt out of his car to see Clunie's, tumbling over and over, bounce off a rock far below and burst into flames.

As it happened, Harry Heslop and his wife Cynthia, a retired couple from Scarborough, who had settled into the cottage adjoining Robert Clunie's a few years ago, were also returning at the time, having had their Sunday lunch at the hotel.

Harry Heslop is a paunchy little man with a bald dome and tufts of white hair over his ears and bushy eyebrows overhanging deep-set steely grey eyes. He talked about that day with an eagerness I found disconcerting, a detached self-congratulation, as in other circumstances a man might demonstrate that his shrewd judgment has proved itself yet again.

"It had to happen, aye! We were about thirty yards behind Big Donald going down that steep bit of road with the bridge at the sharp corner. You know the one? A nasty one that is. And there's no parapet on it! Mind you the steering on that car of his was real bad. Had been for a long time. Even on that very day, when he was moving out of the car park ahead of us, I could see him fighting with the steering! Ah well."

"I suppose you warned the poor old chap about the steering on his car, you being his next door neighbour?"

Harry Heslop knows about cars. He had a garage at one time, and then a second-hand car business.

He said, "You can't talk to these people! You know that. Between you and I they're nothing but peasants, aren't they? They never change."

I had paused at his doorstep. I searched for a phrase with which to take my leave. He leaned closer and spoke confidentially. "Between ourselves, what do you think that cottage of his will fetch? I expect one or two others here have already had the same idea. Of course we are right opposite the Inn, and we have to suffer all that damned disturbance from it, all the noise and racketing about that comes from it, and that lowers the price of our property in this location, you know? It would have been much worse for us property owners here if they had given Bill Walsh his Sunday licence. Never mind, we managed to put a stop to that, a few of us incomers and the church folk. A proper united front. We're going to have to keep it up, that's what!"

I said, "He was a decent old man."

Startled, he showed impatience. "You're thinking that if there had been a Sunday licence here, it wouldn't have happened? He'd have done his drinking here?"

"That thought had also crossed *my* mind."

About to turn aggressive, he altered course. "The chances are that something of the kind would have happened in any case, one way or another. After all it's up to every one of us to protect our own interests, isn't it? And if they won't protect theirs then it isn't our fault."

"Maybe they will begin to do that."

The deep-set lynx eyes studied me. "It takes business folk like us to show these people a thing or two, you'll see!"

I said to Donald, "What time does this pool match start tomorrow?"

"About seven-thirty. Do you want to come later than that?"

"Yes. I think I do. I'll turn up about an hour later."

"Aye – well, I'll wait for ye at the door. Ye know the wee lobby before ye get tae the bar? If ye dinna' see me there it just means I've gone tae take a leak, an' I'll be back in a minute. I willna' leave my post at that lobby for any other reason till ye come. So wait for me there."

The bar and tea-room are in a long low building that had been the stables of the old Inn. Thick walls, as bare on the inside as out, are roofed with corrugated iron on an open timber frame; the floor is of cobbles and stone slabs. With such a casing of hard surfaces the place is a clangorous amplifying machine. Where it stands at the middle point of the arc of land that forms the little bay it is backed by a high cliff of the mountain-side, a huge sounding board that reflects noises and their discordant echoes, downwards to the houses. The first line of houses stands immediately to the rear of the Inn, lining the shore and fronting on to the street.

One enters through a closed-in porch of long panes of glass resembling a small conservatory, whose double swing doors, long out of true on their hinges, often jam tight. Departing drinkers, impatient of such trifles, put their unsteady weight against them to force them open. And the hinges become progressively more of a menace.

"One day," says Bill Walsh, "when I get my new hotel built, with chalet units and so on, it's going to be a proper tourist complex, you see? And this old place – the walls are very sound – is going to be completely done over as an indoor games and sports centre. That'll enable me to extend the season a bit – about a month at either end – as well as giving visitors something to do under cover when it's raining. And the locals too, especially the young folk in the winter time. In the meanwhile I am not too bothered about details like those blessed doors."

Strangely, these doors are set not in the front wall of the porch, that is immediately ahead of the inner ones, but in a side wall. Even someone in control of all his faculties emerging from the bar must overcome the natural impulse to step straight ahead, and instead make a sharp left turn to gain the outer pair of doors.

It was this porch that Donald called 'the lobby'. I arrived there a few minutes after eight-thirty.

When I parked at the Village Hall a hundred and fifty yards away, noise from the Inn rumbled about me as thunder does when it is directly overhead. I walked down the dark street – the glen has no street lighting – and the roar swelled, quietened a little, grew louder still. Guttural voices shouted obscenities with that special ferocity that drink engenders. A woman screamed. Sounds of splintering wood, of breaking glass.

Front doors had opened and people stood in their niches of light, casting long yellow imprints on to the ground before them. They shone torches to and fro like celebrants swinging censers, wondering what to believe.

Recognising me in the chiaroscuro, Harry Heslop shouted, "You hear that! High time that place was closed down altogether, never mind just on Sundays. We can't sit quietly in our own homes any more. That Bill Walsh is incapable of running an orderly house."

I crossed the yard. The sounds of a scuffle inside the building grew louder; the participants were coming towards the doors. A moment later the inner doors were flung open and out burst Angus Logie – a freelance builder and handyman from Glasgow long settled in the glen – an arm protectively round the shoulder of Mary Menzies, the young district nurse. She was shrieking hysterically. Immediately behind them I recognised Ushan Macilroy, the youth who works the petrol pumps at Garroch, usually cheerful and good-natured. Now, his face contorted, he leered over Angus's shoulder like a Brueghel demon, arms coiled round them both. Angus fended him off, snarling and cursing, obviously censoring his words for Mary's ears.

"Ye little bastard! You wait till ah get back! Ah'll smash yer face through the back o' yer heid!"

A mass of struggling bodies burst through the door behind Ushan. He was seized and hauled backwards into the bar.

Angus, obviously well gone in liquor, allowed Mary to lead him away, down the shore road towards the lighthouse on the southern horn of the bay.

Big Donald was not to be seen. Through a side window I looked down the long bar room. Local people clustered along the counter, ignoring Ushan and his group. Others sat at little ingle-nook benches along the walls. Ushan was leaping on to men's backs one after another at the bar counter. Amazingly, not one of them turned upon him. Each simply shrugged him roughly away. In this fashion he cannoned from one man to another the length of the bar till he arrived at the door of the Gents beside the pool table. He lurched towards that door, apparently intending to push it open, when it was pulled back from within and Big Donald filled the doorway.

Ushan's disorganised movement carried him heavily forward and his head butted Donald in the face. Donald grabbed him by some clothing and, straightening a great arm, hurled him backwards hard so that he fell, arms and legs flailing, on top of one of the visiting team, one Charlie Strachan – known as 'a hard man' – to be treated with care. Charlie was bent low over the table, chin on the cue, sighting to make a stroke. Suddenly the whole group at the table coalesced in a furious scrum, blows flying indiscriminately – feet, fists, cues, bottles.

As far as I could see, all of them belonged to the visiting team.

"I suppose," Donald observed afterwards, "it looked as if we had prearranged it all! Och but I really *was* there by chance."

"You certainly put the match to the gunpowder," I said.

Donald made his way down the length of the bar to keep his rendezvous with me.

I moved to a window on the left of the porch and looked into the dimly lit tea-room. Some confused movement there had caught my eye. A separate fight was in progress; I recognised George Macfarlane, Peter Maclean, Matthew Maclellan and about a dozen other local young men. All the tables had been knocked over except one that was stacked with crockery. In a corner just inside the door was a great glass-fronted juke-box. By a strange chance both the table and the juke-box remained immune.

Donald seemed relieved to see me, and a shade surprised too. The tumult inside the bar came nearer. The inner doors burst open to disgorge Ushan and two others grappling with him. They crashed through the outer glass panels of the porch, and thudded on to the ground outside, still contending blindly like great beasts. Badly cut as they must have been, oblivious to everything but the driving fury, they pounded away, knee, fist, boot and head. A few seconds later, as if separation could not be borne, the rest of the Garroch men emerged, crashed through the remaining glass in the same manner, and the battle on the ground enlarged itself.

Charlie Strachan rose up from the scrum dragging Ushan with him. To break free, Ushan delivered a blow to the groin with his knee, and as Strachan doubled up in pain and his head came forward, the knee came up quickly again and thudded against his chin. Blood spurted from Strachan's mouth. He recovered quickly and seized Ushan by the shoulders to 'gie him the heid' – the classic movement of the in-fighter when he pulls the opponent towards him to add force to the terrible collision between head and face. Ushan screamed in agony as he fell back, nose broken, mouth open, choking for breath.

Donald drew me further into the shadow. "Aye – I'm sorry right enough! But it's better it should work itself out that way."

Talking about it the following day, he was especially pleased with one thing. "Och we kept oor ain folk oot of it, as ye saw?"

"You were prepared?"

"Och no, no' really! We had some different ways thocht oot right enough. We had tae improvise a bit once we saw how they were goin' aboot it."

"You seemed to know what they came for?"

Thoughtfully he said, "Aye – there's many interests comin' taegether on this one. Nae names nae pack-drill! As ye know, the main reason they didna' gie Bill Walsh the Sunday licence was 'distur-rbance'? Aye – well, distur-rbance is bad for property values! An' whose interest is tied up there? Och it's the incomers an' the ither folk who've bought up oor houses as holiday homes – as investments. An' then again, them other incomers, the business interests behind the Garroch holiday development scheme, stand tae gain if the Inn here gets closed doon or at least restricted. An' who could ever prove it was the Garroch men – or us – creatin' the distur-rbance?"

I saw how George, careful George, had played his part in keeping the separate, local scrap simmering away all by itself in the tea-room. He had done his duty.

"How did you manage to get George involved in that other fight? He is such a prudent fellow. I never saw him as a fighting man."

"Och I don' know! He can stand up for himself right enough. Och anyway, what's important the noo is that *you* – someone standin' right ootside every interest – *you* witnessed what happened! *You* saw that the folk who created the distur-rbance were the raiding party from Garroch. Aye! Raiding party's the right word for it."

Standing there watching the violence was disturbing. I had no stomach for it. Would no one intervene?

"What's Bill doing?" I asked Donald. "Surely he could have put them out earlier? Before they were as far gone as this?"

Donald shrugged. He seemed to be awaiting some other development.

"Of course," I added, observing him, "they might have turned on *him*! And then you people would have got drawn into a general fight, what you didn't want. All the same, where *is* he?"

"Och I think he got accidentally locked in somewhere. I think in his toilet. Aye – there he is! He's got out at last."

Walsh advanced purposefully through the bar room, in the rolling gait of the burly man. He must once have been fairly strong. Now, in his fifties, he had run to fat. He bulged out of his corduroys and fisherman's patterned sweater. The round open face that usually radiated bonhomie and invited the world to share it, was full of hurt and anxiety.

Donald said, "He was goin' tae put them oot. Anyway he got sidetracked! Och it's just as well. Bill's nae match fer scrappers like Charlie Strachan there. That was the last thing we wanted tae see. No, this way is better."

Walsh emerged and came miserably to a halt before the jagged great hole in the glass, a baggy, crumpled silhouette in the shaft of orange light streaming behind him from the door. Framed in the splintered glazing bars hanging askew, oppressed into silence, he stared out into the dark.

The savagery seemed to impinge on him slowly.

"My God!" he cried, and rushed out, arms outstretched: "Stop! Stop! You'll kill him – stop!"

He seized Charlie Strachan by the arm and tried to drag him away, Ushan sprawled beneath, bloody, mouth gaping, only partly conscious. Strachan knelt upon him, totally enclosed in fury, remorselessly raising a fist on high and thudding it down.

"Come on now – leave off! Leave off!" Walsh looked up desperately. "Help me someone! Help me!"

Gasping for breath, he appealed to the figures framed in the lighted doorways a few yards away. "Please help me! It is your public duty to help. Please!"

From his tone he did not expect much; he was appealing to the enemy. No one moved.

Strachan, straightening suddenly and turning as he rose, swung a fist and caught Walsh a glancing blow on the bridge of the nose. Had he delivered it full on, the consequences might have been serious. Walsh let out a despairing yelp, staggered backwards, and would have struck the back of his neck on an edge of broken glass left in the frame had not Donald sprung forward and caught him and hauled him into our shadowed corner.

It was lucky for the brawlers, especially for Ushan, who was in danger of suffocating in his own blood, that someone had earlier phoned the police station some twenty miles away. Whoever it was – no one will say but I think it was Donald – had timed the call well.

The caller had either been miraculously specific or the police knew from experience what they would have to deal with, for they came well prepared – a patrol car, a van and an ambulance.

Their headlights flooded the Inn yard with blinding white light at the very moment when Strachan, possibly wondering how Walsh had dis-

appeared into thin air, was turning, like a bloodstained ministrant in the inferno, to inflict further torment on the prostrate Ushan.

I spotted Angus Logie and Mary returning. He moved purposefully but with difficulty, for she was using all her weight to hold him back. They approached from the direction of the southern end of the bay where he lives in a caravan on Donald's croft, beyond the War Memorial. On the way there, next to the lifeboat station, is Mary's little granite house.

I have heard a sly aside in the Inn questioning how often she sleeps there alone. But apart from drunken speculation, no open comment. Too many people are vulnerable. Mary is unquestionably respectable.

In any case, so few people feeling secure, the glen prefers the euphemism. It is thought better, for example, to say of a woman, that she is so-and-so's 'common law wife' than that she is 'living with' so-and-so. 'Living with' confers no status. Worse, it takes status away.

Jemima, Duncan Macpherson's wife – they have the croft next along the road to the village from my cottage – gave me a sample of such talk and a glimpse of the visions behind it. They are pillars of the Free Church, sincere, good living people. I enjoy my talks with them, and exchange a word with one or other most days as I pass. She was speaking of Willie Davis, another wandering handyman who has come to rest in the glen. Among other things he helps with boats and fishing and in the bar during the visitor season.

"He came here the other day with the Mountain Rescue Team. It was while you were away."

"Was there a climber lost here? That's unusual."

"Och no!" she laughed shyly, a big girl's busty laugh, "one of our sheep! It got stuck on that ledge up there." She pointed to a crag on Beinn à Shellach. "It's quite dangerous. They say Willie's very good at it."

She blushed unaccountably and added, "It was sad, really, seeing the poor beast up there all that time, getting weaker and weaker."

"How long?"

"Ten days."

"Without food?"

"Aye! They wanted it to get weak. So it wouldn't struggle."

Still blushing a little, she bent her head, retreating into one of her silences, her broad pale face hidden under her dark hair.

"Willie's just moved in tae one of Bill Walsh's bungalows," she said meditatively.

"He's not married, is he?"

To my surprise she grinned mischievously. "Och it's no' too easy tae know such things round here sometimes!"

I smiled too. But for a different reason. After nearly four months, living so near, meeting more or less daily, the ice breaking at last.

I said, "He seems a fairly solitary chap?"

"Yes – and no."

She looked up now, her dark eyes still absorbed in the distant thoughts that always held her.

She went on, "Aye – these mountaineering folk *are* a bit like that. Chummy together. Men together." She bent her head as if to retreat again, but looked up and said, with a shy twinkle, "Och they say he's irresistible tae women!"

Willie Davis is tall, rangy, about forty-five, with shaggy brown hair down to his shoulders. His smooth, pink, girlish face bears a long scar, relic of a climbing fall. He has long arms, and shambles rather than walks. His spatulate fingers, stained from chain-smoking, have blackened fingernails.

She seemed to expect a comment.

I said, "Can *you* see it?"

She laughed. "Och it must be so if they say it, I suppose."

I thought of asking who *they* were but thought better of it. I could guess. Women such as Agnes Macalister for one, a brawny woman of about forty who once rode five miles on her creaky bicycle to 'help' Phyllis Morton do the weekly cleaning in my cottage and to study my books and papers; and who once told Isobel Mackay, the headmistress, entirely seriously, that she would burn in hell for teaching biology in a manner that questioned Holy Writ.

I said, "Why did Willie have to move? He'd lived a long time in that cottage on Donald's croft?"

"Aye. But young Jamie – ye know, Donald's boy – is tae be married soon, and Donald had tae put Willie oot so that Jamie could have it. Aye – I don't think Willie's too pleased about that, for he did so much tae it in the years he was there – put in running water, and a bathroom and toilet and so on. Still, I don't suppose he was paying much rent for it."

She retreated again into meditation, studying her left hand.

She is a big woman. Her eyes are deep, dark, sometimes smouldering with a fire that is belied by her pattern of slow, controlled, seemingly placid movement. She was standing against the Aga cooker in a frilly apron. She spoke with a little sigh. "Aye, ye were asking was Willie married. Well, all I know is he usually seems to live as a married man!"

She stifled a wicked laugh, covering her mouth with a broad hand, displaying the thick wedding ring.

"Where does he get them from? There aren't any single women in the glen, are there? Apart from Morag, I suppose?"

"No-o, I suppose not. Well, there's Mary Menzies, but she's different."

She retreated again.

No one dares classify Mary's relationship with Angus. To do so could endanger her job and the peace of mind of the glen. She is reasonably well liked. However, like her or not they have to trust her, and protect her. As district nurse she knows the inwardness of too many lives. There might be danger in offending her, or worse still losing her. As long as she remains here, and the connecting strands of prudence and mutual forbearance hold fast, confidences are safe. Her predecessor was here for forty years.

Mary is from Glasgow. Her maternal grandmother came from Kintail, not too far away.

"You didn't know Angus when you came here?" I once asked her.

"Och no! I didn't know anybody. It was really quite lonely for the first year or so."

"A strange decision? A young woman. Attractive. Burying yourself?"

"Och it wasna' like that! I knew I would do it one day. Ever since I was a little girl and Granny used to tell us stories of the old life in the Highlands. I didna' feel I had any roots in Glasgow. Och it seemed a worth while thing to do. I'm glad I made the decision to come here."

"Because of Angus?"

I had met her at the shop, and we were walking along the road in the direction of her house. She is one of the very few who walk. Her little car is often left outside someone's house because, emerging from a visit, she has rushed absently away on foot. As we came to the War Memorial she halted and turned to it. After a silence she murmured, "I always stop and think about *her*."

With yearning, with adoration, she regarded the bronze figure kneeling up there, imploring, naked, attached. Of this place.

The wind was sharp. It blew taut the red and yellow ribbon tied to the laurel wreath poised above the soldier's bonnet. Always renewed, the ribbon is about two feet long. It is knotted to the bronze circlet held in the hand of the winged figure. Even when there is no wind – so rarely here! – the ribbon moves gently, responding to the breathing of the sea and the earth. As if breathing with it, the bronze figures beneath seem never entirely still.

Mary dabbed her eyes with a handkerchief, pretending the wind had brought a tear.

She said at last, "Och no, my feeling about being here is nothing to do with Angus. It would have been the same for me whoever it was. Or nobody even. Can you understand that? I think of *belonging*."

She put the handkerchief to her eyes again.

"I feel I knew that woman up there long before I came to this place. Does that sound crazy?"

We stood looking up at the dark, supplicant figure, whose flowing body, even in the inert metal, spoke of life, warmth, hope. The meaning of that posture, the uplifted hands, seemed plain, yet a continuing magnet-

ism drew my thoughts further and further into the enigma smouldering
within it. I said, "We all knew her. We know her still."

She gave a little start, looked at me quickly with a questioning frown,
turned away. She said, "When I stand here looking up at her like this I feel
I belong."

One day, at Duncan Macpherson's house, the talk turned to 'belonging'. Just as it is not possible, with incomers, to avoid the subject of 'them
and us', so with locals the word 'incomer' must crop up.

Duncan likes his dram in the early evening, after he has washed, eaten
the heavy meal he calls his 'tea' and can stretch his feet in red knitted
slippers towards the log fire in the great stone fireplace. He does not drink
seriously, as that would be understood in the Inn – where he never goes.
Still, sometimes when the talk excites him he takes a dram or two 'extra'
and becomes uplifted, as he puts it.

He is tall and spare, with thick iron grey hair, and great steady blue
eyes.

He said, "Och how can they talk of *belonging* here? It doesna' make
sense! There are two ways – and two only – someone can *belong* here. If ye
were born here *and* the generations before ye *or* if ye came here and
married someone who *was*."

"Tell me," I asked him, "what proportion of the people who live in the
glen now were born here?"

"We can count them on oor fingers!" He added pawkily, "Och we'll no'
count the children, only the grown-ups."

"Of course."

"All right. We'll start at this hoose and then go North and work our way
round. Shouldna' take long."

He began running through names on his fingers.

"Wait a minute." Jemima got up and went to a cupboard. "We've still
got that voters' roll. I was helping the doctor when he was returning officer
at the elections."

"Aye all right," he said, "that'll make it easier. We can tick off the
names on the roll. All the same I *could* do the lot on my fingers, believe you
me."

Jemima said gently, "A bit more than that maybe. Och but not that
many more anyway."

It did not take them long.

"There ye are," he said, eyes shining, "ninety-two people – oot o' 1,012
on the roll."

He added, "Aye, and a fair few of them are elderly folk, as ye must
know by now."

His mood darkened. "How can these incomers talk of belonging?
Belonging to what? We are the last survivors. God alone knows how we – I

50

mean oor forbears – managed to cling on here through the clearances! The people were turned out literally on to the heather! Whole families – old people, widows, the sick, the children – put oot with their sticks o' belongings. Nowhere to go; just watch the factor's men pull the walls o' their hooses doon. Some died out there on the hill. Some lived for a time on the shoreline in caves, eating soup made from nettles! They died or went away. Some emigrated. Some went South to the cities. Look out there." He pointed to the upper reaches of the glen. "Ye see those patches of flat ground on the lower slopes?"

I had often wondered about those tiny pieces of levelled ground bitten out of the hillsides. At a central point, on the river bank, stand the walls of a substantial building, the old mill.

"Aye, each one o' them empty plots meant a house and a family! That mill was at the heart o' a sizeable village. That's what I mean when I say *we* are the survivors. I often wonder what my forbears did to pay for their escape from the factor's men! It saddens the heart to think aboot it. Terrible things were done – just tae buy someone's favour and be among the lucky few *chosen*, yes chosen, to keep your roof and your bit o' sustenance."

"Och Duncan, don't say such things," Jemima protested.

"Och dear, some things have to be said – sometimes – so that we willna' forget! *Something* must have been paid, *some* price, tae be left in your home when everyone around ye was being turned out on tae the hillside. We know the kind of thing. A daughter, or a wife, slept with the factor, or the laird – who knows? Other favours, other things were done – bloody ones. Aye – it was a wild time. If only those stones out there could speak! But a price was paid every time, you can depend on it. What can *we* do about it? We mustna' pretend it didna' happen! We must live with the knowledge."

He turned to me. "Have another dram with me. Go on! This subject always churns me up." He drank and drew in his lips angrily. "And *they* talk about *belonging* here! I ask ye? What is there left here for them tae belong *to*?"

Quietly, he added, "Or for *us* tae belong to?"

Mary had spoken wistfully, renewing the dream, protecting it.

Belonging. Somewhere.

And when the dream can no longer sustain you – what then?

About thirty, Mary is small and sturdy, with broad features, high colouring, long tawny hair usually arranged in plaits wound round her head. She presents herself as tough, a protective aura.

Like Doctor Boddie, and the school-teachers Isobel Mackay, Betty Vallance and Jessie Thoms, her official position insulates her. And isolates her.

As Isobel once put it, "We can never be 'locals' and we are not incomers. We are simply *the* teacher! *The* doctor! *The* district nurse! You see, in theory our masters can post us away from here tomorrow! We *could* be here for the rest of our lives – my predecessor spent her whole teaching career here. But we shall still be neither one thing nor the other."

I said to Mary, "Angus doesn't belong here either. So few do."

"I *know* that." She said it with impatience.

Prosaically she added, "His people came from Fife."

The irrelevance nettled her. She rushed on, "It's – oh, it's hard to explain. It's the Highlands. Life is *closer* to you here, the real things of life, I mean. Ye feel ye know *who* ye are. Yes, that's it. Ye have tae *belong* tae know who ye are."

Glasgow and the other cities nourish their pockets of nostalgia. Alas for these Highlanders, and Highlanders in spirit! The glen – and many another glen – sings a siren song.

Angus had tried to do his chivalrous duty. He had escorted Mary away from the fight, out of danger, intending to return quickly for vengeance and for the ardent fulfilment of a fight. But Mary had frustrated him. Distressed now for him, she was intent on stopping him. She pulled at him, dug her heels in, tried to hang dead weight on him.

The scene drew me back to Glasgow in the old days. I had seen it so many times, a woman doing exactly that, trying to stop her man going to the pub, usually without success.

Angus insisted, dragging her along behind him. Her loosened hair streamed about her in the night breeze.

"Oh Angus, Angus! *Please* come away. Don't go back there! Don't! You'll get hurt for nothing. Oh Angus!"

They were only a few paces from the Inn yard when the police head-lights filled the street with white light. Angus stopped. Quickly she turned him about like a sad child and led him slowly away.

Donald spoke close to my ear. "Go please! *Now*. At once! Don't be seen. Go that way. Quickly!"

He pointed to a dark area at the back, along the edge of the knoll, where boats loomed – high, dark shapes, laid up on cradles.

The police vehicles entered the yard with a throaty crescendo of engine noise, rattle and bang of car doors, shouts of command. The cries of battle were superseded by resentful snarls and curses as the fighters were separated, soon dominated by police voices, solidly confident, jaded, impatient, concerned.

"Och come on now Charlie, ye're in trouble enough already, man. Och no ye don't. Ye know what ye get for assaultin' a police officer!"

"Och now this young lad *is* in a mess. Better get him away in the ambulance. Quickly now!"

I glanced back. Donald knocked at a window of the tea-room, a sharp treble knock. The rough and tumble inside stopped. George Macfarlane and the rest seemed to take but a moment to put the room to rights. They straightened their clothes and hair, lit up cigarettes, and stood chatting amiably.

At the back of the Inn stone steps lead down to a narrow causeway that crosses the gently sloping shingle at low water – as it now was – and gives access, on the other side of the little basin, to an incurving spit that forms a protected mooring.

In the gleam from the sea I could pick my way without using my torch. I climbed to the top of the spit, turned to the left and crunched along the gravel surface to where it joined the shore road near the War Memorial a few hundred yards from the Inn. The noises from there, thinned by distance and the night air, were here overborne by the insistent surge and murmur of the sea.

I climbed up on to the levelled promontory and stood in the shadow of the Memorial figures. I needed to hear other, eternal voices.

I contemplated the dim outlines of the mountains against the cold stars, great sad figures leaning their heavy heads meditatively across the dark world.

I thought again of Jamie Macleod speaking of the old Highlands and the men going off on their forays. Donald had referred to the Garroch men as a 'raiding party'. Had things changed so little? Were the old currents of feeling the same as they had ever been? Were they flowing as strongly as in those far off days?

True they were now mixed with other, 'foreign' influences, with the calculations of businessmen like the Garroch financiers, like Harry Heslop. Yet surely these had done no more than deflect, not change, the deep need of the spirit still cherished in the glen by the true inheritors, to affirm a special identity in the stirring of the blood?

Someone once said, perhaps cynically, that a high point of English genius in Scotland was the channelling away of this energy in raising the Highland regiments. Violent action of some kind might be necessary for its fulfilment, who knows? Yet the essential need is what it had always been; loyalties, crude or not, that uplifted the heart. That primordial hunger retains its driving power. It is still near the surface, too near perhaps. The pity of it is that it can be so readily manipulated, if Donald is right, and steered to meretricious fulfilment in squalid forays like this one.

At the Inn a heavy vehicle started up and trundled out of the yard. The ambulance. There was much excited talking. People must be competing to give the police their separate versions of the 'disturbance'. I wondered what Harry Heslop's would be.

I walked slowly back along the road. To get to my Land-Rover I had to pass the Inn. I did not want to be caught up in that clamour of self-interested evidence.

I too had been manipulated. Thinking back, I saw that I had been more than half aware of it. I had no one but myself to blame. Donald himself had been a little surprised to see me keep the rendezvous.

Was it simply the confidence of hindsight, or had I too foreseen tonight's enactments? Yes, I had foreseen them, more or less. Why then had I come? And, having foreseen them, how could I be impartial?

As for testimony, I would have to give it. I would have to say what I had seen.

But let it not be tonight.

I was sad at heart.

Lost in thought I must have shut out a dim awareness of low voices in the darkness ahead of me. The winding road here passes through a defile between a huge rock and the steep mountain-side. It then follows the curve of the little bay past the Church of Scotland and the Inn to reach the street. At the far end of that were the Village Hall and my vehicle.

In the deep shadows of the defile I stumbled into Angus and Mary, and realised it must have been the murmur of their voices I had heard. He was slumped against the rock, disconsolate. She stood in front of him, between him and the direction of the Inn. They were totally engrossed.

She said, "Angus, you couldn't do anything! It's all over and done with. I'm glad I stopped you when I did. You'd only have got taken by the polis. I don't care what the likes of him says."

"Ah still can't understand how somebody managed to bundle us out like that! Ah wasna' as drunk as all that, was ah? Och if only ah'd stayed! Ah could have smashed him – the filthy little f . . ."

Had I walked straight past them I doubt if they would have noticed. But I couldn't.

"I'm sorry," I said, "I didn't see you. I was thinking . . ."

"Look who's here!" Angus seemed to brighten up. "Where did *you* spring from?"

"I was outside the Inn," I said. "I came away when the police and the ambulance arrived. I came round the back way. I saw most of what happened from outside."

"Ah had to get Mary oot, ye see?" he said thickly, protecting his honour, "but ah wish ah *had* got back there in time to smash his face in."

He was appealing for comfort.

"You mean Ushan?"

"Aye."

"What did he do?"

"Don't say it," she pleaded. "It doesn't matter now. It really doesn't."

He turned his back to her as if to shield her from his words. He needed to tell me – anyone.

He said, "He came up behind Mary as she was standing at the bar with me and he . . ."

"No, Angus. Please!" Mary said, her voice trembling, "He didn't really touch me! It was – oh, it was the idea of him! Oh, it doesn't matter what people like him think?"

She needed to make it prosaic, something belonging to her alone, to her vision of herself – *her* vision of the world. In doing so she could remain in possession of herself. To let *him* do battle for her, give him the heroic role, would be to give him suzerainty over her. Her dream of 'belonging' did not include that ancient ingredient. She could not go that far.

To find that she could not do so must have come as a shock; it was out of keeping with her dream of herself as 'belonging' here – a woman of the glen more or less like any other.

Angus shifted position. He put his shoulders full against the rock and stared straight past us.

Because she had forced his heroic anger back in upon itself, he chose to stand alone, keeping his spirit, his honour, pure. For him, reaching out to 'belong' here too, the old tradition is strong – the woman feeds her man's masculine image. In him, over and over again, the old heroes must be reborn. That, for him, is part of the atavistic dream that draws him on like a shining light in the mist. In it he too is reborn. He 'belongs'.

He is a big man, about forty-five, with ice-blue eyes, fair hair turning grizzled and receding, large hands. It is his habit to speak the rough Glasgow 'twang' but he changes to normal speech from time to time and back again, perhaps to suit his mood or his company. Behind the rough diamond exterior there resides a certain simplicity, a softness that yearns for an answering voice.

He is another of that strange fraternity, the old campaigners of mountaineering, that has wandered into the glen. One day I asked him, teasingly, "What happens to professional mountaineers when they get too old to climb? Do they, like old soldiers, simply fade away?"

"They become teachers at outdoor schools," he answered with complete seriousness. "You know, by an odd coincidence all of us ex-mountaineers in the glen were once on the staff of the same outdoor school! Though not at the same time. I only found that out when I came here."

He thought again, and went on, "After a time at that sort of work you realise if you've got any sense that you're getting too old even for teaching the basic techniques up on the rocks. You get rusty, you know, creaky! No longer as precise and sure in movement and clear in assessment of problems and methodical in the execution of manoeuvres as you should be.

And then one day you have to say to yourself, 'If I go on like this I will have an accident and maybe involve other people in it as well!' I've seen a few accidents on mountains. Aye! Ah've got a few dead ones down an' some who'll never be the same again! Well, at that point some of us pack it in and take to the road. We are restless souls. We need to feel free! So, some of us end up in places like this as 'handymen', turning our hands to the odd jobs of life!"

He said it with an edge of bitterness, but added quickly, "At least you can try to be your own true self here, out of the rat race."

He went on, the bitterness now tinged with envy, "Some of them, take Duncan Burke, for example, with his boat hire and marine equipment business and I don't know how many other enterprises, and Adrian Templer with his arts and crafts workshop, have really turned themselves into businessmen pure and simple. They've sold themselves to the capital- ist system even though they continue to talk like socialists. Mind you, Adrian was a renegade from the upper class to begin with, so I suppose you can't count him. He has simply reverted."

No one knows much about Angus, or indeed about any of the incomers. They maintain a rule, as used to be said of the French Foreign Legion, 'You do not enquire about someone's past.'

They have no past, only a search for a lost present.

He belongs to a visionary Socialist tradition that grew up on Clydeside and other industrial areas, which links emancipation with a 'communion' – the only word for it – on the high crags and peaks, in sharing danger, linkage of thought, necessary care for each other, closeness of bodies in bivouac, camp and hut, sweat, earthiness. He remarked once, "There's no such thing as class on the mountain."

The tradition contains, too, an association of ideas with the tang of battle, the mind of soldiering. The very language of mountaineering has the military ring: 'reconnoitring', 'assault route', 'attack on the moun- tain's defences' and reference to the mountain itself as an enemy to be outwitted if not defeated.

There is also a feeling, perhaps the strongest, of moving out to the fringe of nature, there to refresh one's vision. On the mountain, the nearest savage frontier, the dedicated ones search among the elemental forces for a dreamed of essence of being, a lost starting point for a purer pilgrimage.

Angus and Mary were silent. No one approached the defile. All the life of the glen seemed to centre upon the events at the Inn. We stood joined together in the darkness, casting about among our separate thoughts.

Angus said, grumbling aloud, "I still can't understand how I came to be bundled out. I don't think it could have been the Garroch men."

I knew. But how could I say it? Donald had done it. The glen folk wanted this to be their *own* affair. In a delicate issue like this, when they

56

had even contrived to segregate their own younger men – to allow an incomer to fight for the honour of the glen would have been to diminish their own heroic image of themselves. Angus would not understand this. He would see this as a declaration that he did not 'belong'. And he would be right.

Dimly, I fancied, he perceived this, just as he understood, in his heart, that his 'belonging' was a myth of his own creation. And Mary had denied him the 'right' to fight for *her* honour! Her action, it would seem to him, underlined the verdict of the glen.

They were both silent now. The evening's events, though extraneous to them in origin, had shaken them both, in ways they needed time to understand.

I said, "I must be getting on. I'll say good night."

"Oh please stay!" she breathed.

"Aye, don't go!" he rumbled, relieved too. "Och I don't know what's happened to us – to everything. That business has changed something. No, stay with us for a bit. We'll go to my cottage! Let's forget about the lot of them! Come on!"

"No – no, come to my house," she pleaded. "I'll make some tea! If we go to Angus's it'll only be another dram and he's had more than enough for tonight!"

"Aye," he said sombrely, "maybe ah have at that."

They needed me as insulation, from each other and from themselves. Each needed to be alone, but not yet.

We turned and walked back, away from the Inn. The police were still there, and I was not sorry to have an excuse for not passing by there just yet.

We walked in silence. Ahead, seeming to rise up out of the enclosing sea, the lighthouse stolidily swung its probes of light through the night; two long white beams held fast across the wrinkled water, then a short green flash. We were a mile or so away from that headland that marked the limit of the curve of the great outer bay. As the white beam completed its swing over our heads its fleeting radiance outlined the coastguard radar station and the nearby white lifeboat shed.

Here, I reflected, lay yet another strand in this complex knot of conflict. It was in this southern part of the wider bay that Bill Walsh planned to build a yacht marina, as part of a grand design for an international holiday resort, complete with helicopter pad to bring the jet travellers from Inverness. Later he would have a landing strip for his own feeder aircraft. If he were to get even a nucleus of enterprises under way here, he could begin to draw the market to him, and the Garroch interest, with similar plans in train, would stand to lose heavily.

Again Mary picked up my thoughts. She said, "I have been wondering why this happened *tonight*. It wasn't by chance, you know? I am sure of that."

"Wasn't it?" Angus took it up. "Maybe I did have a few drams too many then! What do you mean?"

"Oh, I happen to know," she said airily, needling him, "that the Garroch company wants to develop a yacht marina there too. If they can get the opposition built up against Bill Walsh's plans here, they hope to force him to abandon this scheme and sell up and go. And then they'll have a clear field!"

"How do you know all that?" Angus asked suspiciously.

I said, "It seems to be an open secret." She looked at me gratefully.

"You mean," Angus said, oddly slow in his thinking, "the whole performance tonight, the fight and so on, was a put-up job?"

"Och I don't know," she said, going into retreat. "You know there's been a lot of disturbance in the last few months?"

"Aye, there has been. But I thought . . ." He broke off and was silent, then exclaimed, "I see now. Good God in Heaven! I see."

"What?" she asked cautiously.

"Yes! God curse the lot of them."

"What?" she asked again.

"There's no escape then," he muttered angrily.

"From what?" She turned and faced him. "What?"

"Yes, I see it now! The bloody capitalists and the church lot always do get together! The local property owners and the incomer investors are in it too. It all comes together, don't ye see?"

"I don't see it, Angus, I must say," she said.

"It must be that! It must be. The whole thing adds up to a dirty united front!"

"Why should you get worked up about it?" she said evenly, going against him still. "It is the way of the world! Why should *you* care about Bill Walsh's interests? *He* doesn't belong here any more than you do. He's been here a shorter time than most of the incomers if it comes to that!"

"Don't rub it in about not belonging, Mary," he admonished her gently. "And it's not Bill's interests I care about particularly either. I feel like this because even in this out of the way place we can't feel free. The f . . . . . . capitalist bastards! The forces of religion and capital working together, feeding on the ignorance and primitive loyalties of the working class!"

"Oh, Angus, it isn't as complicated as that surely? It is simply business! And why shouldn't people do the best they can for themselves? And loyalties? Oh surely we need *them*! Badly. There will be always good and bad in us – and we need loyalties, a sense of *belonging*, to show us the difference. Without that we are *nothing*!"

58

Four

Incomers and dreamers

Cruachan Castle, built under a lower cliff of Beinn à Shellach, dominates a gorge of the river, the Allt à Shellach. It stands on the opposite side of the glen to where, on the slopes of Beinn Dhu somewhat higher, General Wade pushed through his road to be free of the gorge and to dominate it if necessary.

Sited where the glen opens out to the flat land and the sea, Cruachan held a strategic position on the ancient drove road that came through here and then wandered on over the saddle of Beinn à Shellach and made for the south: for here was the first suitable watering-place for cattle as the drovers made their way inland after the strenuous sea crossing.

Standing at this spot one can see how a band of determined fighting men, skilfully deployed, could have dominated this once important trade route, and when necessary destroyed more powerful forces. It would have been simple to trap sizeable herds of cattle here and hold the drovers to ransom.

Levying tribute in such a fashion on the trade that passed his gates, the Wolf of Cruachan grew rich, fed and armed a formidable company, and built up a power.

In its heyday the great keep was joined with a high wall that formed a large protected area well able to accommodate booty of cattle, as well as retainers, their families and chattels, horses and other beasts in the recurrent troubled times. The wall is now visible only as a line of raised verdure. It comes down the steep bank to the water, which here forms a wide pool, clear, sparkling, that ripples with the force of the tumbling stream above. At the seaward end, the outflow falls away through a screen of huge boulders into a muddy delta where it mixes with incoming sea water.

The formidable building itself is in fair condition. No one can say when it was last lived in. For many years it has served as a dry store – hay, potatoes, logs, fencing and building materials, farm implements, spare house furnishings. Perhaps as a result of such thrifty usage it is one of the best preserved examples of this type of Scottish stronghold.

Now, after passing through several ownerships in the last two hundred years, it has come into Robert Wallace's hands with a parcel of land he has recently added to his croft holdings.

One day I stood at the side of the military road, contemplating the square grey keep across the glen. Robert drove up. He was returning from work in the forestry plantation and the rear of his little car was packed with logs, small off-cuts and loppings.

March was well advanced and the days were longer. The capricious weather smiled and frowned. Rain clouds rolled across the glen, slipped low into the folds of rock and down towards the road, then as suddenly wafted away and a weak sun shone through.

The river was in spate. It grumbled and clattered in the echoing ravine at my feet.

"Penny for your thoughts," he said.

"The Wolf of Cruachan. You are his latter-day successor!"

"Aye. What a thought!" He laughed a little shyly. "Still, I do sometimes think about him and his times. Yes, especially his times. Some things were a lot easier. You knew where you *belonged*. Your place was set in the order of life. And that told you what you had to aim for. I mean as a person, the sort of person you should try to be. And on the whole the common people kept to those rules. Now these signposts are down. You don't know where to fix your sights any more. Aye! You don't know what to do for the best – for your peace of mind as well as for your stomach. So it's not really freedom at all."

He stood for some moments studying, with the critical detachment of the proprietor, the great stone walls.

He said, "You know, I suppose I shouldn't say it, but I sometimes say to myself: 'If only I could use that place half as profitably as he did.' As things are I do get a bit irritated sometimes, when the visitors go clattering through the place when I'm wanting to get at my stores or do some work there. Still, they always have been free to go through there."

"You could make a little money out of the building itself – an admission fee?"

"Out of that!"

"Lots of owners of historic buildings do it. Why shouldn't you do the same?"

"You mean I should stand at a little gate there and take money for them to go round the place?"

"Perhaps not you personally. Maybe your wife could? But who actually takes the money is not really the point."

He lifted a foot on to a bit of the broken roadside wall, and leaned on his knee, looking across. His denim trousers had so many holes worn in them they could have been hit by a charge of shot.

"Och it doesna' seem right," he smiled ruefully, "to take money from people without doing anything for it. It's difficult to put into words. I wouldn't be – how shall I put it? – proving myself. It wouldn't be money that had anything to do with *me*. And there's something else. Simply by accident, Cruachan is on my land. But any value it may have is because of its history, the memories and associations attached to it, and these things are the property of the people – the ordinary people – who *belong* here. How could I turn all that into profit for my own pocket? How could I look folk in the face if I were to do that?"

It was some weeks since we had talked seriously about a way forward. We had met in the interim, at the shop, by the wayside as we had now, and passed the time of day. I had a feeling, this time, that he would reopen the subject.

He said at last, "I've been giving a lot of thought to the talk we had that time at my new house. You remember?"

"Yes."

"I've decided that the bakery idea is not for me. It's hard to explain. Ye see, I came back tae the glen tae make a living as a crofter, a man of the land. So I want to look for ways of making a living *from* the land."

Did this mean that he really was thinking and planning, or was it an excuse for inaction? They had given me so many.

I said, "Whatever you do has to be your choice. But you must do something. Time is running out for the glen."

"You know," he said after a silence, "how the glen's been full of talk about community co-operatives recently?"

"Yes."

"What do you think of the idea?"

I know that look by now, seemingly innocent but keenly observant. The locals never tire of the game of 'Will you trip up this time?' or 'Can we get a rise out of you?' You, the outsider. It is like the children's game of trying to catch the grown-up off guard; except that this one is deadly serious. However well they might know you, the probing and the search continues, the recurring test will be sprung on you.

That other voice, heard beneath their words, speaks to you in a minor key. Fail this test and our faith is lost yet again. Faith in you, in our judgment of you, of anyone. And who can blame us, then, for closing in on ourselves once more, strengthening our grudges, bending to the wind but holding fast, scanning our stars?

The question itself, like this one, is seemingly straightforward. The subtlety and the danger are in how they read the tea-leaves of your answer. Are you with us or against us? Have you shades of motive that do not have our interests at heart? The tea-leaves or the answer? In my melancholy moments I feel that the tea-leaves concern them the more.

With us or against us? What does 'with us' mean? To answer that I need to know where they want to go. Murdo Macfarlane warned me that to seek that knowledge has its perils. 'If you succeed we will never forgive you!'

Why should they fear that discovery? Did they nurse some secret resolve so awesome that it must never be uncovered?

Murdo, that steady old campaigner, does not utter empty words. In all this seeming inertia, fatalism, righteous maintenance of old fires, pride, grudges, is there a dreadful determination concealed? 'We live life *our* way – or not at all!' After us, failing a miracle, nothing. We, the true local folk, will not – in our hearts – ever compromise. And we despise those who do. We will go down if necessary, but we will not make ourselves over into another kind of people and take on another emotional life – which is what matters to us – as the price of survival.

Could that be the truth I must not uncover? Have they placed too high a price on retaining their identity, their view of themselves? Inescapably committed to it, all lesser offers cannot save them from the abyss?

Malcolm Macgrath, restless, kindly spirit, has more faith than most. For him it is not a matter of silently holding on, with the old values tightly enclosed and inaccessible. He fights, quietly and strongly, to reinspire the *will* to turn to them, be united with them, once more.

Malcolm has a croft of his own. He combines work on it with his job as local road maintenance man, filling in pot-holes, mending retaining walls and fences, clearing ditches and other minor repairs. Partly because the task demands special vigilance but also because of his own sensitive personality, he moves through the glen like a benevolent spirit, sensing every shift in affairs, every change in attitude, receptive, sympathetic.

His narrow red road-roller, and the trailer carrying the tar boiler, announce his presence from afar.

Inevitably he can never be abreast of the work. The great timber lorries thunder through with loads many times heavier than Wade's engineers ever dreamt of; it surprises me that this humble single track retains any level tarmac at all. Today he was working on the pot-hole near the old Church of Scotland manse, at a bend where the surface never remains whole for very long.

I last saw him a few days ago at the annual general meeting of the Community Council.

"What were your impressions of the meeting?" I asked him.

He is a small man in his fifties, with the build of a wrestler. He leaned on his pick. "I think that some people bring trouble on themselves, that was clear enough."

I knew at once the part of the proceedings he had in mind. The Chairman, Calum Johnson, running through the preoccupations of the year, had begun to talk about the dispute between the people of the glen, represented by the Council, and Bill Walsh, over Sunday opening for the Inn, when Bill interrupted. "Mr. Chairman, excuse me for interrupting, but I feel that people should be informed of the latest position . . ."

"That is what I was doing," Calum cut in acidly.

"I am sorry, Mr. Chairman, but I have something to say that should change all that. I now have a table licence for Sunday – enabling me to serve drinks with meals . . ."

"We know that. You had that before."

"No, no! That is not so, with respect. I had only a six-day licence. The table licence you refer to is indeed a seven-day one but it is for the hotel, and it will only be legal when I have completed the hotel – which I hope will not be long delayed – and this place will then have a hotel once again, which it should have . . ."

There was a rippling murmur of dissent, echoing in the bare room in loud discord with the crackling hiss of the Calor-gas heaters.

"Please! May I continue? Some people may disagree, but there is surely room for more than one opinion in the community! The young people, and the visitors, need that facility, and I intend to provide it. And so I have withdrawn my appeal for the Sunday *bar* licence. So Mr. Chairman I want it to be clear to you and to everyone else – perhaps you, in particular – now that I can serve drink with food on Sundays, that I do *not* want to open my bar on Sundays, and that as far as I am concerned *that* question is now closed."

Murdo Macfarlane, sitting next to me near the back, shook his head slowly, frowning. People around us whispered, hunching their shoulders, drawing together. Disbelief, perplexity, hostility, hung powerfully in the air.

Calum had remained standing, pale, holding himself in check. At last he spoke.

"At this meeting the Council dissolves, as I said, and who knows who will represent you on the new Council. But whether I am one of them or not, I shall continue to press my view, which I know is supported by a large majority of the folk in the glen, that the Sabbath day should be one of peace, quiet, of respect for what the Sabbath means, and that we should allow nothing to happen that would encourage the young folk and the children to turn away from these traditions of ours."

He paused. It was plain that he was controlling his emotion with difficulty. "I for one," he went on, "like the majority of the *local* folk in the glen, rejoice in the fact that I was brought up in these traditions – and I feel that to retain *one* day, the Sabbath, when we as a community affirm these principles strongly, is an important means of upholding, to put it at its lowest, the moral principles we have faith in, and protecting ourselves and our children and young folk from the corruption and debasement of life that we are aware of in the cities. In fact it is the very failure to do so that has brought about the slackening of moral conduct and the evils that flow from it in the world as a whole. And so I for one, as I say, will continue to resist with all my strength any encroachment here."

I admired Calum then. He spoke, in the end, calmly enough, fairly and squarely, in a mode seldom heard today from a layman. Plainly too, his words resonated closely with the feelings of all but a handful of the people in the hall – the few incomers. And even some of them looked shakenly at one another, as if old voices within them, dismissed as dead, had made themselves heard once again, and they felt the Eumenides coldly pursuing, awaiting their moment.

"Tell me, Malcolm," I said. "Surely Bill is not a fool. He must have known there would be opposition to him, what he stands for and what he wants to do, in a place like this? And once here he must feel the strength of it. And the dislike too. Why does he insist on fighting the storm! It can't be pleasant to be disliked so? And to meet those who dislike you, day after day, at every turn?"

"Och I don't know about him. Aye – he's a decent enough man," he said carefully. "People like that, coming from places where these things are not important, think that oor ways havena' got any strong feelings to back them up. And that all ye need to do is to keep on pushing and we'll give up and do what they say! But we *have* strong feelings about things! And they refuse to learn. But I'll tell ye something else. I think there is a movement – I don't know whether it will succeed or not – in the opposite direction. I mean back to the old Highland ways. With us – and I think *you* are seeing it in us – it is no compromise. It's all or nothing!"

"The old Highland ways? What do you mean?"

He smiled, shaking his head slowly, then suddenly turned to listen. From beyond the bend in the road, in the direction of the upper glen, came the sound of steady footsteps.

"That'll be old Jamie Macleod. I know the step. Let's see if he agrees with me."

Jamie came up, and Malcolm told him of our talk and my question.

"Aye! I think I know what ye'll say!" Jamie's red face wrinkled in a fatherly smile. "Anyway, go ahead an' I'll listen."

Malcolm turned to me again. "It's a strange thing to talk about. Everything is getting more expensive. Oil, the basis of so many things we have been taught to 'need' is running out. Energy is running out!" He pointed to the ragged hole in the road. "All these cars and lorries eating up the land and fouling everything around us. That'll all be a thing of the past for most folk before many years have gone by. We will have to tighten our belts, live modestly, go back to being dependent on ourselves, on our own resources, learn to make and mend all over again, as we used to do. We have been taught to turn away from difficulty, to want the easy life! But the easy life cripples ye even if ye can afford it. How many of us *walk* – like Jamie here does? How many people use their muscles if they can get a machine? Hardship is relative. Who can prove that *so-called* hardship – absence of luxuries like hot and cold running water, a room tae yourself, new clothes, money tae throw away – stops you from living a good life? Aye – it's going tae be hard tae learn these truths all over again! 'It's an ill wind that blows ye no good!' So it may all be for the best – as the new Minister preached the other day! Our life will have to be tailored to *thrift* as it used tae be – tae what we can safely expect the land and the sea to give us. And for all that we shall need tae return tae the very stuff of life itself, *closeness* of living, of family, of kin, of community."

He set his jaw and looked away from us. He had spoken sadly, with insecure conviction. Beneath his words echoed the question, 'Could it be too late?'

That too was unacceptable.

He sighed. "Aye – well, practically speaking we are going tae have tae re-learn, and teach oor young folk and children the old trades and crafts, tae feed and clothe ourselves as we did in the old days out of what we can produce. But the pity of it is that the young folk are still being taught tae demand an extravagant life – by the radio and television and by the great people who are supposed tae be our leaders. But even so, the shoe is beginning tae pinch. The truth is forcing itself upon us all. There is just a chance – a sma' chance right enough, but a chance all the same – for us tae turn back in time."

Jamie listened with bowed head. Long after Malcolm had finished speaking, he continued to stand in that intent attitude. He spoke at last, "Aye – I don't disagree with ye, Malcolm. These are things that will have to happen if decent life of *any* kind, not only ours, is tae survive. And there's the rub." He shook his head sadly. "You're a younger man! You have faith in the possibility. I haven't. We are stubborn folk. We would sooner give up everything, become extinct, rather than change willingly."

Malcolm listened respectfully. We stood there in the middle of the road, Jamie squinting eagerly about him, nursing his thoughts; Malcolm looking sombrely into the distance, leaning on his pick handle. From the copse at the manse, a woodpecker hammered, the first I had heard this year. From near at hand, at Duncan Macpherson's, there wafted the sharp tang of sheep-dip.

Malcolm said, "Aye – well! Ye may be right, Jamie. I suppose I want tae believe. What you are saying, really, is that if the folk here genuinely were willing tae do something tae help themselves they'd have done it before now anyway!"

Jamie nodded. "Och – I didna' think it oot like that but – yes, that probably is right."

Malcolm wanted to push the thought away before it contaminated him. "But there are still pockets of the old crafts and trades left! All we need is a bit of push."

Jamie smiled at me. "There ye are ye see? Push! That word again, it hangs about like a blight."

Malcolm shifted the pick and said, musingly, "Och there's not that much difference in the skill between making a fiddle and making a boat."

"What do you mean?" I asked.

"There's a man lives near me who makes fiddles! Aye – an' he builds good boats too!"

"Does he sell them? The fiddles, I mean."

"No, he doesn't. Not yet anyway. They are good fiddles, though. He gave one to a nephew in one of these musical groups and it plays fine."

Jamie looked amused. "He's Malcolm's brother, Roderick!" he said.

Roderick is tall and brawny, about sixty, with a broad black beard. He has the distant, clear gaze of a man of the sea. He came back from the sea when still a young man to take over his father's croft.

His cottage is on the edge of the sea, in a cove on the far southern side of the Point. The houses cluster beneath terraced pastures rising to the foot of a group of rock buttresses. Before most of the houses, between them and the water, a strip of grass looks as though it has been regularly cared for, shaved, rolled, cherished. Even before I learnt more about the cove from Roderick, I had the sense that it was a place whose life was stilled, caught in amber.

He sat on an erect-backed wooden bench near his front door, in a minute garden, looking out on the sea. It was a calm day and the water rolled steadily, reflecting in yellow gleams the afternoon sun. He talked with enthusiasm about his fiddle-making and how he came to it. "Aye – I always wanted to work with wood. But my father wanted me on the croft and so I never went away for the training."

"How did you learn?"

"Och, ye learn things – if the will is there – by watching, being with the other folk, seeing them work, trying your hand! That was always the way crafts got passed on here."

"Malcolm tells me you make boats too?"

"Aye!" His laugh was easy, a surge of pride. "Ye might think it's a world apart from a flimsy thing like a fiddle, where the wood's got to carry sound and tone instead of people and goods and the strain of wind and water! But really the judgment, the craft, the feeling, ye might say, for the materials and how they must perform, is the same!"

"And you sell the boats?"

"Aye – when someone comes tae me tae make one. People tell other folk about my boats."

He talked on steadily, softly, as if each boat had been nurtured close to his heart.

I said, "This place used to be well known for boat building. What are the chances of reviving it?"

A little sharply he said, "Och ye don't know what they did tae us? Last year the incomers got this place listed for landscaping!"

"Landscaping?"

It had been listed as a place of great natural beauty where 'development' cannot take place without special permission.

"The incomers got it through against the wishes of us local folk. They packed the meeting, even people with holiday homes who only live here for a few weeks in the year! They organised the whole thing so that it was over, wtih the decision against us, almost before we realised what was happening. So now I can't even put up a new boat-shed without asking for special permission – which I can't afford to pay lawyers to do – and it's practically certain I wouldn't get it anyway. Ye've got that much chance," he snapped his fingers, "of getting it."

"What did your local M.P. say? Did you try to get his help?"

I saw it was a naïve question.

He looked at me tolerantly. "Ach – it's pointless hoping for anything from that quarter. No. All that these official people are interested in – what all their fine talk amounts tae, whether it's London, Edinburgh, the Highland Board and so on – is tae keep places like this just ticking over! So that incomers and holiday-home owners can enjoy themselves on our backs; and all we are here for is to provide a few services and a picturesque background!"

"Ticking over? That has to mean renewal too?"

He shook his head. "I don't see how renewal can happen. Even without the freeze on this place I've just told you about, the young people are going, as you know. So where is this renewal tae come from?

"Aye – some things have gone for ever," he said. "Look over there," he pointed to the south and the narrow entrance to Loch Aillse. "When I was a boy you could walk over the loch dry-shod, so closely packed together were the herring boats. And here – you see this neatly manicured grass verge? All along here were the fish tables with the women working at them, and us boys, and many of the girls, helping with the boxes and barrels. All that has gone. Finished. The factory ships have taken over. Our boats have gone. The men who sailed them are dead or gone away."

He talked on and the evocation was strong – even as *I* had known it, all those years ago. The bustle, the noise, the chanting of the women that chimed with the vigour of their movements, and the smells, of fish, of brine, of boats, of wet wood, of decaying fish.

The stage was now deserted, cleanly swept – too clean.

"Aye – they've cleaned it up, as they call it! But where is the sense – if the life goes out as well?

"Take one example of how these people over there think." He gestured behind him to the world beyond the mountains. "This idea of the community co-operative that the Highland Board is pushing hard. The motives are either hypocritical or the obsessions of political cranks. But one motive is clear and cynical – to keep communities like us in a sort of preserved state, only just existing. A necessary part of the tourist shop window!"

His words took me back to an elegant room in Edinburgh, an eighteenth-century room with appropriate furniture gleaming, a large and ornate writing table, a splendid carved fireplace, the room of a highly placed personage. He was a dignified man, in well-cut tweeds and shiny brogues. In a corner rested a piece of luggage and a gun-case. Being Friday he would be off shortly to 'John –'s place'; he referred to his weekend host, bearer of an ancient title, familiarly, as he did to other great hereditary landowners whose names cropped up, placing himself on their level. When he referred to 'the people' he plainly saw them as the lower orders.

"You know," he said, "a bit of tourism does them good! It encourages them to keep their houses clean and tidy, and their door-steps well scrubbed."

He added, "About this community co-operative affair, well of course I know that some lefty evangelists have taken it up, but they won't get too far. And in any case I myself don't expect great things from it. But it might do the people in these declining places some good, give them a bit of community spirit they badly need, just enough to hold the remnants together. After all we do need the people, don't we, otherwise the tourists wouldn't find anyone left to give them bed and breadfast, would they! That and a bit of atmosphere!"

His is the assured style of a member of an élite of power, who feels he can speak freely within its ranks, relying upon its solidarity against the lower orders. To the outside world the ruling sentiments would be concealed in a different language.

Even so, the true word filters down. And in any case Roderick and Malcolm and Jamie Macleod and the rest can read the inner intention of words and actions as well as anyone else, as they often remind the outsider a shade resentfully.

I said to Roderick, "But if the locals will not have anything to do with the community co-operative idea, who is behind all the talk about it here?"

"Incomers of course." He laughed without humour. "You must think we talk overmuch about the incomers? Still, they *are* leaning on us, aren't they? At one moment they are blethering away at us with flattering nonsense about the simple beauty of our way of life and the next minute they want tae tell us how tae live! Aye – it's them that's pushing the community co-operative. In it, one or two o' them see a way of carving out comfortable jobs for themselves with oor money! And positions of power! At the same time proclaiming their gospel of socialist enterprise, the simple life and drugs! Wonderful, isn't it? Many o' them havena' got any solid economic basis here. Some live on social security, at oor expense ye might say! That doesna' worry them. And life here is easy for them by city standards. 'We don't have to keep up appearances here,' they say. In other words, *our* opinions and standards don't count! And yet they have the cheek tae lecture us about the simple life and village co-operatives! I sometimes marvel at our patience. In the old days we'd have run them out of the glen as soon as look at them, or thrown them into the loch more likely."

Roderick's mention of drugs chimed well with the day's news. Police and customs officers have found huge amounts of cannabis 'washed up' or 'discovered' (the reports vary) on the West Highland coast, not many miles, as it happens, from the glen. The locals talk of it eagerly, with oblique but transparent references to certain incomers.

"Aye – I wonder how long it will be before the polis come to them!"

"Och we've had a good idea of it for long enough! D'ye never hear that old Land-Rover of his coming in during the night? Aye, it's usually about four in the morning. He switches off the engine and runs quietly doon the brae – or as quietly as that old tank will go!"

"Aye, an' I'm not surprised. That one is very fond of taking his boat out fishing on moonless nights. An' he often goes down that way!"

I thought of Adrian Templer even though he dramatically diverges from Roderick's words in some important ways. Thus, following his back to nature dream he does not drink or smoke and forswears all but natural products in food and clothing. And as for drugs he is sternly against such decadence.

Adrian, like so many incomers in the glen, strikes one as a figure from another age, in this case from the world of Dornford Yates or John Buchan and the old Runagates Club. His customary dress is a vaguely military one. Calf-length boots, with khaki trousers thrust into them, a broad leather belt, and a fleece-lined leather jacket, whose pockets hang low with the weight of cartridges, pliers and other hand tools, even on one occasion a can of corned beef. In spite of the picaresque aspect, the old Wykeham-ist shines through. His is a mixture of cool charm and steely egoism.

"Follow?" I asked Adrian one day. "That's a bit strong?"

"Why not?" he raised an eyebrow. "They won't do anything on their own. Their initiative has been crushed by generations of being ripped off by the landowners. I've got lots of ideas for self-sufficient enterprise. All I need is some money. I'm going to persuade them to subscribe to a co-operative scheme so that I can get started. One big obstacle is Calum Johnson! That man's got the biggest power complex I've ever seen. Well, we'll see about that. The Community Council election's coming up and there will be a move to unseat him. We have to break through here somehow. Inflation and energy prices are going through the ceiling because of capitalistic greed. Community action is the only way. They'll follow us sooner or later – and the sooner the better."

I had a vision of a partisan leader in jungle boots, gun belt and bandolier, thundering at the peasants for their conservativism and sloth.

He speaks like a man who believes in his star. Perhaps there is no other way to survive when the world has cast you up on this shore? For such as he, the glen's general protective tolerance is a marvellous thing. Long ago, it is clear, folk decided not to 'mind' his idiosyncrasies. But woe betide him if what Roderick calls his 'lecturing' goes too far.

We were standing outside his workshop on a misty April day. Buds were bursting on the horse chestnuts. The dead greens and browns of winter had changed imperceptibly, signalling renewal. In the meadow near the great old manse, Duncan Macpherson was ploughing. Fresh smells, sounds and echoes of the awakening earth were all around us.

The form of co-operative that the Highlands and Islands Development Board is trying so hard to 'sell' to these remote and fading communities contains some of the elements of the village soviet and the kibbutz. According to it, members of a community should subscribe money to run an enterprise the proceeds of which are not returned to them in the form of interest or dividend but, as the Board's leaflet says: '. . . the co-operatives' surplus or profit is reinvested in expansion, on new community ventures, or in improving social facilities.'

I said to Robert Wallace, "In my discussions with Highland Board officials I never get a satisfactory answer when I put the central issue to them like this: 'You say that a community co-operative enterprise must be commercially viable. That is perfectly right, for you are using tax-payers' money! But if it *is* commercially viable, why can it not be set up with venture capital in the normal way and return a profit on people's money in the normal way? Why should you expect participants to take their savings out of, say, a building society or the post office where they do get some return on their money and put them into a community co-operative where they would get no return at all?' "

"Are ye connected with the Board then?" he put in quickly, "as they said about ye in that *Glasgow Herald* article?"

I have still to live down a statement, in a *Glasgow Herald* article about me, to the effect – based on a misunderstanding, it seems – that the Board is financially supporting my field work. That statement is not true. I was out of the glen when the article appeared. When I returned a few days later the whole place buzzed with it.

"Oh, come now, Robert! I seem to have answered that question so many times. I have no official connection with the Board or any other such body. I am lucky enough to be completely independent. If I weren't I couldn't be impartial, could I?"

"Och well." He brushed it away blandly. "Don't take any notice. Ye hear so many rumours. A man like you has never come into the glen before, who has these visions of rebirth and wants to help us with no benefit to himself! *And* who has no official strings attached to him. Believe me, we *want* to hear that you are impartial and disinterested. We can't hear it often enough! All the same ye *are* an unusual person, ye must admit, and folk can't help wondering about you."

"One can never stop reassuring people!"

"That's right. Och it takes a lifetime, doesn't it?" His face clouded. "Anyway, about the Board. Ye're right. Who do they think we are, talking down to us like that? Who are *they* to say we shouldna' make a profit with our own money? They play a different tune when the incomers go tae them for help in *their* investments, don't they? Take Duncan Burke, for instance. They didn't insist that *he* shouldna' make a profit when they gave *him* all that money to set up his boatyard business. And then all those other businesses?"

For the locals Duncan Burke has become egregiously symbolic. He is certainly 'pushy', an alert businessman. Rumour has it that he has had more money out of the Highland Board than anyone else in the whole district; and with that support he has set up a number of linked enterprises, boat hire and repairing, chandling, weaving. He employs a few local people. He would be resented no more than any other incomer but for one thing – his insensitive attempts to intrude into local affairs.

"What have oor affairs got tae do with him?" asks Malcolm. "We *belong* here. *They* can up-stakes and move elsewhere any time they choose!"

"You mean more than that, don't you?" I said cautiously. "If the incomers interfere, as you put it, they may get things done, bring about changes in the glen, that will express *their* view of life and not yours – the locals, the people who do belong?"

"Aye – ye've hit the nail on the head! *We* are the folk tae decide that. We don't want *them* tae impose a way of thinking, a way of going about life, they have brought from the city. And it's strange, isn't it, that it's these very ways they *say* they have turned their backs on? It's as if they carry the stain of the city with them, like the Mark of Cain! If they want tae live *their* way they shouldn't *be* here! This is *oor* place where oor view o' life must prevail, not theirs. They canna' have it both ways."

He added, "They canna' even argue that what they contribute justifies them having a say! They bring a completely insignificant amount of employment – *and* their disturbing presence and confused ideas forbye! We could do just as well without them, better in fact. We wouldna' have the aggravation for one thing!"

Duncan Burke is in his late forties, tall and spare, with long blond hair down to his shoulders and a straggly goatee. He bought three adjoining houses near the lifeboat station and converted them into one long and spacious one. It is expensively carpeted and furnished; and centrally heated, a rarity in the glen. In the drawing room hang a Braque, a Matisse and a Modigliani. He drives a pale blue Lamborghini.

Flora his wife, is a petite and shapely brunette of about thirty-five. Her hair is cut in boyish style. She is fond of wearing a full kilt of the Buchanan tartan. Taciturn at first, she warms on acquaintance, and then her words are direct and shrewdly aimed.

One day she said, in a bored voice, "He wants to get involved in community affairs just to prove he's not here simply to make money."

Her words upset him. He turned to me, "I feel I should identify more, not simply *take* from this place but put something back through communal service."

My expression must have troubled him, for he went on quickly before I could say anything. "Do you remember the day last year when you first came here? You had only just begun your travels along this coast. I may have talked . . . I mean I may have said things that gave you a wrong impression. Perhaps I may have talked about selling up and moving on? Do you remember . . . perhaps not?"

He ended lamely.

"Yes. And I remember being surprised, for you said you had had a goodish season?"

"Not bad, I must admit. Still . . ." He looked across at her signalling for help.

She stared past him out of the window. Woolly clouds hung low over the racing sea. Here and there gleams from the sun, higher now in the advancing spring season, touched the troughs of the waves with molten gold.

He went on doggedly, ". . . there are days when you feel out of sorts with a place, you know? When the vibrations are all wrong."

"I do remember thinking it was early for you to be moving on."

Duncan and Flora have a history of moving on. They come to one of these remote places, 'do up' a run-down property in conjunction with a business, then sell out at a profit on the improved value and goodwill, and move on for a similar 'development' somewhere else. Since the strategy hangs on financial assistance from the Highland Board, his concern to give an impression of enduring commitment to the locality of the moment is understandable.

One day I was having tea with Isobel Mackay, the headmistress, in the handsome granite school house near the old port, when Duncan arrived unannounced. By an odd coincidence she had just been complaining about the locals' habit of assuming that she had nothing else to do but sit waiting for them to knock at the door and burden her spirit with rambling tales and complaints – seldom relevant to the school – yearnings, dreams, disappointments.

"I know, in a way, why they do it to me! Being an outsider, and being reliant on their goodwill, they know that I wouldn't dare pass on what they say! So they feel safe. I feel, sometimes, that I am a substitute for the minister! But I have an advantage in their eyes! If they went to *him* with such talk, most of it pretty trivial stuff I must say, he would either give them short shrift or some good advice! I don't dare throw them out . . . and I know they don't want good advice anyway. So I sit and pretend to listen.

"Do you know," she added, "there are times, if I have a lot of paper work to do, I take refuge in the school in the evening to do it! Just to escape! I know they won't disturb me there."

"I wonder if it isn't a compliment?" I said. "That's how they drop in on each other. They've accepted you."

Statuesque, straight-backed, her fair hair worn in a tight bun, of a certain age, serious, innocent but firm, she seems to me a figure out of the Victorian age rather than of the present day. I can envisage her in high-necked bodice and whalebone, a text in a sampler frame visible behind her on the schoolroom wall. I wonder, sometimes, whether her decision to work here, in this stronghold of old orthodoxy, had led her to present herself in this image from the past? Or was this her true self, that can find expression, she hopes, only in such a place?

The same yearning that brings so many of the other incomers here?

She smiled sceptically, "I wonder whether it is such a compliment! It's more like treating me as a dog's-body at their beck and call! They wouldn't come in to the doctor's house in that way – or the minister's! Oh, no! They know it wouldn't do. They would phone up first to ask. They've nearly all got phones now – or can get to one easily if need be. And I'll tell you this. When it *is* something to do with a child, it's nearly always so minor that it could just as easily, and far more quickly, be dealt with by coming to see me at the school! I've explained that often enough.

"I know why they won't phone up beforehand," she added. "They think I'll tell them some story to put them off!"

"I suppose you've tried," I ventured, "putting up a notice in the school – or sending one round to the parents – saying you are available to them *at the school* at certain times?"

She pouted. "Of course I have! Useless. They simply ignore it. They come hammering at my door just the same, plank themselves down here and start talking!

"What I resent more than anything," she went on, "is the way they take me for granted, like a piece of furniture. I'm not really one of them, because I don't *belong*! That is always made clear, not maliciously, simply as a fact. I still remain an outsider. Not an incomer – an outsider. And yet I am not allowed to live like one – to come home and be my own private self at the end of the working day – and it's a hard life you know at a little village school like this where you're on the go the whole time. It's not like an ordinary town school with set periods and free periods! No, they won't let me close my front door and have some peace. Do you know, if I want to be sure of having an undisturbed day at the weekend or in the evening when it's light, I have to get into my car and leave the glen? Like a fugitive!"

A car door banged and the gate to her garden squeaked. Feet crunched urgently on the gravel, the door knocker sounded a brisk rat-rat-tat.

She rose, giving me a self-mocking glance of despair. "I think I know that knock – and the car door! I know them all. It's Duncan Burke."

I heard his impatient voice in the little hallway. "Isobel, I wanted to talk to you . . ."

He pushed open the sitting-room door and halted, disconcerted by my presence, and seemed about to retreat. He thought better of it. What he had come for must be important.

"Well, well, you do get around!" He tried to be patronising, but instead the words came out tartly, with an almost feudal air of displeasure. "How is the famous investigation going?" he went on.

Isobel, perhaps taking courage from my presence, interposed. "Is it something urgent? I was not expecting you."

"Urgent? No. Important – yes. I'm all for spontaneity. When I decide to do something it seems pointless to wait. Anyway, well . . ."

He glanced pointedly at me. Seeing that I made no move to rise, he continued, less confidently, ". . . the fact is that a little group of us are thinking that we would like to help the school?"

I sensed a charge of electricity in the air. As a cat stops quite still in a room, a paw in the air, ear flickering, the searching eyes narrowing, then places the paw down with precision, Isobel asked carefully, "What kind of help?"

"That's really what I . . . I mean. Let me put it this way. Is there, for example, any special equipment you need?"

"No. We happen to be rather well supplied. In fact so well that our problem is lack of storage."

There was a twitch of mischief in the corners of her mouth. The temptation to tease him was great.

"There you are, Duncan," I said, "there's your chance! You could club together and buy the school a storage shed. You could have a commemorative plaque over the door, 'Presented by the grateful parents . . .'"

"What a good idea, Mr. Burke!" she said, placing emphasis on the formality. "We'd be so grateful. But I'm afraid you would have to give me time to apply to the director of education for permission to alter the design of our school buildings. I could write tomorrow. Yes, and he would have to apply for planning permission. It will probably take at least a year I should think."

"Wait a minute, that's not . . ."

"Duncan," I interrupted him, "what an excellent opening for *you* to make your mark in the glen! The delay will give you plenty of time to raise the money."

He said tensely, "You're talking of a lot of money!"

"If you really want to help," Isobel put in evenly, "then oughtn't you to think of giving us what we *really* need? A shed, as it happens, is what we really need."

"Nothing else?"

"Nothing else."

He was silent, biting his lip. "What we are thinking of," he ground out at last, "is a group that would collaborate with you, you know?"

"Collaborate?" She was deliberately misunderstanding him. "You mean take over some of the teaching?"

He hunched his shoulders deeper into the chair: "No! I mean we could – through a parents' association . . ."

"You mean parent-teacher, surely?" Her voice had become husky with controlled rage.

"No. Parents in the first place. We could ensure that the parents' views are properly represented . . ."

"To whom? And about what?"

"We have nothing specific in mind, but in general . . ."

"If you have nothing specific in mind, what is this all about, Mr. Burke?"

He looked happier. Opposition suited his purpose. Aggression would be justified at last. "Do I take it," he said softly, "that you oppose the idea?"

"Yes. I see no reason for it, Mr. Burke."

"Duncan!" he said.

"Mr. Burke," she firmly repeated. "You say you want an association to represent the parents' views?"

"Yes, I mean . . ."

"One moment. To whom do you want to represent them?"

"Well – to the school."

"That is to me and my colleagues, and to me in particular as the head teacher?"

"Yes, but . . ."

"Then let me tell you this." She shot me a glance. "Every parent wanting to discuss anything concerning their child has free access to me, and curiously enough I was explaining this when you suddenly arrived. In fact my whole time, in school and here at home, at almost all hours, is freely made use of by the parents. And that is the way they have been used to doing things for generations! I am sure many of them will be furious to know that a group of incomers wants to interfere with that immediate and personal relationship! A parent-teacher association might be useful in a big city where this close personal contact is impossible. But to impose an impersonal way of doing things in a tiny and traditional community like this, and I am not going to mince my words on this, is preposterous. So there must be another reason."

He lost his look of satisfaction. Her shaft – 'a group of incomers' – had found its mark. The prospect of finding the local parents ranged against him was daunting. He got up. "I am sorry, Isobel . . ."

"Miss Mackay."

"Miss Mackay. I am really sorry you feel like this. I had hoped otherwise . . ."

She interrupted. "There is something else I must say. You came in here and talked about 'help' and 'equipment' when your real purpose was transparently different. If any child in my school – even one of yours – were to behave like that they would be punished for being deceitful. In fact it would be the kind of behaviour I would probably decide to talk to you and your wife about . . . in private! Would you like your David or Maria to behave like that? Would you?"

"That was a mistake. I apologise," he said with sudden gentleness. He glanced at me, this time with a plea for solidarity. 'What I am doing,' he seemed to say, 'is surely the modern, progressive way! You must be on our side in this?'

He turned to her. "Anyway, I feel I ought to let you know, as a matter of courtesy, that we *are* calling a meeting of the interested parents."

"To which I and my colleagues are invited?"

"No."

She got up. He took a step backward as if afraid she might strike him. Her eyes flashed fire now. "Do you mean to tell me you are calling a meeting with the object of 'collaborating' – as you say – with me and my colleagues, and are excluding us?"

"Well, at this meeting . . ."

"Mr. Burke. I have heard enough. More than enough. I warn you that I shall take advice about this."

He looked alarmed. "It really is all right! Isobel – er – Miss Mackay – there is no need to bring your teachers' union into this. There's no need for hard feelings I assure you!"

"I certainly hope not."

He hurried out.

She remained for some minutes in the hallway after the front door had banged behind him. The only sound was her quick breathing. I wondered whether some instinct, or the glen grapevine, had prepared her.

At last she came in, sat down very erect, and stared out of the window, palms upward in her lap. Without turning round she said very quietly, "I am glad you were here. It may do some good, who knows? But as you *are* here, please do something else for me. I need to talk. And I am going to have a drink – and I do not want to drink alone. Will you please pour me one?"

She took a deep breath and looked down at her hands, then suddenly smiled. "My hands are shaking!"

She pointed to the wall cupboard beside the fireplace. Set between the chimney-piece and the outside wall, the cupboard stretched from floor to ceiling. Its five deep shelves were surprisingly well stocked, but it was not the store of a committed drinker. There was a fair range of spirits: malt whisky, a blend of Scotch, gin, vodka, brandy, some sherry, various aperitif drinks, even some cans of beer. A drink, it seemed, for every mood.

"What kind?" I asked.

"Oh, I think I will have a malt. You will have one, won't you? Just to keep me company."

"Perhaps a sherry."

I handed her a well-filled tumbler. She stared into it, sipped, and looked out of the window. Out at sea the clouds were high and scudding fast. On the mountains across the Sound the sun moved in yellow bands, momentarily lighting up the deep corries. A white sail leaned over before the wind, the first herald of the new pleasure season.

"Why does he want to do it?" she asked. "Oh, I think I know. He wants to be somebody – chairman of something – and so get himself on to a level with the doctor, and the chairman of the Community Council!"

She took another sip. "It's his way of doing things I hate so," she added. "I suppose I could apply for a transfer, but it's not too wise to do that with all this cutting back by the education authority. It really is going to be so unpleasant to be hounded by him and that crowd of misfits from the South."

"You're not really thinking of opposing him?"

"What else can I do?"

I thought of the fight at the Inn and my failure to stand back from it, to be impartial. Could I, should I, try to be impartial this time? Did it matter to me who won this new battle, whatever its motives?

In an open fight, she could only lose. Her opposition would inspire him and his group. And even the locals might be drawn in against her, relieved to direct their amorphous resentments against an identifiable scapegoat close at hand. And so the remnants of known and trusted ways of living would be frayed still further.

Everyone would lose.

I said, "Forgive me, but would you let me offer a little advice? I know how you can beat them. But you will need a lot of self-control."

She swung round to face me fully, spilling a little of the honey-coloured liquid. "How?"

"By being Machiavellian!"

She drew back a little. "I don't want to do anything underhand!"

"Wait a moment. It's not quite like that. *You* call the meeting!"

"How can I? He knows I am against it."

"That is the point. He won't know what to do!"

"But the locals will think I've gone off my head!"

"They're not as simple as all that! The word must have got around by now. They must know what he's up to. As for him and his group, they'll have lost the initiative. When you have been pushing at a door and it suddenly opens you fall flat on your face!"

She became very thoughtful, and drained her glass. "You mean kill it from inside?"

"Not immediately perhaps. It may tick over for a bit. But if *you* call the meeting, they can't exclude you, nor of course can they oppose it! And with you inside, all sweetness and light and helpfulness, you will disarm their aggression. And the locals will still want to come to you directly as they always have done. So nothing will have changed. And after a time the steam will go out of Duncan and his crowd, on this idea at any rate, and you will be left in possession of the field."

"It goes against the grain even to pretend to do what they want."

"I know."

We sat in silence.

She roused herself. "I never bargained to have to fight like this when I applied for this job. These people come from the city and want to structure everything as it is in the city! They can't *bear* the simplicity they say they came here to find! They want to pressurise you with their woolly ideas about children and imagine that they are being extremely responsible parents! But what they are really doing is to hand over some of *their* parental problems to the teacher! At least when the locals come here individually they don't try to advise *me* – it is I who advise *them*! So their parental responsibility remains where it should be, with them!

"I must admit," she went on, "that it was to get away from such pressures in the city – all the falsity and twisted values – that I thought of coming here. And now look where I am!"

She smiled ironically and held out her tumbler. I replenished it.

At last she said, "I think you are right. They don't deserve any better! I think I will follow your advice."

Five

Connal's way

Some days I feel that all is static in the glen, that nothing will ever move. That I too am caught in the coagulated substratum of bygone time, a sticky fixity from which all action and thought must take its cue. Will the pattern change? Does anyone want it to?

Will Morag stay or go? Will Robert Wallace make a move to put into practice any of the schemes we have pondered together? Will Nellie Templer, who has talked all these months of starting a bakery, ever do it? The Templers are among the longest established of the 'new white settlers' and, as she says, mentally acclimatised. Will the jetty ever be rebuilt? Will the rubble of the burnt-out Inn ever be cleared up? Will Angus Maclintock ever start his joinery shop?

Spring is fully here. The earth proceeds in the ordained movement. In the crisp air the silences are intense. Folk move slowly, or perhaps they only seem to move. The appearance of tranquillity is misleading. Perhaps there was a time, long ago, when they *were* content to know that up there on the high tops, just out of sight, gods and heroes moodily ruled their destiny. Did they try to turn away and seek an easier scheme of movement through life, demanding no spiritual effort, no self-questioning? And then, in punishment, did the gods enchain their will?

Is there a wish, now, to turn back, to acknowledge the old powers once again? To have no moorings at all is frightening. To affirm the immutability of things offers a perverse comfort. Nothing changes, only the forms do, not the substance. Or, alternatively, what I am thinking of doing is of a piece with the past, therefore it is safe to attempt. But wait, who can tell?

To speak of change, they seem to say, is as good as making it happen.

Robert Wallace, looking across at Cruachan, muses on, "Aye, there's more than one kind of Wolf. You called me his 'latter-day successor'! I know you were only joking. But in different ways someone is still doing what he did. What about the Garroch company and the fight at the Inn? We all know what that was about, don't we? The incomers prey on *us* the whole time, one way or another."

Their convoluted thinking, once I am attuned to it, is not too difficult to live with. The evasions are. They raise doubts in my mind. What do they signal? Are they saying, 'No – we will do nothing'; or 'We want to do something – but on our own'; or 'We don't know what we want to do, but just leave us alone'?

Should I try to push, cajole, still their doubts? It is *their* life after all. If, dismayed at the fading of their world, they feel too weak to infuse it with life once more, who am I to press them on?

And what of my impartiality? I thought again of my remark to Murdo Macfarlane about being an 'active catalyst'. To interfere, intervene, presume? Rejuvenate the glen: yes, it seemed a just cause. But could I be accused of arrogance?

"Provided," Murdo cannily observed, "ye know what rejuvenation means!"

"To answer that, one needs to dig down into the remnants of the culture to define what people want from life, their values in fact."

"Och but what do ye mean by culture?" he asked. "I know what *I* mean. I want to know what *you* mean."

"By culture I mean the pattern of behaviour, the principles, rules and organisation, together with their ways of expressing them, that people evolve to pursue fulfilment in life as *they* understand it."

He sucked on a pipe, "Aye – those are fine-sounding words! Still, I see what ye mean, and I think I accept that definition. I don't know about having a 'right' to intervene. If you feel these things are important, go ahead and do what ye can and good luck to ye. *I* think they're important! So do most folk. But we want *our* values, not other folk's! Nor do we want tae impose oors on them. Aye – values are going down all over the world. We need some men of honesty and goodwill tae help us. Only . . ." he pondered something, "let me give ye the advice of an old campaigner." He gave me a piercing look, "Ca'canny!

"Maybe," he added, "as an outsider ye might have an advantage over us in seeing the right road. Your sight won't be fogged up by old memories, animosities, grievances, regrets. I know ye are troubled about not remaining impartial. Take my advice." He pointed the stem of his pipe at me. "I wouldn't have said this to ye when ye first came. But if ye take an honest and level-headed view of things, that is the best any man can hope for. Ye spoke of looking for the heart in the onion. Remember? Well, as I said to you then, I dinna' rate yer chances very high! All the same, as our new minister said last Sunday, every man's got a duty to side with the good against the bad and take his chance! As he says, it isn't the judgment o' his fellow men that matters, but the judgment o' God."

Even Murdo, for all his shift towards frank goodwill is still saying, with his emphasis on 'honesty' and 'level-headedness', "We are standing back and watching you! Don't push us too hard or too fast."

Their change towards me is like the April weather. The glen has grown softer and the air is full of a shimmering light that penetrates, but whose warmth is hesitant, retreating unexpectedly then cannily moving towards you again. The sun is higher. At last the north-facing slopes are out of the shadow, but their verdure still displays the dull and unawakened shades of winter.

The lambing has been good, with many twins and one set of triplets; but on the debit side each day leaves a number of dead ones on the roadside, slaughtered by passing cars. The flow of early holidaymakers and visitors leaves its mark.

"We lose enough from the foxes," says Duncan Macpherson savagely. "We could do without the visitors running them down. They won't *try* to understand how they should behave here.

"Just like some of the incomers," he added.

Murdo had not risen to my mention of 'the active catalyst', but his sharp glance told me he had noted the implications. For me to assume such a role is a decision the locals have already taken for granted.

Isobel unexpectedly explained this. I met her walking away from the new Free Church manse, a modest stone house above the great pool of the river. "You are having an effect on the place! You mentioned being a catalyst, didn't you? I've never seen so much ploughing. They're cultivating bits of the glen that haven't been turned over for years!"

"I haven't said anything about that to anybody!"

"Maybe not in so many words, but people have been talking to *you* about that, haven't they, saying that some folk have not been cultivating their land?"

"So they think *I* have provoked all that? H'm, I think I can see how it worked. People who for reasons of their own wanted to be critical of the non-cultivators implied that it was *I* who brought up the subject! In that way they got their criticism across while putting the responsibility for it on to me, the outsider."

I added, "So all that talk comes through to you too?"

"Aye, well, everything gets chewed over and passed on. As I told you I get it all sooner or later. I know, for instance, what Calum Johnson and Jamie Macleod and Alistair Macduff have been saying to you about that."

"You really think that is why they are doing this unusual amount of cultivation? As a demonstration for my benefit, as a reaction to my being here? The catalyst stirring them to action?"

"I can't think of any other explanation."

She became thoughtful, "Do you think they could be afraid of something you might report about them to the world outside?"

The unease stirring in the glen is touching her too.

Since the evening of Duncan Burke's visit I sense in her a subtle

82

intellectual shift. Perhaps to comfort herself in her feeling of being attacked and isolated still further, she appears in some moods to share with me the viewpoint of an informed, detached observer. Perhaps, through our talks, she sees the glen, and her position in it, more clearly.

Now she seems to swing the other way; she must not draw upon herself any anxiety my presence might arouse.

I said, "Perhaps the older folk, disheartened by the glen's decline and seeing the younger ones treat the land with scant respect, are using me to fight back? Custom, the manners of the glen, prevents them from openly lecturing the others. But here I am – with who knows what means of influence in the world outside! Why not use *me* to put pressure on them, invoking guilt, and the desire to show the powers that be that they *are* doing their best with what they have?"

"Possibly." She was pensive.

Her mood changed. Colour rose on her high cheekbones.

"You remember," she said, "the parents' association affair? I took your advice."

"I know. I saw the notice you put in the shop window."

"There's Jamie Macleod coming along," she said quickly, animated. "I would rather not talk about it here. But I'd like to tell you. It's amazing, really. Come in for a cup of tea later if you can spare the time."

She went off in her long, swinging, flat-heeled stride.

I continued on up the glen. Jamie stopped me. "I hear ye've been cracking with Murdo about rejuvenation. That is an old one."

He said it kindly. In his reflective yet direct manner, he showed sympathy. But Jamie is a pragmatist, a highly analytical one.

Over the years many people have come to the glen with nostrums; promising fulfilment, bringing disappointment.

"It isn't that the folk here *knew* that the schemes were wrong in what they were aiming for or that they couldn't work anyway! The truth is much worse than that. None of *us* is sure what we really want tae happen! Ye look surprised? Let me try and explain it tae ye."

With an old man's circumspection he unslung a small sack from his shoulder and laid it on one of the broad stone slabs that crown the meandering roadside wall. He called his brindled dog to sit. He put a foot up on the wall.

"The politicians after the Great War thought they were being very clever. I was a lad of eighteen or so. And everywhere one heard the fine words, 'Homes for heroes!'

"Aye – and other cries too! From every quarter the parties and the cranks and self-seekers set themselves tae win some advantage out of all the confusion. And nobody knew what the world was going tae be like. We felt sure of one thing only. It would never be the same again. At least we *said* that – though we didna' *know* what we meant! Look at the War Memorial. Every family in the glen. Two of my brothers, an uncle, four cousins. And in many a family – some o' the lucky families!", he grimaced, "somebody came back a cripple! Or under sentence of death, like my father. Looking back on it, that was a time when folk were frightened tae even *try* tae go back to how things had been before, because that past was – how can I put it? Well, you couldna' *think* of the past way of things without thinking of the people who *belonged* tae that past world and who would never come back tae be part of it. Do you understand?"

"You felt you had to turn away."

"We didna' *know* we were doing that! All we knew was that it had tae be different!"

In a shared reticence we looked away from each other.

In the clear air, with high thin cloud showing hints of blue, the far uplands shimmered in delicate tints of lilac and misty green. Nearer, where the narrow glen made one of its great sinuous curves, the steep side of Beinn Dhu reared up like a wall; and from a dark copse beneath it a cuckoo clamoured insistently. Below us two herons wheeled above the river.

He said, "Aye, and that is a state of mind when people are easy prey for fine-sounding schemes, plans, slogans, easy answers tae life.

"You see all this land?" With a sweep of his arm he took in the whole glen. "All that was then one farm. Aye. And farmed well I must admit – by one man. Old John Findlay. My father worked for him as a shepherd, besides having a plot of land and a bit of grazing for himself."

He bent his head and I fancied his lips moved. He could have been in prayer.

He sighed. "In those days, among my father's generation, they still talked about the Crofters' Revolt of forty years before, argued about it, fought the old battles again. It's hard tae speak about all that now, all that heat, all that strong feeling, yes – even the fighting spirit – it was all real tae us! We youngsters were brought up in all that. And so we joined in the new upsurge of the shouting about 'crofters' rights' and so on even though we didna' understand *any* of it. All we were doing was repeating the talk we had heard ever since we were children. What did the likes of us know about 'People's rights to the land'? It sounded fine tae us! Even though things in the glen were not really too bad, by the standards of the time, ye understand? Well, with the old world broken. With the men coming back from the trenches and the great ones in London frightened, the canny ones – aye, and some hotheads too – saw the chance tae win easy favour among the common folk by bringing up again the old crofter's cause. And so the shouts went up: 'Land for the returning heroes!' 'Break up the big estates!' Crofting is the answer. Make a man independent. Give him back a stake in the land! And so on. And the politicians thought: 'Ah – here's oor chance tae solve the Highland problem! We'll buy up a few farms and grazings with money from the taxpayers' pocket and distribute them as crofts! We'll throw the barking dogs a few bones tae keep them quiet and then forget all about it!' Just think, after nearly two hundred years – since the '45 – there was still something called 'the Highland problem'!"

"Are you saying that the distribution of land in that way, as small crofts, was wrong?"

Eyes deep in the wind-reddened face, he gave me his piercing stare. He bent over to hitch his thick green stockings over the buttons of his heavy knee-breeches.

"For sixty years I've been turning that question over in my mind. It's hard for me – *even* for me. For I am one of the few survivors of the whole upheaval. It's hard to think of the changes separately from other things. By other things I mean something more than the details of the changes themselves, the legal things tae do with our position on the land and so on, but other changes that can never be avoided when ye upset the way folk have looked at life through the generations. Things we can't explain but in the end make us the people we are! I'm searching for a way of explaining it to ye. When ye put on a new pair of shoes ye feel all of a sudden that ye canna' walk exactly the way ye used tae, and ye have tae walk a bit differently, and not only that, ye have tae put your mind tae something ye took for granted – walking! But then ye force the shoes tae your will, and in a few days ye are as ye were before. But these upsets were stronger than *we* were. *We* had to bend tae *them*, in hidden ways that we were not aware of, but these *were* the really important things. And if ye balance out what was destroyed in *that* way against what we got in the way of livelihood and the famous 'independence' the hotheads blethered about, there's nae doot, looking back on it. It was all wrong. *We* didn't win! Folk like us never win. The politicians won.

"Aye!" He shook his head in reminiscent sadness. "For us young folk it all looked fine enough, even though looking back I think we did feel something in oor bones, a kind of fear we didna' understand, a sort of shiver in oor hearts like the shiver ye feel when someone walks over your grave. Looking back, though, I think we *did* know, somewhere in oor hearts, that *we* were trampling over many things we could never put back the way they had been! Life never lets ye do the right things at the right time. Or at least ye never know whether it's right or not until it's too late! The changes were out of their proper time. The war had destroyed not only flesh and blood but oor roots as well. We didna' know that at the time. For many folk, not for lads like me because we didna' *know*, everything had become soiled, dirty, unreliable, without hope; and even the land and the old ways – I don't know how to put it in words – ye might say the understanding that life, and proper conduct, and the land were one and the same thing. This too was not to be relied on any more as we had grown up to believe. And the proof of that came before very long. Aye, the young men back from the trenches tried the crofting for a bit. And then the restlessness, the disappointment, the sadness in their hearts got too much for them. They ran away, to the cities in the South, or they emigrated abroad. Remember, at that time there was government propaganda – and financial help – for people to emigrate? To Canada, for instance. For them it was as if nothing *here* was worth rebuilding – or even trying to carry on with – so throw it all away and start again! But life doesna' allow ye to go on like that. Only a child thinks like that. Ye don't *get* another chance.''

Duncan Macpherson drove up on his tractor. He must have sensed that Jamie was in serious vein. He approached respectfully. Jamie acknowledged him with a nod.

"Aye, so for a lot of people. Aye, and for a lot of places. Yes, it was a mistake, a big mistake. Old John Findlay was a good farmer, as I say, and a good man, one o' the few that cared well for the land and what it stood for and for the folk on it as well. For myself I canna' be sure if I gained from it. I would have worked just as hard if the break-up hadna' happened! And maybe I wouldna' have had so much sorrow as bit by bit the old life fell away leaving us only memories tae live on. That wouldna' have happened, or at least it wouldna' have happened so fast maybe. No, they shouldn't have broken up the glen into crofts. Aye, and gey small ones at that! Maybe the break-up had tae come because it was of a piece with the breaking up going on in the world? Anyway, even then, sixty years ago, many a man couldna' make a living on his croft, and things in the glen were better than in some other places.''

He turned away. The lines round his mouth were etched hard. The effort to make words express the long years of contemplation, to relive the sadness, had become too great. And Duncan Macpherson stood there as a challenge. Jamie faced round again. He spoke to me, but the words were aimed at the other.

"What sickens me is the way folk like us get taken in. Every time. The way our lives are nothing more than the tools that the great ones make use of tae build up their position in the world. They pretend that it's *oor* lives they care aboot with all their big talk. It's no' true! We are just the stepping-stones they use! And the pity of it is that us here, the wee folk trying tae live a good life the best way we can, *we* believe them! That is what I canna' get over. How can it happen? Take these things – the agitation, the land break-up – they were just things that came usefully to hand, for selfish people to make *their* way to high positions and public honour. Och it's true that many landlords were bad men, stupid is more the truth of it. But that wasna' really the point. It was that something had happened tae the world we had known and we couldna' make oot what it was. And the great ones tried tae make us believe that nothing important had changed and a few touches here and there would put everything right! Well, the truth soon showed through. The men back from the trenches didna' talk much about what they had gone through. But somehow we *knew*. We felt they looked at things, at life, in a different way than when they went away. We *knew*, without knowing why, that the trenches had thrashed out of them what they had learnt at their mother's knee. They didn't *trust* the old way of looking at life any more. They spoke tae us from another world. Aye, another world! They were sad men. They lived only for one day at a time, and tomorrow was far away. The trenches had taught them that. They thought ye could buy a good life with money, that ye shouldna' have tae wait. And you needed a lot more money to buy it with than you could get from working a croft."

He turned towards Duncan but changed his mind: he addressed me again. "Aye, I learnt about all that slowly. For me, when my father got the croft. He died a few years later . . ." His whole frame seemed to shrink. Then he straightened up. "You see he got gassed in the trenches. Well, when I took over I didna' have those ideas. I worked hard. We always had done. I got married and my wife helped, of course. She was from the island, from hard-working stock. We lived as folk like us always had done. We made a simple livelihood. Had our ups and downs like anybody. But, looking back over these sixty years, at the way things have gone, at the way things are now, I've got tae answer ye straight. I think the whole crofting scheme after the war was a trick! In the world as it turned oot tae be, and with the old ways of looking at life gone for ever, it couldna' work. It gave nobody what they needed. Och it was all too late. So many things were wrong. Some crofts were barely two acres, and a bit of grazing on the hill. And for another thing, tae be set doon to work all on yer own in those conditions was too much of a strain for many o' those young men back from the trenches – pitifully ruined in themselves as so many of them were."

He turned sharply on Duncan. "You don't remember any of this – but your father was one o' the few who did get through all that. Aye, an' he had a gey hard time of it!"

Duncan was uncomfortable. "Och ye're saying they should amalgamate the crofts into big farms again. But where would folk like us be then? Workin' for wages!"

Jamie faced me again. "I said 'another world', didn't I? Aye, now it's *me* that's from another world! Folk think in catch words! Wages – as if tae earn wages is a crime! As if *anything* we earn with the sweat o' oor brows isn't a wage!"

He shifted to Duncan. "A *shared* wage, if ye like? What's wrong with that? Why can't we just work hard and try tae live a good life, and no' pretend tae be more than what we are – wee simple folk? The trouble is that folk forget that the war-cries o' the crofters' movement belonged tae a way of thinking that harked back to a *feudal* state of affairs! They talked of 'rights' – but they forgot that each man paid for his so-called 'rights' with his blood in the fighting, and the blood of his sons. Aye, and very often with the bodies of his womenfolk too!"

"Och but Jamie," Duncan protested, "I never said anything aboot rights."

"Aye, I know," the other grunted, piqued at the interruption from the younger man. "Ye talked aboot wages – as if that was bad – and that thought harks back to the old romantic rubbish about the Highlander's famous independence! Och I'm tired hearing of it. The Highlanders have been befogged by the story-tellers! We've never faced reality. Who ever said that the Highlander *should* have land? We common folk never *had* land in the modern sense of holding a piece of land independently! The only thing that matters is tae work in partnership with the land and with everything on it. Life is hard in any case. Always has been. Aye an' always will be. It's the partnership, or the want of it, that matters."

"And ye'd have us at the mercy of the landowner again – or the farm factor?"

Had all this been said in a different setting, I felt, Duncan would have accepted much of Jamie's vision. But he was irked by the old man's jaded putting down of cherished Highland prejudices. And he could not – or would not – rise to the other's transcendental level.

Jamie sighed again, this time because the talk had fallen away and because the younger man made him feel his age, when all arguments have been heard before.

"Duncan! Ye take me back to yer father's time with this talk! But ye are old enough to know that wee folk like us are at the mercy of someone, somewhere, *always*! The *names* dinna' matter!"

He picked up his sack and swung it carefully on to his shoulder, called to his dog, nodded and said, "Good day to ye, then," and strode away.

The names do not matter. Over our heads the great forces contend for ever.

We watched him walk down the road, which here passes through an arching avenue of chestnut trees. In the clear blue sky the westering sun beat through the overhanging trellis of great leaves and filled the avenue with a vibrant green light. Jamie leaned a little into each step in the steady, undulating, economical gait of the old-style countryman, his white hair, flowing out from under the frayed deerstalker, fleetingly touched by golden rays coming through the enclosing green. In the brilliance of the declining sun he moved timelessly.

The glen belongs to the sea

. . . and to the encircling mountains

. . . and to the clear silver light and slow-moving shadows where
Fionn and his band go hunting on the wind

. . . and folk dream on the once bustling shore

Skeleton of a small trading ship, left – like the community – to moulder on the shore

The school sleeps under the mountain. Shadows from the age of optimism – of plain living and high thinking

The shape of the past lingers on

Sometimes it is stubbornly maintained, as in this fine 'black house'

The sea replaced. A load of timber going 'out' over the bealach

The machines are there – but only one small hay-rick

Deserted sea lane – empty
land

Where once the herring
boats crowded the bay and
the shingle rang with the
business of boats and fish –
now there is a handful of
pleasure boats, and silence

A sign? The glen holds its first cattle sale for over fifty years . . .

In early spring the shadow of the mountain recedes. The left-hand slopes have seen no sun since November

In the middle distance are terraced areas bitten out of the mountain-side, where once several hamlets flourished

The venerable steading glows in the fading days of summer, and
seems to beckon another life

Empty road, empty sea and the far gateway between the mountains.
Will no one come back?

When he had gone out of sight, Duncan turned to me as if released. "Aye, I respect old Jamie. But he makes it hard tae talk tae him sometimes. He tears every idea to pieces before he'll look at it! He takes nothing for granted. Maybe he has good reason, who knows?"

I saw why Jamie, always kindly, humane, profound in his sympathy, sometimes talks to me with the same weary scepticism.

"Och I am no' against what ye are trying tae do. But I canna' honestly say that I am in favour either. Ye talk of rejuvenation? For that tae have any chance, ye would have tae have enough folk left – not old ones like me – who *know* what it is tae belong, and who feel that there are enough roots left here, living roots, to make it worth the candle – people who have the will, aye, and the courage, tae look at life steadily, as it really is. I dinna' see any o' that here."

Jamie sees man as facing life always with inadequate means; his vision always incomplete, unable to comprehend the higher powers controlling his destiny, his only guide a continuity with a proven past.

For him the present-day world, refusing to 'look at life steadily' and to build upon the past, has built upon dreams, fantasy, the incomplete vision, the mirage dimly seen, on hope without substance.

How then can one presume to 'intervene'?

Action seldom turns out as planned. Even if it does, what other consequences, impossible to foresee, may it also bring? 'Better the devil we know . . .!''

And how can the outsider, however strong his sympathy, understand our course of life better than we can – who we are and where we want to be?

When Robert Wallace, and other locals, resume their plaintive grumble about the hardships and disappointments of their condition, life dropping away, the future empty of fulfilment, and genuinely seem to want action, is it real or is it shadow-play? When the time comes for action, will their fatalism take control? Will they draw back from decision?

Even if the fatalism is only a mask for frailty, have I the right to break through it? It protects them against making hasty judgments or offering hostages to fortune. It has proved its value over the generations. Have they not a right to cling to it?

There is that other enigma, the bland politeness, seemingly full of acceptance, which one finds in so many places in the world among people of the land – deceptive, impregnable, and dangerous if one fails to interpret it quickly.

'Yes – it is very interesting. One day, quite soon, I will do something about it . . .'

Smoothly, often with much charm, the politeness plays for time. It avoids the effort of explaining doubts and fears about the proposed course of action, or why they cannot overcome their inertia – difficult and sometimes painful to examine in oneself. One day I *shall* be sure enough to act. Meanwhile I do not want to say 'No'. That would be a definite judgment too, and I am not ready for that either. How can I explain all this to you? And why should I have to? If you have any sense you will give up and leave me in peace. If not you are a fool, and fools, in the end, must suffer for their folly.

Weeks ago, talking to Robert, I suggested growing table vegetables under glass. The Gulf Stream swings in towards the land here. The glen is noticeably milder than the region beyond the pass. It has many advantages for such cultivation.

He became enthusiastic. He talked expansively about what he would do. He would go away and think about it.

Today he came back to it. He drew me into detail, fuel efficiency, markets, delivery routes, even the merits of certain sites on his land.

And then, as the glen itself changes and the clouds gather quickly on the hill bringing rain, he changed too. He drew back. Blandly, as if we had been talking of Cruachan for hours, he nodded across to the grim keep. "Ye know, I did make a little money out of it once. In fact I still feel a bit guilty. A film company wanted to use it for a day – and paid me twenty-five pounds for it."

"Twenty-five!"

"Ye don't think it was enough?"

I hesitated.

"Ye don't, do ye?" He was gentle about it, hastening to forgive me.

"It does seem a bit low."

"Och I felt as though I was getting money for nothing!"

Sadly, he added, "Ye must think I'm no' much of a businessman?"

"I wouldn't say that. There's no reason why you should understand how the film business works."

"How much should I have stuck out for?"

"Was it a feature film?"

"I think so."

"H'm – you might have got a bit more. Still, that was an isolated instance. When I suggested you might make something out of the castle, I was thinking of something properly organised – on a continuing basis – for the visitors to pay to look over the building; maybe adding some features to interest them, displays of weapons, for instance, old agricultural implements, harness, wagons, old furniture, pictures, that sort of thing. Something like what they've done at other old buildings of importance in the Highlands."

He was silent, chin on hand.

"There you are," he said, "that just goes to show you. We aren't business minded. We think," he added tensely, "of more important things – that's our trouble."

They return again and again to this fiction of being above the money-changers. Does it serve their pride so well?

Others take a different view. John Connal, like Jamie Macleod, was born in the glen and lived through the great changes. He still holds his croft here though he is primarily a businessman with interests outside. By local standards he is very rich.

"I knew Robert's father. His son's the same – a good man and a hard worker but . . ." he prodded the ground with his crook and shook his head, "och well – likeable enough – a good husband and father. Aye, he'll just keep goin' on right enough."

John started off as a shepherd here over fifty years ago while still only a youth. Then he began to deal in livestock 'on the side', as he put it with a sly twinkle. Now he owns several farms beyond the mountains, and has an interest in a large broiler plant on the East coast; rumour also credits him with shrewd dealings in property and machinery contracting in the hinterland of the oil business in Aberdeenshire.

Hard grey eyes assess you from afar. His speech, larded with sharp wit, seems designed solely to beguile you while he schemes, refines, plots his next business move.

Alone among the locals, he bestrides the two worlds; the one beyond the mountains and the old one in the glen. His attitude bluntly affirms that he has challenged that other world and beaten it at its own game.

"I've got nae time." he says, "for the folk here who go around greetin' about the incomers being too 'pushy'! Let them get off their tractors and look aboot them, and feel the ground under their feet. Your feet can tell you a lot!" He prodded the soil with his crook again. "They need to look about them, and look slowly – aye, and get their brains working – and see what can be done, work oot some ideas and go and do it. That's what I did. But . . ." His breath whistles between his teeth, "ye canna' remake folk.

"Ye know what I do sometimes?" he added. "I take away the ignition keys from the vehicles and tractors and tell my men tae go aboot on their two legs and come back with ideas! And I promise them ten pounds for every idea I put intae practice. I do that for a few days." He grinned wolfishly. "Ye'd be surprised how many tenners I pay oot that way! Worth every penny of it."

"Talking of tractors," I said, "what do you think of this? I saw Duncan Macpherson and his son in the big field down the road today – with two tractors, one fitted with a mechanical shovel, the other with a hopper and spreader for fertiliser. And they had . . ."

He interrupted with a growl, "And they'd emptied all the fertiliser out of the sacks in a great heap on the ground and were using the mechanical shovel tae scoop it up intae the hopper on the other tractor?"

"Yes."

He swung his great grey head wearily. "What's the use of talking! They're drunk with machines most of them! They want tae be in step with the great modern world! Aye, it's pitiful. Ye're asking me why they don't just empty each sack direct into the hopper? Because machines and machinery have got them by the throat! In the old days when all ye had was the sweat of your back it was as much as yer life was worth tae waste yer strength doin' daft things like that! Ye never had enough strength tae waste. Ye'd use your heid. Ye'd think oot the easiest way! Nowadays they don't stop tae think. They have forgotten that life doesna' give ye something for nothing. With everything ye *think* ye gain there's a loss tae be balanced oot against it! It's true that sometimes it balances oot the right way but" – he pushed his lips up and shook his head – "more often than not it doesna'. And as far as that goes machines have changed nothing. I'll tell ye this much. If I ever found any of my men doing a daft thing like that I'd have them off my land before they knew what day it was!"

He looked about him in exasperation. "I used tae try talking tae some o' the folk about ways of working – trying tae improve things. I gave it up long ago. They dinna' want tae think any more."

For Calum Johnson the malaise is in the spirit. "Och they dinna' want tae feel themselves as part of the workings of the land! That's how I have come tae think of it. They want to draw a wage packet from the forestry and let the land go sour. Shall I tell you something?" He pointed to the vegetable rack at the rear of the shop. "I may be speaking against my own interests but never mind. Take potatoes." He paused and said slowly, for emphasis, "I sell nearly every potato they eat in the whole glen! If someone had told me that would happen I wouldna' have believed them. Potatoes! They used tae say when I was a boy, 'You can grow potatoes here with your hands in your pockets.' But they won't plant any. Potatoes used tae be almost all they ever ate – that and fish! Maybe that's why. Maybe they want tae put that as far away from them as they can. They prefer tae buy from me. Aye, explain that one? It seems tae me, sometimes, that they want tae fancy themselves on the same level as people in the city – take their wage packet and go and pick the produce off the shelves – as if the land it comes from isnae' any longer any concern of theirs."

John Connal has little patience for detached analysis. "Och that's just playing about with ideas. There may even be something in it. I'm not saying there isn't. But Calum has a short memory. Five years ago the price of potatoes went so high they were like lumps of gold in your hand! Everybody put in potatoes as soon as they could. It was the old story. Next time round they couldna' afford tae lift them out o' the ground. They were worth nothing! No wonder they turned their backs on that."

"But to plant none at all? Not even to eat in the house."

"Aye, well, I see that."

He said it vaguely. His attention had flown. His grey eyes veered away towards the high pass.

"Aye, I'm going tae tell ye something that will surprise ye. That forestry up there – people say it's the saving of this place! They're wrong, ye know? It's the killing of it! Most of the younger men do a bit on the forestry – and it's a regular pay packet – and then again if they're on the felling they make a lot more than the basic pay. And what happens? They come back home at four in the afternoon, and have their tea, and become crofters! The land takes second place. How can that work? Anyone who has learnt *anything* about the land knows that you have tae be thinking, scheming, looking about ye, working things oot, noticing things that need to be done and doing the right thing in good time, watching points, searching for opportunities – the whole twenty-four hours o' the livelong day. As it is the forestry takes pride of place. And the land is not much more than somewhere that gives them a roof over their heids – aye, and entitles them tae some bits of government money, subsidies, grants for this and grants for that! Mind ye, I'm no' saying anything against getting the subsidies and grants. I'd be the last one tae do that! Whether they do any good with them is another matter altogether. But it's their way of *thinking* that does them no good. That's no' the way tae live with the land. You've got tae have a business heid on yer shoulders. If ye put yer trust in a wage packet from the forestry – where there's no call tae use any business heid ye've got – well, like everything else in nature, what ye don't make use of will in the fullness of time become useless!"

"Your views must make you pretty unpopular in the glen?"

He grunted. "I'm long past minding what they think here! I did once when I was a youngster – once! – when I should have backed my judgment and done what my heart told me tae do, and I've mourned that day for long enough!" He cleared his throat heavily. "Aye, that's another story. But as for what they think *now*? The auld ones we all respected as youngsters – aye, and obeyed too whether for good or ill as I said" – he shrugged and clicked his teeth – "are all gone long ago. And as for the folk now, what *are* they? Lost souls! Feather-heids drifting this way and that with nae pride in themselves. I started with nothing – and I mean *nothing*! Just the rags on my back. I put my heid to work. Aye, and my back too! Well, where are they and where am I? I could buy and sell the lot o' them if I had a mind tae. And they know that too."

He caught my eye and grinned, a rascally look, with a baring of tobacco-stained teeth. He savoured a subtle, convoluted, bitter joke –

partly against himself, partly against them all, against the world he had risen above and which had fallen away around him, with no one left to acknowledge his triumph.

Only a man of wit and quick insight, of calculation, with sentiment under tight rein, could risk such detachment.

One thinks of the great generation of Scottish merchant adventurers, aloof, cool, clever and determined, as men of this stamp.

He changed tack again. His eyes tilted once more towards the dark ranks of close-planted trees on the far slopes. "I did once think of seeing what I could do in the timber line but I got oot before I got my fingers burnt. Aye, it's well seen that only the government could stand for those un-businesslike ways of working. The costs are crippling! And yet it could all have been . . ."

A cloud rolled across his face. The windy scarlet became a deep russet, the eyes dull. He opened his mouth with the lips taut, defiantly dismissing a sombre thought. Then his bulky frame straightened; a fighter squaring up again.

"I'll tell ye something else. D'ye know aboot the auld stone jetty?"

"Wasn't it below where the War Memorial is now – where those bits of stonework have fallen away on to the shingle?"

He sighed again, looking weary, "Och come on over here. I want tae sit doon."

He moved away from the fence where he had stood looking down the long sloping meadow. A dozen black cattle, with calves cantering round them, converged slowly towards the river. All around us the colours had brightened, and the earth was turning before our eyes. And the sky, lifting high, dazzling now as the sun pierced through thin cloud, beckoned the mind.

He led the way into the deep wooden porch of his house, and subsided into a heavy oaken rocking chair. He looked older.

"Ach!" It was an exhalation of relief. "That's better. Well, as I was saying – the old jetty. That's right, it used tae be doon there, below where they put up that War Memorial. It used tae stretch oot intae deep enough water for the steamer tae come in every day. Well, I was still in my teens then. It must have been in about 1923 or '24 – when some of the grand folk hereabouts started a fund tae build a memorial tae the fallen."

He shrugged with a tilt of the head. "Ye see, that has a particular meaning for me." He pressed his lips together. "My family was more or less wiped oot. Three brothers, and then my father; he volunteered, told a lie about his age and got torpedoed on convoy duty. I was still a boy. I got work with the sheep and had tae look after my mother. Well, anyway, while the money was being collected there were two opinions about it. Some folk said, 'We should use the money tae rebuild the jetty. It's falling intae ruin.' Others said, 'No, let's have a proper War Memorial like other places are putting up.' That group was led by the gentry. Somehow they won the day – I don't know how – and so they put up those great dark lumps of metal that nobody could tell the meaning of, and they put underneath the names of the men who never came back frae the war and that was that. And not long after that, a bit of the jetty fell doon in a big storm, and what was left got too dangerous tae use. The steamer wouldna' come alongside it any more; she had tae stand off and folk had tae go oot tae her in small craft tae board her tae get tae Mallaig for the train tae Glasgow or tae get goods on or off. Sometimes in bad weather we couldna' get oot tae her at a'. And then the time came when the steamer stopped coming altogether. And that was a bad blow. And folk said, 'Oor men who went tae the war and got killed wouldna' have wanted that tae happen tae us. They'd have wanted us tae have the jetty!' "

He fell silent.

"There's another way of looking at it," he said after some moments. "If that jetty *had* been rebuilt, I could have taken all that timber away cheaply by sea! It wouldna' have needed the tremendous cost of all those great vehicles and all that road mileage and fuel and so on. I could have got the logs on tae low bogies and run them straight on tae a ship doon there! Aye, and used the jetty for wool and machinery and livestock and quite a fair bit o' other trade as well."

"I had been wondering about that myself," I said. "Why don't they transport the timber by water? Using modern methods and materials they could put a jetty there at a once for all cost that would be far less than all that heavy transport is costing over a period, to say nothing of the road maintenance. And as you say the jetty would have other business uses too. In fact, taking everything together it would bring some life back into the glen."

He had swung back to the smooth arrogance of the successful business-man. He greeted my words with a curl of the lip, not directed at me but at the blindness of officialdom. "Aye! It's not too hard tae work that oot ye would think! Well, who knows what will happen? Ye know that they are closing doon the paper mill at Corpach? What's going tae happen tae the forestry jobs then?"

"I hear there's a delegation from Lochaber going to see the Secretary for Scotland about that – to persuade him to keep it open."

"Aye, I know. But what's the use? That paper mill's been losing money hand over fist. And *we* pay for it in oor taxes! And what are we doing anyway, taking years and years tae grow those trees just tae make them into newspapers, use them for a day and throw it all away?" He shook his head. "Leaving business out of it, ye must admit that we human kind need oor heids looked at!"

"I've been wondering about trying to use the timber locally. You could set up a small plant to process it, bond it with other materials, and make it into such things as building units."

He became thoughtful. "H'm – ye think it could pay on a small local scale like that?"

"Nowadays, high technology can be scaled down in ways that were not feasible before. The idea that everything must be done on a mass scale is out of date."

"Have you talked to anyone else here about it?"

"Not yet."

"They used tae be good workers in wood here." He was chewing over an idea. He slapped his knee impatiently. "Och why should I bother my heid about a' that?"

He continued to meditate.

"H'm, if that Corpach mill fizzles out," he remarked, "the forestry's going tae have tae scratch its heid about what tae do with a lot o' the timber round here. And then I suppose if somebody offered tae take it off their hands at something near the Corpach price there might be business tae be done?"

"Either way, the government should be on the look out for ways of running the whole forestry operation more profitably.

"Aye. Maybe ye're right. Maybe not!"

That 'maybe not' sounded hopeful. His is the businessman's instinct, while hot on a scent, to pretend total lack of interest. He was thinking hard.

"You'll take a dram?" he said suddenly. "Go in there and fetch the bottle and glasses. Ye'll see them on the dresser. There's a good lad. I'm a bit tired in the legs at the minute."

A widower, he lives alone in the old croft house when he is in the glen. He works the croft with hired labour. His sons run the farms beyond the mountains. The wife of one of his labourers comes in and cleans the house and cooks.

By his scale of commercial operations the croft is insignificant; its importance can only be emotional.

The walls of the little sitting room are almost totally covered with large family photographs; dominated, near the fireplace, by two-foot high enlargements of his father, brothers, cousins, in uniform. Over the mantelpiece a tinted picture of the old stone jetty shows the packet boat *Glencoe* alongside.

I handed him the glass, and he looked up at me shrewdly. "I bet ye're wondering why I bother with the croft, the way things are with me?"

"You were reading my thoughts!"

"Aye, I'm no' bad at that sometimes. Well? Why do I do it?" He sounded roughly jovial. But he was sombre beneath.

"Dare I suggest this" – I watched his face – "you feel a spiritual *need* to look for what remains of firm ground here? Though so many things have gone."

The rough grin vanished. He quaffed the pale amber liquid, brows knitted.

"Och I didna' think ye'd see that," he grunted, "and I didna' expect ye tae call it spiritual! I dinna' want ye tae think I'm greetin' about the way *my* life's gone. I've done a damn sight better than any one of them who were lads here with me. Well, as ye say, what *is* left? Nothing really. Only shadows of what's gone. And ye mustna' think I go around brooding when I come back here. No, that's not good for a man. All the same, when I look at that picture over the fireplace I see my father on the deck o' the steamer. If only – well what's the use of saying it? Anyway, I will say it. I wish he could have seen what I made of my life. Aye, and I wish a few others could have seen it as well. But then again, who knows? If he *had* come back maybe I'd have turned oot differently, stayed on here as a crofter! He was a strict man and I worshipped him and I think I would have followed what he wanted me tae do. But those were unsettled times with those island folk coming over here and taking over crofts when Old Findlay's land was broken up. And who knows how things might have turned out? Aye – Findlay's land wasna' the only thing that was broken up in that time. Ye talk aboot the spiritual? I know you didna' mean something religious. Still I wouldn't have thought of calling it a *spiritual* need."

Wearily he leaned back. "Aye, you go and talk tae Annie Dalrymple aboot a' that. Aye, Annie Dalrymple! I courted her once – or I tried tae! But I was just a poor shepherd boy with a widowed mother tae fend for. Still, never mind about that."

He pushed his chin out.

"Anyway, ye've given me a few things I want tae think aboot."

As I was leaving he said, "Don't tell Annie Dalrymple about any of this."

Which 'this' did he mean?

I set down the bottle on the low table at his elbow. On it there was a red telephone and a dictating machine. He replenished his glass and leaned back, and rocked gently, and stared hard towards the forestry plantations.

I looked back again as I was closing the little iron gate. He had lifted the telephone and was dialling.

Annie Dalrymple, a noted Gaelic scholar, is something of a recluse in her granite house near the old Church of Scotland manse. She is an alert woman of about seventy, slender, supple looking, with clear blue eyes. She speaks with the precision of one whose concern is language.

"I hear you have been having some profound talks with Johnnie Connal?"

I have ceased to marvel at the sensitivity and speed of the grapevine. Had he picked up that red telephone to forewarn her? No. That had surely been in pursuit of some business scheme.

She said, "Johnnie's one of the most wonderful men I have ever known! Oh, he was a fine young man! So strong and bright eyed and quick! Had things been different between our families I would have married him. But I was an obedient daughter. It wasn't possible as things were in those days. You are surprised at my frankness? Well, an *old* lady may be permitted certain freedoms!" She laughed gaily, "Oh, yes! At my age I look at so many things with a clarity and a detachment I wish I could have possessed then. Johnnie's a very close and warm-hearted friend. I must admit I feel sorry, sometimes, that being so successful, he is so unfulfilled."

I had met her briefly, at the Village Hall, at the shop, enough for recognition and a few politenesses. This time, I felt an immediacy, eager, free-flowing, as if we had talked in this way for years. I had come to her from him, carrying a link of sympathy.

"I have known Johnnie since 1924. My father brought us here from the Island when he took over a croft after Findlay's estate was broken up."

I said, "Forgive me, but you yourself mentioned John Connal and family opposition, so could I ask you this: was the difficulty partly due to local hostility towards people from the Island?"

"You do not need to be so delicate." She smiled easily. "No, the opposition, certainly from *my* family, was largely to do with money and status. Though, now you mention it, yes, maybe that *was* an element in it. Johnnie *is* a native and I *am* from the Island! Still, to be honest the basic trouble was money. Johnnie was a shepherd with his tiny wage, the sole support of his mother. How *could* he take on the responsibility of marrying the genteel Annie Dalrymple, the apple of her father's eye? To be fair, though, there was also religion. We were Free Church and he was Church of Scotland. People still felt passionately about schismatic issues."

Only twenty years earlier, in 1904, the government had sent a gunboat to the Island – with a hundred police on board and a regiment of soldiers held in readiness at Fort George – all because of squabbles between the schismatics. Even now, after more than three-quarters of a century, the differences remain sources of disquiet, if not of passion.

"Many locals did object to us island folk coming into the glen." She went on, "And some of the older folk are still bitter. Even in the younger people an emotional undercurrent of 'differentness' persists. I am sure you've heard the locals use the expression 'the new white settlers'? They refer, of course, to the recent wave of incomers from the South, though the expression contains many other meanings, jibes at colonial attitudes and so on. The main point is this: the word 'new' distinguishes them from *us*, the people from the Island who came to the glen in the Twenties. That graft never took. Perhaps that was to be expected. They had lost so many in the Great War. They forgot perhaps that so had we! Our presence, filling vacant places in the glen's life, was salt in their wounds."

She added, "Many of the natives who were left were elderly. Their sons having been killed in the trenches, they had no one left in the family to take on a croft. But there is another reason, sadder still in its way. A number of natives refused the chance of a croft, and chose instead to take a regular job in the forestry. They turned their backs on the land and what it stood for in life. In that respect the Islanders did cling more strongly to tradition. They did stick to the land, and so to the continuity of their values. Only later did some of our men take on supplementary forestry work. Whether the whole crofting system should have been extended, as the politicians did after the Great War, is still debated! It certainly was not the great emotional and economic liberation the demagogues proclaimed it to be. But that is by the way. Slowly the tensions and antipathies sank beneath the surface. An arm's length relationship – a working relationship quite amicable as far as it went – evolved. Gradually that changed too. People drew together, a little closer, in a common defensiveness against the outside world. One thing to be said in favour of the old mutual antipathies is that they rested on something healthy, a strong feeling of identity! Alas that has gone, or nearly so. What remains is so diluted that it does no more than feed the younger people's discontent. It is not a heartening picture."

I said, "These were massive shifts. A collapse of confidence in attitudes towards life that they had inherited from their forbears?"

She nodded, then said with a little toss of the head, "I always have seen life in terms of attitudes, emotional points of view. They shape life. They are the sinews of a culture. Please do not misunderstand my view. I am not one of those who bewail the loss of a static past. The past was not static. Movement was always there. But up to recent times it was usually very slow in its transitions – slow enough to permit new grafts to grow firmly on to the trunk of the past. Even in my time, however, movement has been so fast that there has been no time for that, and the trunk itself has withered. I have spent my life trying to keep the sap flowing. *That* has become my great sorrow. The forces of indifference, of despair, are so strong. Yet it is strange and tragic that the young do have an insight. It tells them to seek spiritual roots; for without them they experience a frightening desolation. To seek these roots through Gaelic can help them. But it is so hard when their families – and their environment – offer little or no sympathy for the quest."

"Talking of emotional shifts," I said, "what was the most crucial?"

She was silent. The little square room, brightening and darkening as the clouds passed, became still. The only movement, an apt one, was in one of the bookshelves, where stood a gleaming video-tape machine whose red digital clock mutely flicked away the seconds.

"The glen ceased to be an island," she murmured. "You may think it strange for *me* to say that! But it's not. When we came to live in the glen all its links were seaborne. Its thinking, its life, its attitudes were bound to the sea. Coal, for instance, came by sea; the puffers unloaded it on to the shingle. We got the mails by sea. We could get 'out' only by sea, unless you were very hardy and had plenty of time. Then you could push a bicycle up the unsurfaced road over the bealach, or travel over in a pony cart – in winter often impossible! – and then try to get a bus; and the buses were very few and unpredictable. In ordinary speech people expressed their feeling of living on an island by referring to the country beyond the bealach as 'the mainland'. It was not simply a feeling we Island people had. The natives did so! People said it without thinking. And visitors used to be puzzled and amused. Only in the last fifteen years or so has the feeling slowly changed, especially after they surfaced the road, and gradually more of the people got cars. For people of my generation particularly, and even for some much younger, it's hard to have to remind ourselves, even now, that the sea and what it means to us – all our dreams, fantasies, legends; its moods, its demands on our intuitions and our sensibility, its influence on our *picture* of the world – is no longer our link with that world.

"Of course, the island image is symbolic of profound attitudes," she mused. "The island viewpoint protects the inherited values. The mainland dilutes and corrupts them. We have ceased to be an island. The mainland has not yet totally drawn us in. Where then do we *belong*? I am speaking now of attitudes in the glen as a whole among both Islanders and natives.

"In that respect," she added, "we are at one with the natives. After all it is more than fifty years since we came. And we do consider ourselves to be locals now."

She coloured, and wonderingly shook her head, "Hearing myself say that, it's strange."

"The links with Island are still there?"

"It's not only that. You mean family? I thought you might mean cultural links. No, the family links are now distant, a matter of second cousins and so on. There is a difference, a deep one I believe, between us and the native born locals, and you may think it strange for me to speak of it in this context. It is in the attitude to Gaelic."

She has written an important book on Gaelic legends, several plays and

100

a number of children's stories in the language. For many years she travelled widely advising on the teaching of Gaelic.

"We did care more for the language than the native-born folk here. That is undeniable. When I was a girl it was common for Gaelic to be spoken in the house, amongst Island folk, I mean. But very much less among the natives. This was a profound separation. And it separates us still."

"Still?"

"Yes. They have forgotten how fiercely Gaelic and its culture was suppressed. They do not want to remember. For many years it was official policy to persecute Gaelic speakers in the Highlands. Teachers used to punish children in school for it. No doubt some teachers genuinely felt that they acted in the children's best interests – forcing them to concentrate on English so as to give them a better chance in the world as they saw it. My niece, for instance, who went to school in Inverness, was strapped mercilessly for speaking Gaelic. Such punishment was certainly condoned by the authorities, to put it no higher, for a very long time. As for the native locals here, they simply gave in, most of them. But we defied the persecution. Nowadays, you may well say, there is no persecution, in fact the reverse because Gaelic instruction is now *permitted* in the schools! But that is not because the dominant attitudes have changed. It is because the suppression succeeded. They now permit the teaching of Gaelic because they believe it is a dead language and presents no cultural threat. With that suppression they also killed off much of the spiritual and emotional in life that Gaelic used to sustain. And as I said, solid values do not grow quickly enough to take over when old ones wither. You are left with a terrifying vacuum! And like any other vacuum something rushes in to fill it; ready-made 'values', if they can be called that, which cannot provide the spiritual certainties that have gone, being as trivial and as temporary as the fleeting fashions that produce them."

I said, "Does nothing remain? Is nothing being recovered, regrown? A lot of people buy your children's books from what I hear. And many schools use them."

She began rolling a cigarette, using black paper reminiscent of Balkan Sobranie. She did it with grace and concentration and licked the edge to seal it with a flourish. Then she fitted it into an amber holder and lit it with a gold lighter. She held the lighter in the palm of her hand and said, in a mixture of pride and irony; "That was presented to me at the Mod for endeavour in the cause of Gaelic culture."

"The odds are heavy?"

She leaned back and took several long draws. The little book-lined room filled with the sharp, throat-catching tang of dark shag.

"Open the window, if you like. I can see you are not used to this

101

tobacco. It is the same as my father used to roll his cigarettes with."

I opened one of the long sash-windows and breathed in the concentrated sweetness of broom. All over the glen in recent weeks its deep burning yellow had sprung out, by the roadside, on the steep lower slopes, and even in the meadows nearby, tell-tale sign of land long out of cultivation.

She said, "Of course the odds are heavy. I go on doing what I can. So do a few others. Forgive me, but I must say this. Many people do not realise that the cause of Gaelic has changed from being a true social movement into being an abstract and, in a sense, political one. Here is an example. In the school here the parents, the locals – and let me be clear, in that term I am now lumping together the true natives and us of Island origin, to differentiate from the new incomers – practically without exception put their children down to do Gaelic. I see the forms, so I know. Well and good, you say. And so the children do a bit of Gaelic in class. But it is very uphill work because out of the whole glen perhaps in only two or three families is Gaelic spoken at all! And even then by no means regularly. So it has no chance of being a true 'mother-tongue' any more. And then, when the child is twelve, and has a faint understanding of the spoken language and a tiny grasp of syntax, and it is time for him or her to go off to the secondary school, lo and behold the parents put them down, not to continue Gaelic, but for French or German! 'Because,' they say, 'Gaelic will not help my son or my daughter to get a job."

"You mean they put them down for Gaelic here in the primary school simply as a pretence of attachment to the cause?"

"I can think of no other reason. It's political. They are staking a claim, nothing more, feeling in their hearts that as a language its place in their life is ended. If I say to them, 'You are cutting off your spiritual roots,' they nod in a kindly, patronising way, as if to say, 'Don't worry about that. We don't want to spoil our children's chances against the world.' "

I said, "*Against?* So it is a confrontation still? That means that there *is* a sense of identity – a differentness they cling to?"

"The question is how strong? Oh dear! I have lived through so many cultural false dawns! The Scottish Nationalists, for instance, try to make use of the Gaelic movement; it suits their book to do so. But it is for them, too, of limited use. For of course, as you know, Gaelic was never more than a regional culture anyway."

"You remind me of Jamie and his poor opinion of the politicians and the crofters' movement."

With the amber holder touching her lips she pondered that. "I see the parallel. And I think his views are apt for the Gaelic question too. Where I differ a little is in this: so long as there is a straw to clutch at we must reach out for it. But we must not make the mistake of fighting the wrong battles. Gaelic can help to fill the vacuum of identity but it can do so only if other things – the way people live, for instance – are right for it. The cities are losing their attraction and there are the beginnings of a movement in reverse. Yes, I think that is true: faint beginnings but they are there. People in the cities are looking wistfully for ways of living in smaller communities once again. Never mind that they do so for the wrong reasons, perhaps. They are feeding the general re-examination of life and how we are living it, the slow awakening to the view that the sophistication and anonymity, and seeming freedom from responsibility that the city offers are not the answer. That new perception *may* swing the balance for localities like this one; young people will not be so certain that the answer to all their perplexities is to get 'out' to the city as soon as possible! And *then* – who knows, I say it with so much caution now! – then they *may* turn back and try to grasp the fuller identity, the sharing in our ancient understanding of life, that Gaelic offers. I have no great hopes! No. I simply keep on this course because . . ." she grinned at me girlishly through the smoke, "because I can do nothing else now!"

Six

Wind of unreason

Summer has come too soon, for it is only early May. The glen is full of golden light. The air is soft, though in the high corries there are long streaks of dull white snow, reminders of the grip of the dark days.

There is an unfamiliar excitement. All the hamlets are astir.

Nothing new, they say, has happened.

And yet something has happened.

Their very reluctance to turn to it is an accolade. For everyone knows, and yet will not say, that the event is important, and not only for what it seems to signify now, but in the evidence it holds up to them of profound movements, beyond vision, the dark forces working in the earth and in the air around them – whispers in the wind; not understood but recognised, respected, feared – elements of themselves.

A little white car buzzes about restlessly. It radiates a curiosity, a concern that is unfamiliar in the glen. Out of it steps a tall broad-shouldered man in a dog collar, with a heavy black greatcoat and a square-looking black Homburg hat. Beneath the hat is a face of serenity and strength. And, unusual in the ministry in these parts, he wears a full blond beard of patriarchal majesty, its thick curls hanging down to the heavy silver watch-chain slung between the lower pockets of his waist-coat.

In the few weeks since he came, he has visited every scattered house. Everyone, local, old incomer or 'new white settler', knows the face, and the deep strong voice, of this ardent spirit ceaselessly on the move.

The Reverend Alexander Mudie, the new minister of the Free Church, has made a powerful impression.

There is much oblique talk about him. Perhaps not so much about *him*, as about what his coming means, now and in the days to come. There is wonder, and there is a disquiet. Everyone is aware that the forces that brought him here are at work within themselves. That awareness is perhaps the most disturbing of all.

And no one will be the same again.

Part of this awareness shows itself in the form of anxiety and attack.

And the attack often betrays the earlier spiritual commitment – abandoned yet still tugging at the heart.

A startling example of this came from Jessie Thoms, one of Isobel Mackay's junior colleagues at the school. "He's finished here!" she said vehemently. "He'll never last here. You mind what I say."

"But why? He's only just arrived."

"Och he's too modern! Folk here will never stand for it."

Jessie is about thirty, small and square, with the open, concerned expression of a sixth-form girl. Her red hair is worn in a thick page-boy bob. She has the pale almost translucent skin and the engaging freckles often seen with that colouring. And her temper, they say, is as fiery as her hair.

The words came strangely from her. To the locals, especially the Free Church adherents, she herself is far too modern. She of all people, they say, should know better.

"Aye, and she comes from a strict Free Kirk family herself! Aye, and her father's a minister, ye know?" They shake their heads. "Aye, it iss as they always say, 'It iss the son or the daughter of the manse that gey often takes the longest steps anyway'."

Her home is on one of the smaller islands, where the fundamentalist stance of the Free Church is maintained in something like its nineteenth-century rigour. She never misses a service on Sundays. But she goes to the Inn and that is doubly wrong; because of the strong drink and because it is 'secular'. The Free Church frowns on secular activity, a term that includes even the Women's Institute gatherings in the Village Hall. Condemned, too, is her smoking – though to be fair she sticks to the old-fashioned principle that a 'lady' does not smoke out of doors – her wearing of slacks, her painted fingernails.

The Reverend Mudie impresses me as sincere, gentle, well-intentioned, a man with a powerful sense of mission. And he has that rare gift of speaking always as if no part of life is trivial, as if everything, every thought and action, must be looked at *sub specie aeternitatis*. Rarer still, he does it with a light touch.

He came into the glen before Easter to take over the vacant 'charge'. The last Free Church minister went to France in 1914 and was killed on the Marne. The glen has 'made do' with missionaries ever since.

Sixty odd years – two generations and more!

I thought of Jamie Macleod's poignant words, '. . . Ye couldna' *think* of the past way of things without thinking of the people who *belonged* tae that past world and who would never come back tae be part of it.'

Had it been, unknowingly, a sanctified despair, a fear of desecrating memory with 'normality'?

'We didn't *know* . . . All we knew was that it had to be different.'

105

Did they simply wait? Or not press hard enough? Did they hope that an 'interregnum' would show them the way – not having the heart 'to go back to how it had been before'? And did the interregnum, the period of 'making do with missionaries', simply prolong itself? Missionaries came and went, year followed year.

And how did the old forces, slowly shifting in the depths of the earth and heart, break through the inertia at last?

I am given reasons of a kind, patently incomplete, uncomfortably expressed, evasive.

Since 1843, when the Free Church emerged after much feuding, proclaiming itself to be 'the unvitiated Constitution of the old Reformed Church of Scotland' its adherents have lived through battles of many kinds, prolonged legal strife, bitter antagonisms that overflowed into many areas of life. There has been spiritual frustration, communal tension. But for the traditionalists in its congregations the Free Church's fundamentalism must have been a source of strength and support as these declining communities tried to hold fast. Whatever these gains, this history of conflict, together with the pastoral deprivation for the better part of this century, have left an atmosphere of defensiveness in the glen.

I sense, sometimes, that the glen has lost its grip on the cause being defended. The ramparts are manned but the fortress is empty.

Outwardly the Reverend Mudie's coming was certainly an extraordinary event. At his Induction the tiny Free Church was filled to bursting, not only with Free Church adherents. And not only from the glen. People came from the whole region. Dignitaries travelled from Edinburgh and Glasgow and London. And from far beyond the seas, from Australia, Canada, America.

For everyone in the glen – not only of the Free Church, but of the Church of Scotland as well as all the 'others' – the event has driven deeply into the long accumulated sediment of life, unfinished emotional business, postponed, forgotten or sleeping.

Even now, so many weeks afterwards, the excitement is almost palpable. Indefinably, in invisible but decisive ways, the familiar world has moved, nudging everyone out of accustomed postures. And not in spiritual attitudes alone.

The Church of Scotland folk feel a sympathetic elation, but some misgiving too. With a new spiritual leadership, seemingly a powerful one, they too will be forced to move, re-examine their position.

Even the lapsed church people sense that this new momentum will take them along too, that their fancied 'solution' – a free-flowing secular world without serious values – will no longer do.

The atheists affect indifference, but not with conviction. They have a sense, inexplicable, alarming, that they too will have to ask themselves

106

where they stand, and that the answer may be nowhere; not in the glen, anyway.

Do they, I wonder, looking back on the fight at the Inn, detect an early sign of reawakened identity among the locals? Do they, and the others, too, see Bill Walsh's retreat on the Sunday licence issue in a different light, as recognition of a strengthened local resolve? Do they remember Calum Johnson's powerful re-statement, at that Community Council meeting, of an older morality? Do they remember how strongly it was endorsed then? And, later, in Calum's return by an overwhelming vote in the Community Council elections, and his re-appointment as chairman?

Do they wonder at the fact, strangest of all perhaps, that several non-Free Church people, including Nellie Templer who used to proclaim that she had 'no time for churches', have been attending Mudie's services in recent weeks?

Among the Free Church people there is a vibration, a sense of being once more connected.

Why then should they 'bother their heids' to analyse the event for my benefit?

Talking to Jemima Macpherson at her gate one day, I remarked, "Not to have had a minister of your own for all that time must have been depressing?"

"Och well, missionaries were cheaper, ye see? My mother used tae talk aboot how things were after the Great War – all those men lost. Some families left without a breadwinner at all! And then the Island folk coming in, and nobody knowing how things were going tae be. It wasna' so much that folk turned away from the Free Kirk. Well, maybe some did, everything being so uncertain and folk feeling, God forgive me, hopeless. Anyway, I suppose folk just waited tae see! And so things went on from year tae year, waiting. And then again, for long enough there wasna' enough money coming in here in oor congregation for the General Assembly tae let us issue a 'call' for a minister of oor ain."

She quickly changed the subject.

Jamie Macleod was typically blunt. "Och why should they waste a minister in a place that's going downhill like this?"

And he too switched to another topic.

Malcolm the roadman was more expansive but could not, or would not, throw more light on why, after a deprivation of more than half a century, the glen now had a minister of its very own. Probably he knew and yet did not *know*; only, as he was to say, 'The time had come.'

"Och well, the Assembly made a special resolution in our favour, tae allow us tae 'call' a minister. Many of us felt we had tae do *something* if the glen was going tae have a chance again. Ye remember me talking to ye aboot a movement to 'get back to the old Highland ways'? Ye were surprised? And ye're no' the only one tae wonder! Well, who knows what will happen? But we couldna' do much without a minister of oor ain tae help us rally oor strength again. Well, that's one way of putting it; perhaps I should call it helping people tae hope once again? And hope comes from *inside*, as the minister himself said last Sunday. Aye" – he sighed, "though it's hard sometimes. Anyway, so we made a special appeal tae the Assembly. Ye see we hadna' enough money, even though we sold oor auld manse for a good price. And it nearly broke the hearts of many of us, especially the older folk, tae do that, and selling it, as we did, tae folk frae England who only stay in it for a few weeks a year. Aye, it was a fine old manse that! It meant something tae every single one of us. The manse and the church! In one way or other all our lives were tied up there – tae them two places."

"But you had to use some of that money to build the new one."

He gave me a shrewd look. "Aye, well, that's right. But it's only a wee bungalow. It didna' cost us that much. It'll do the minister well enough for the time being."

"You mean there's a subsidy from the Free Church headquarters?"

He did not answer directly. "Aye, well, they made a special arrangement for us."

Phyllis Morton put it on a somewhat dampening basis: value for money. "Ye see, we used tae get missionaries tae come for different periods. Well, I don't know but they seem tae have become very expensive these days!"

Malcolm smiled when I mentioned this, but he would not be drawn further. "Och the main thing is we've got a minister at last! And we're going tae build on that. Who can tell what ye can do here till ye make a start?"

Colonel Marriott was typically sardonic. "I suppose you realise that the Free Church has been fighting a guerrilla war since the middle of last century? Since what they call the Disruption. Know what I mean? Now look here. If you could only deploy a very limited number of troops, and if you had insufficient supporting resources anyway, where would you put in fresh fighting men?"

"Where the opposition is weak."

"You've got it in one."

"Is it so weak here?"

"Frankly, yes, though it isn't the Church of Scotland padre's fault. Dunnett's getting on, and he's not a well man. Crippled with arthritis, poor chap. So there you are. There's no doubt there's been some drifting away, but then who am I to talk! Apart from that our family's from a different tradition. When we live at our place down in Hampshire we're C of E. When we're up here we go – when we do! – to the Episcopalian Church though I must admit it's a bit of a sweat. I'm not keen on driving eighty miles round trip for that, now my eyes are playing up a bit. Know what I mean?"

He gestured in a resigned way, and his eternal cigarette dropped its long ash on his pale grey waistcoat.

"Frankly I've never been keen on Church matters at the best of times." He continued, "Well, of course, when we were children it was a case of family prayers with the padre in attendance! Church on special occasions of course. Know what I mean?"

I pressed Jessie Thoms to explain why she damned Reverend Mudie as 'too modern'.

We had met as she walked away from school. As she came out of the playground, the little iron gate creaked on dry hinges. All sounds had the muffled, distant tone that comes with summer, unfamiliar now so early in the year. Far away, beyond the lighthouse, someone was burning off stubble; thick blue smoke floated darkly in the clearer blue of the cloudless sky.

We are in an unseasonal heat wave. No one can remember a May like this; such a heat and such a drought. We have had no rain at all for a month. The hillsides are turning a premature brown. The river is drained down to a trickle. Even the great pool below Cruachan is so low that I can see the foundations of the perimeter wall planted in its rocky bed.

"He's wearing a tie!" she said as if no further evidence was needed. She thought better of it and added, "And no hat! *And* he hasna' got a black suit on either!"

Earlier that afternoon I had spotted Mudie hurrying from his little car to take his weekly Bible class at the school. Of this astonishing innovation I shall speak presently. Usually he is to be seen in the standard uniform, black suit with clerical collar and black Homburg hat, with his black greatcoat in the cold weather. Today he wore a suit of dark 'clerical' grey, a white shirt and black tie and no hat. The air was still, oppressive, more like the dogdays of summer. He mopped his brow with a gleaming white handkerchief.

"But in this heat," I said, "the poor man's doing his best, surely? He's wearing a very proper clerical grey suit, and the tie is a black one!"

She shook her head. "That's not good enough. He's letting the standards go. The folk here can't abide changes like that. They want a minister not only to *be* the right type but to *look* it! Otherwise they'll think – well, if that's the way he goes about, not *seeming* to care, then he can't be the right man *inside* either! You'll see. He won't last. Not unless he changes his ways quickly."

She added, frowning, "And no hat of all things!"

Her disapproval was too emphatic. Lurking behind it, there must be a powerful unease.

Half to herself she added, "Aye, appearances do matter. They do have a meaning."

She stopped with a little jerk as if she had physically tripped. She questioned me with her eyes. "Have you been talking to him then?"

"Quite a bit, as a matter of fact," I said, thinking of our long discussions. "He's a man of very wide learning and a thinker. He's a very good and sincere man I feel."

She pressed her lips together. "I thought you probably have! You seem to be . . ." She frowned and looked away.

I wondered if her outburst against Mudie had been a symbolic cry for help. A daughter of the manse, her uncertainty hurts more. If the minister, himself a sign-post of certainty, seems to waver, that is frightening.

She said, after a little silence, smiling timidly, "I was thinking, since ye know so much about the way things are here – especially because you can stand away and not be directly involved, impartial in fact – that you could perhaps help? He may not realise that these little things, the appearances as ye say, might put some folk against him before he has a chance to do any good."

The appearances 'as you say' – she had forgotten already that it was she not I, who had said, '. . . appearances do matter'.

Mudie was born on one of the outer isles about forty-five years ago. His speech is guttural, deliberate, muscular, containing an engaging re-arrangement of the customary stresses, as if he had taken the language to pieces and rebuilt it brick by brick to transmit his evangelical vision.

"When I received this call" – he drew out the word so that it sounded like 'ca-w-w-w-l' – "I heard the voice of God sounding in my ears. I felt I *must* come *here* and do His work! And that is why I came."

He came to the glen from a missionary assignment in India.

One day, when he had been here only a week or two, I said to him, "Tell me, do you intend to give any religious instruction in the school?"

He stood for some moments in deep thought. "Aye, well, I am here to do God's work! In the school too, I would hope. Aye."

He added, "I have not yet called upon the other minister, of the Church of Scotland, I mean. And I must talk to the mistresses at the school. It would be unfortunate if there were an accidental clash."

"I imagine there will be no difficulty *there*."

He caught the emphasis. "You mean there might be óther difficulties?

"May I say," he added before I could reply, "ye have been here for some time I understand, observing? I am pleased tae learn all I can from ye."

It was said with a delicate inference. I could speak freely.

I said, "Reverend Dunnett tells me that he goes into the school to give religious instruction two or three times a year."

He drew in his breath so sharply that a whistling sound emerged. What was visible of his face above the beard reddened. "I think I understand," he said with care.

I thought of Colonel Marriott and the fresh troops going in.

Mudie said, "Och I am well thankful tae ye. I must follow the voice of God tae the children too. What you have told me will help me tae do God's work among them. Ye mentioned another type of difficulty?"

"I am going to pull your leg a little."

He smiled faintly, watching me. "Aye, go on then."

"I am told that there are *three* religious groups in the glen, not two."

"Three?" He said it from politeness, playing the game.

"Yes, three. The third is even more passionately dogmatic than the other two."

The faint smile remained. He waited patiently.

"I'm thinking of the atheists."

"Aye?"

"They are violently against any form of religious activity in the school, even the singing of psalms. They pounce on the poor teachers, plague the life out of them! Isobel Mackay and her colleagues, conscientious and hard-working, are caught in a cross-fire. Between the atheists on the one side and the Church of Scotland and the Free Church people on the other."

"Aye, and those two groups are divided as tae what should be included and how it should be given tae the children?"

"So I understand."

"So the teachers try tae play safe?"

I did not want to be drawn on that. It would not be fair. "I'd rather the teachers spoke for themselves on that one."

He nodded his bent head. "Och it iss not an uncommon predicament. I have known teachers, in my own village for instance, who say, 'We'd sooner no' be involved in religion in the school at all. Then we'd have a chance tae get on with oor job and have a quiet life!' The question is . . ." he sighed heavily, "what iss their job! Tae so many teachers the education of the young iss a *secular* task! And nothing more than a 'task'. We are in a secular age. Once upon a time it was understood that teachers should be committed Christians! And it was their bounden *duty* tae instil the word of God in tae their charges!"

He mused for some moments, then roused himself. "Aye, there iss much work for me here." He sighed again, "Aye! And anent these atheists, as you call them, do they declare themselves tae be such?"

"It seems so."

"They are among the incomers only, I would suppose?"

"Yes."

"H'm. Certainly God has called me for a great work in His name here."

I was glad that he had not risen to my sally about the atheists being a 'religious group'. He is too serious a man to be lured into an arid debate. He keeps the talk on his own ground, his mission, the need for the Church to be closely related to daily life.

"Or rather," he corrected himself, "I should put it the other way. Many preachers forget that the common man and woman need tae have dogma made explicit. Och I know ye won't think I'm being superior when I talk like this, as befits men, shall I say, of learning and of goodwill? Every action, every thought, in daily life must reflect the Word of God."

He talked of the history of the Free Church, of its fundamentalism.

"Ye see," he wound up in the deep resonant voice, "we are the undeviating bearers of the original Reformation message."

"You continue straight on from John Knox?"

He considered that, as he does most remarks, for some moments.

"Aye, ye could say that. One moment." He searched among the heaps of books scattered over his modern steel desk. "Ye may like tae look at a history of oor Church. And here is a short biography of oor great leader in the early years, Thomas Chalmers."

We come together fairly often, sometimes on the road, for he is an indefatigable visitor. A superficial view would be that he is determined to 'play himself in' quickly. That would be less than fair. He is patently sincere.

When Isobel Mackay went down with 'flu, in the very first days of his settling in, he hurried to call upon her, and busied himself with arrangements for hot meals to be sent in to her and for general sick-room care.

News of this action echoed quickly through the glen.

"Aye, he must be a good man!" said Morag, blushing. "There was no call for him to visit her even!" Morag's family are staunch Free Church people. Isobel Mackay, Morag was saying, is 'only' Church of Scotland after all.

Isobel herself was full of it. "He didn't mind catching my 'flu himself! And considering he's got young children too! But anyway there I was, lying there, you know aching all over and the door knocker went downstairs and, thinking it was maybe Jessie Thoms coming in to make me a cup of tea or something, I called out – or rather I could hardly call out! My throat was sore. But I did my best to say loudly, 'Come on in – the door's unlocked.' And the next thing I hear is a man's step on the stair! And I think – my goodness! – what will folk say? A man coming in up to my bedroom! And me in my nightie! They'll be writing to the director about my goings on."

She laughed at the thought, not altogether dismissing it.

"Aye, then there's this timid knock on the door and a deep voice I'd never heard before says, clearing its throat; 'May I come in, Miss Mackay?

It's Mudie – Reverend Mudie. I hear ye are not well.' I felt better then about it. The new minister! That's all right then. But the Free Church minister? What will they say about that? So in comes this great bearded face, and he tiptoes in and takes a chair quite near the bed. And he was so *sweet*. He didn't stay long, just long enough to ask how I was and whether Doctor Boddie had been in, and what I'd had to eat. And then off he goes and comes back again a little while later with some hot soup his wife had made for me."

She added, "That's a new thing for the glen. Or rather it's going back to something older. I would never have thought it."

I see him just as often at his house. As I pass his gate on my evening walks, he may come to the window, perhaps welcoming the interruption. "Come on in! Have a cup of tea with us!"

His wife sets out her sumptuous baking, with a pot of good strong tea. She is a charming sloe-eyed woman from the Border country, of few words, of radiant sympathy. She sits at her knitting and listens as our talk rides over the horizon. Listens, too, for the restless noises of her four children.

"Four!" I showed my amazement the first time she mentioned her family. I had stopped at their gate to pass the time of day. She was hanging out washing in the blustery March sunlight.

"You think I'm too young!" she said happily. "Och they all say that. We have two sets of twins. Twin girls and twin boys. I never thought that God would bless us that way twice. But He did."

She studied me. And she read my thoughts.

"What shall I do now?" She spread her arms a little to the side; and her thoughts took her away, and she coloured. "I love children! But it would be difficult if . . ." She smiled shyly. "God must be our guide."

In their little sitting room, with its flowered carpet, cane furniture and lacquered tea trolley, she gently presides. Mudie returns again and again to personal responsibility in the following of God's word.

I talk of the crumbling community, weakened identity, fading certainties, Jamie Macleod's hard view.

Mudie sees only one answer, or rather only one road to an answer. "The road of God's word must save them. Aye!" he clasped his hands, chin sunk on his chest, "there isna' any other way."

"You do not feel, perhaps, that things here have gone too far, as some of the folk say?"

"Too far?" He looked up in puzzlement. "There is no living soul that is beyond saving by the word of God."

"I mean in economic and social terms. The young can't get jobs and so they go away, or long to go! As you know the crofting economy cannot keep them. The feeling of identity with the glen is fading. We have talked of these things many times. Take young Morag, for instance. She dearly longs to go. She told me a few days ago that she has heard of a job in Glasgow learning the hairdressing. Yet she is torn, for in her heart the idea of going, of severing her roots, saddens her. She knows, too, that if she goes she will never come back – not, that is, to *live* here again in the closely joined way she has lived here all her life."

I am aware that his mind is hovering above these secular matters, looking for a spiritual perch and not finding it.

I said, "In the city such spiritual links as survive are weak. Even here in the glen such strength as remains is more in the memory, the folk memory you might say, than in the present reality. It is backward-looking, abstract. People talk endlessly of how things *were*; sure sign that the present is rejected, and that the bridge with the past has fallen down. You preach here *now*. But as the locals die off, as the incomers increase the strength of secular attitudes by their very presence, who will be left for you to preach *to*? Forgive me for putting it so bluntly. But I believe you and I have a purpose in common."

Mairi Mudie put down her knitting and leaned forward, joining in his meditation.

He surfaced, and looked up, and his gaze penetrated right through me to some far horizon, beyond the sea; backwards in time I felt. Perhaps, I wondered, to some far corner of his life.

"Aye, in a way I agree with ye. We talk, I hope, always with oor hearts open tae each other! And so I'll say this to ye. I have tae tread carefully, an' if I were tae interfere in secular matters many folk wouldna' stand for it! An' that's a fact! Still, I must find a way. For if congregations shrink because people go, where do I stand then? The malaise, then, will be the dispersion and isolation of souls, a condition in which belief in the word of God is much harder tae sustain as I well know."

'As I well know'. What crisis had shaken him? How did *his* revelation come to pass?

Like many of his colleagues he came to the ministry after some years 'out in the world'. He had been a solicitor for ten years.

"Aye, ye ask what can be done?" he said after a silence, raising his head and looking about him, mouth open like a swimmer surfacing from a dive.

I said, "You feel that if the spiritual force is strong enough the inspiration for secular action will come from within?"

"If ye want tae put it that way – yes! If God wills that they are prompted tae stay, and the community tae thrive again, and that they *will* arrange matters tae that end, then they will find a way for His will tae come tae pass!"

I wanted to say, 'But has man *no* free will? Must we believe that the decay here in the glen is God's will? And that there is *nothing* we can do?'

I must not say that. For me to introduce that old controversy, with

114

echoes of Arminianism and its fierce condemnation by Calvin, would be a tactless challenge.

Still, it is far from a dead controversy in Scotland today.

He rose to the hint of it. "Och ye are disappointed? Ye feel that each soul has a will? You want my help in stimulating that will to act in a certain way. I have wrestled with that dilemma for many years! But I too am but dust. We are all dust!"

His chin sank once more to his chest.

"Can we not see it as our duty?" I said. "Folk here know in their hearts that their chances of rejuvenating the glen are fading day by day. And yet they will not compromise. It is as if they were saying, 'It is all or nothing.' And if other communities are anything to go by it *will* be nothing! They are expressing a kind of despair. Should we not help them to overcome that?"

He wrung his hands, nodding dubiously, "What have ye tae suggest?"

"I was wondering whether one could gather together a small group – no more, say, than six people – to examine the possibilities of renewal? At the very least that coming together could start ideas moving. And then, individually, initiatives could follow. There are many areas in the glen's economy where enterprise, and adaptation, could be fruitful. We've talked on these lines before, haven't we?"

Mrs. Mudie smiled encouragingly and picked up her knitting again.

After a longer silence than usual, he said, "I feel that there is God's will in what ye say. I feel that ye speak from the heart. As for me, I am a new soul here. As always I look for a sign of God's will. But ye have planted seeds. Let me try tae find the way."

It is a holding statement. Nothing more. 'Interference' or intervention is not in the tradition. Grandeur of preaching, uplifting influence from the pulpit, nothing more is expected.

Mudie looks back beyond John Knox to Calvin and even to Saint Augustine. Man's natural will is perverse, disinclined for good. 'We are all dust' is in some ways a fully protected stance, one that allows you to avoid direct moral responsibility. Dust, after all, can have *no* will!

The strength of a silent, unreflecting tradition, the 'dust' holding fast, came through to me when Isobel Mackay described the parents' meeting at the school.

I had wondered why the atheists had made their assault on the old ways at this time. Had they, too, sensed the dark powers shifting in the earth beneath them? And, fearing them, did they too question the answering tremors in their own hearts?

> And what rough beast, its hour come round at last,
> Slouches towards Bethlehem to be born?

For many of these 'new white settlers' the great attraction of the glen had been the decay of its traditional values and the seeming openness accompanying it. They would not have expressed the feeling like this. They saw the decay, with its relics, as they thought, of a serene simplicity, as naïve charm. The openness, in reality a mixture of traditional politeness and the quiescence of despair, they interpreted as carte blanche to realise their dreams. But if old values were to rule again the 'openness' would go. Intolerance would ride roughly over them. The glen would cease to be the refuge where, unhampered by the prejudice of others or the debris of their own past, they could fashion a freer, purer life.

In aiming at a secular influence in the school – a strategic position – had they instinctively hoped to hold tradition at least in check, if not to push it back?

Isobel sat erect in her leather wing chair in reflective mood, seeming to be happy with the result, but there was a hint of unease too.

She said, "First of all it's only fair to give *you* the credit. It was your suggestion that *I* call the meeting and I . . ."

"Come now," I protested, "the idea could have come to you anyway. And it was *your* decision! But tell me first of all what happened. If it was a good idea that is all that matters."

She smiled faintly. The unease seemed to come closer to the surface.

"All right then. The amazing thing was – guess who came along and didn't say a single word?"

"Burke himself?"

She pouted. "Someone told you!"

"You gave it away! The way you said it. It had to be the chief instigator. Did they shout him down?"

"Och no! It didn't come tae that. He just sat there huddled up, looking worried – aye, and I think a bit frightened. He must have felt the hostility. Och the old ones – they were marvellous! Ye could see their eyes piercing straight through him like swords. Talk aboot discretion being the better part o' valour. Och but you're making me tell the story back tae front!"

"I'm sorry. I side-tracked you! I'm listening."

"Aye, well, I'll start again then," she looked down at her hands, cheeks flushed, the excitement returning. "I was not too sure myself what tae expect. About forty or so parents came. That was a surprise to begin with! I've given up calling meetings for things. The only things they'll turn out for are film shows or Bring and Buy Sales in the Village Hall, where there's tea and cakes and they can have a good old gossip. But that's not all – about twenty grandparents came. *And* two great-grandparents. Would you believe it!"

I pictured them sitting defensively together in those moulded plastic chairs of shrieking yellow in that stark modern assembly room – old women and their married daughters or daughters-in-law, withdrawn faces outlined under close-fitting woollen hats. The hissing of the radiators echoing forlornly. And on the raised platform – too small to be a proper stage, as Isobel often complains – with its litter of old desks, netball equipment, books, dressing-up boxes and two battered upright pianos, Isobel presiding primly at a high old-fashioned oaken desk.

"The old guard turning out in force! And what about the atheists?"

"The really militant ones no! Apart from Burke. The word must have gone round that the locals were going to turn up in strength. So only a few of the moderates were there with him, a sort of token appearance! I started off by saying more or less what I had written in the notice calling the meeting: 'I had been approached . . .' – and before I could go on, old Maggie Macvoe – she was one of the great-grandmothers there – interrupted me: 'And *who* approached ye, Miss Mackay?' All very proper with the 'Miss Mackay', it's usually 'young Isobel' when she meets me on the road! And I said, 'Well, Mr. Burke did for one.' And she snorted and looked round as if to say, 'We'll see about that!'

"So I went on, all sweetness and light, saying that though I thought the existing direct contact between parents and teachers was satisfactory, my colleagues and I would not wish to stand in the way of new ideas that *might* be helpful and so on and so forth. As I talked, Maggie and the older locals got more and more restless. At last Maggie said quietly, but knitting her brows fiercely, 'Miss Mackay! Ye're surely not in *favour*!'

" 'Well, Mrs. Macvoe,' I said to her, 'my colleagues and I want to help in every way we can. That is our duty. If you, the parents and members of families, *want* a parent-teacher association – then *you* must decide.'

"And then all the locals – they were sitting together in a solid group – turned and stared at the little handful of incomer parents as if *daring* them to open their mouths!"

"And did they?"

"Just about! But not *him*. Talk about someone's face being a 'study'! He didn't dare look at anybody straight, not even his own followers."

"The old guard was meeting his challenge with drawn swords!"

"Aye," she said a trifle sadly, "you were right. If I had let *him* call the meeting, the old folk – the old guard as you put it– mightn't have turned up in force like that. Still, I felt a bit sorry for him all the same."

"Even though *he* was attacking you? You are a generous soul!"

"Och well, maybe I am too forgiving?"

She looked away from me. Outside, the darkening clouds were piling up over the sea.

She brightened a little as she turned back. "Aye, well, there *was* a bit more – in fact the most interesting part really. One of the incomers spoke up – oh *so* quietly – saying, 'We just thought it might be a good idea for parents' views to be heard "educationally".' And Maggie growled at her, 'And what, pray, do you know about education? That's what Miss Mackay and the other two went tae college for! We don't want folk using oor children tae make experiments with new ideas they don't understand themselves! If a child o' oors is not doing well enough at school, or is being a rascal and making trouble, we go and talk it over with the teacher and see what can be done – and that's that. Apart from that we let the teachers alone tae do their proper work in peace. We will *not* have them interfered with!' And she looked round at the other locals sitting together with her and they all nodded their heads and after that it all sort of fizzled out."

"Just like that?"

"Well, there was a bit of talk then – I myself started it simply to save people's faces, and perhaps to cool tempers a bit – oh about the school play, and sports outings, and collecting money for the hire of a coach for the outings and so on. And then – oh yes – I said, just to put my own final word on things, 'We can consider, next term, whether you want to meet again on this subject. If you do, let *me* know and I shall be happy to call another meeting.' There was a confused murmur, which amounted to, 'Maybe'. And that was that."

"Next term? That is *this* term? Has there been any word from anyone about another meeting?"

"Not a sound."

She was silent, and looked far into the distance. An unseasonal rainstorm now battered the window panes. The meadow, carpeted in buttercups, blazed in waving gold. Round the house the foliage seemed to thicken before one's eyes. The differing shades of green grew more vibrant still. In the pasture the lambs, now solid and strong, the size of lean young terriers, ran about on stiff legs and looked up at the rain and shook themselves.

"Do you think," she said, "that anyone could suspect that you had a hand in it? I mean in the way it turned out."

"Is what you did so much out of character that they would suspect another hand in the game?"

"If you put it that way, then I'm not sure. But I must tell you something else that has happened in the school and I'm amazed that I haven't had coals of fire on my head from the atheists about it! I've been bracing myself for it every day, and still the attack does not come."

That straight-backed look of hers is poignant in its innocence! It seeks in vain the signposts of a surer world.

"Tell me."

I wondered as I spoke, and then I knew.

"I fancy you can guess." She smiled ruefully. "Mr. Mudie came into the school at the beginning of term, and after chatting generally for a bit, asked if he could meet the children in class. He would like to talk to them now and again about God. Now to me it was significant that he didn't ask *any* questions at all about whether the Church of Scotland minister was giving religious instruction, or how often, and so on. He knew already! And he knew something else – something many people *don't* know. You may not believe this but religion is the *only* 'subject' the school is obliged by law to teach!"

"No, I didn't know that."

"I'll dig out the document and show you it. Anyway I suppose, come to think of it, *he* should know the regulations about that! He skilfully inserted the fact into our conversation. And then, gently but with unmistakable firmness he said that he would come in once a week."

"I'm sorry," I said. "I see you really *are* concerned. But surely they can't get at you now? Especially after that meeting. You had a good turn out of the old guard. And they showed that they had closed their ranks and are ready to fight? Most of them were Free Church I fancy?"

She nodded, and looked down at her hands open in her lap.

"And now," I continued, "this new broom of a Free Church minister comes in to the school and claims the right, under the law of the land, to give religious instruction! You've got powerful forces ranged on your side. Duncan and his crowd dare not challenge *them*. That is why they're quiet!"

She said nothing for a time. Then she began to speak in a different voice, softly, timidly, as if daring to summon up thoughts out of the far depths. "Sometimes I get a feeling that great and terrible forces are gathering around me. Perhaps it is my isolation here? But I wonder why all these things are happening at once! It is unbelievable that there should be an 'awakening' in this place! And yet these 'awakenings' do happen. My father has often talked of the great 'Lewis Awakening' thirty years ago. And there have been others in the Highlands, even in the last few years. The descriptions are terrifying. People going into trances, throwing themselves about and so on. My father has seen some of it in nearby parishes. Of course there are people who say it isn't religious at all but mass hysteria! But then they always say that, don't they?

"That doesn't make it any better!" she went on. "*Worse* if anything. More frightening. If it were to happen here I feel they could turn on me! Simply because I stand away from them. I try to bring reason into their world. After all they did do things like that in remote places like this in the old days; the teachers represented the forces of unrighteousness!"

She too has listened to those whispers on the wind.

Here was another's intuition to set beside my own. I could question mine, for perhaps I *wanted* to feel that an 'awakening' could be on its way? But for her it is certainly not wish-fulfilment. Her fear is real.

119

Gently I asked, "How worried are you?"

She looked away out of the window. Outside, for an instant, the world was silent. The rain had stopped its rattle on the glass. The road was quiet. No vehicles or tractors could be heard. Quietly the great trees swayed and shed heavy drops with a plop and patter on the garden flagstones. And then bird song sounded out again and the broad chestnut leaves glistened as the sun came through.

Without turning round she said, "I don't think I would feel safe if the old guard, as you call them, turned fanatical and took some of the younger ones along with them. The 'wind of unreason' as my father calls it, is dangerous. I *am* a believer – in my own way. But all that tumult, all that wild emotion, all that hysterical ranting of people who have lost all control of themselves – that frightens me so."

"If it is the only way for the glen to break out of its inertia? What then?"

She turned slowly and her expression was of wonder and sadness. "There would be no place for me here – any more."

In seeking sanctuary in the glen, she had wanted to come *closer* to the old certainties, not to escape them. In her innocence she had brought with her the world of reason, of enlightenment, *her* hard-won world, and sought to fuse the two, an alchemy of the soul and the mind, that soaring Renaissance vision. That was her dream. The violence of an 'awakening' would tear and trample it. She, a 'new woman' born long after her time, could not then be at peace here. She would stand out against the 'wind of unreason' and she would suffer.

Her simple spirituality had made her flee from the nihilism of the city. And now she sensed the gathering of primitive forces, indifferent, intransigent, menacing, futile to oppose. She would have to flee once more.

And where, this time, could she go?

"Perhaps," I said, "it won't happen the way you fear? If at all."

She shook her head. "I feel it will! My father says, 'Keep your head down and let the "wind of unreason" blow itself out!' I doubt if I am strong enough to do that. I always felt I *was* strong enough to stand up for my principles. But that is all very well if you can meet reason with reason! I have never had to face this sort of test. I can feel it in my bones getting nearer and nearer. It is a shock to realise how naïve I have been all this time."

Later, I mentioned Jessie Thoms. "Perhaps, as she says, they'll send Mudie packing and that will be that?"

She thought about it. "Jessie's torn, like me! We're both daughters of the manse! Except that her father's Free Church and mine is Church of Scotland. Jessie knows she's back-sliding. And she's afraid that Mudie's influence here will force her, too, to stop drifting, to make up her mind

120

where she stands spiritually. And that upsets her. And so she finds something to damn *him* for, not realising that in doing so it is her own traditional upbringing coming to the fore!

"And then again," she added, "she may be right about his modernity. I never have understood the Free Church mentality."

I said, "I also have a sense of change impending. How much has it to do with him? Certainly his presence is felt all over the glen."

"I didn't know," she said wonderingly, "when you came in just now, that I was going to talk about all this. It must have been on my mind." She pressed her lips together. "Perhaps I shouldn't? But then, there is no one here I *can* talk to, in this way. That is what I meant when I said I am isolated."

Mudie's bungalow is almost next door to the Free Church, a stark, barn-like building on the edge of a piece of waterlogged land below Cruachan. The walls, painted a dazzling white, accentuate the darkness of the low slate roof. Its few small windows are of plain frosted glass. The roof guttering, drain pipe and the single square door are of a sullen green, the colour of the brooding pines and firs on the plantation higher up. I stood contemplating its severity one day when he came up.

"Have you heard any references?" He looked well satisfied with himself.

"References?" Then I caught the meaning. "You mean the school? I did hear you had gone in. No, I've heard *no* comments. Tell me about it."

The bushy beard parted in a grin. "I am giving a class once a week. But I am puzzled. Not a word from any parent. Even when I visit they say nothing about it. And there has been nothing from your *third* group!"

"Maybe they're all recovering from the shock! You simply marched in and started?"

"Very nearly! It iss clear that the teachers are glad tae have the responsibility taken out o' their hands."

"One way or another!"

"Aye. As ye say, they feel they might be attacked any time either on sectarian grounds or by these confused people you say call themselves 'atheists'. They canna' defend themselves. But my position iss strong because I serve God, not the State, and so I can be a shield for these well-meaning ladies, the teachers."

"That explains the atheists being quiet! They are doing some hard thinking. They could find themselves in head-on collision with you and your Church."

"They may still." He sounded as though a fight would be to his liking.

"All the same," I said, "that doesn't explain the silence of the locals. Wouldn't some of them be pleased? And tell you so? Though I suppose the Church of Scotland adherents might raise sectarian objections."

"That, too, might not be unwelcome." He grinned again. "But, ye know, when the children go home and talk about it they might make their parents uncomfortable. Children are inclined to give their parents harsh reminders on moral matters! Still it iss my mission and I am bound tae proceed with it come what may."

Again I hear the undertone of belligerence. This is no meek pastor. He sallies forth fully armed. He will lay about him.

He certainly thunders from the pulpit. Jemima Macpherson told me that on his first Sunday here he had shouted out, 'Think! Think of it, my friends! If you do not make your answer – *cursed for all eternity!*'

The believers are stirred and comforted. They hear the bugles as the relieving forces march.

And Jessie hears the trumpet of retribution.

But Isobel feels the earth tremble and the walls shake as the 'wind of unreason' gathers strength.

In our conversations Mudie is gentle, polished, forbearing. I had yet to hear him in action.

I said, "I have been thinking of attending service in your church. I thought I would mention it to you first."

"Och it iss public worship of God. You will be welcome at any time to come and take part in it."

Conflict between the adherents of the two churches, Maggie Macvoe declares, has hurt everybody.

"When I was a girl before the First War, aye – and afterwards as well, the adherents of the Free Church and the Church of Scotland lived in a harmony that doesna' exist any more. I will chust give you an example. At the Communion time the two had their Communion services on different Sundays, and folk crowded into one another's church. The difference didna' worry anybody. Well then, the time came when a Free Church missionary – I forget which one but it was after the last war anyway – decided tae change all that. From then on, the Communion service was held on the *same* Sunday as the Church of Scotland! Aye, and naebody went to the other's church after that!"

She speaks in the tight, clipped fashion often heard on this coast, among older people whose first language is Gaelic. At eighty-four she is sturdy, bright-eyed, and active. She looks after a couple of cows and a great black horse, one of a very few in the glen, which draws a little springy two-wheeler when she goes visiting.

She prodded the fire, still kept going for her though it was so warm outside, and then tucked stray wisps of silvery hair under her close-fitting red woollen cap.

"Aye, they split families too. Ye see many o' the folk who came over from the Island after the First War were Free Church, and some o' them married Church of Scotland persons. So they put husband against wife sometimes, married children against their parents. They even set children against each other! For sometimes the father – or mother – wouldna' go intae the other's church tae hold the baby for baptism! And so the child chust grew up, not knowing anything about the reasons, and in later years many of them didna' go tae church at a' because o' the way their minds had been confused. And so they were lost!"

"Why did they do it?" I wondered aloud. "You would think they could have known that would happen?"

She was listening to something outside. Her house is the middle one of a group of three, isolated on a knoll beside the river some way above Cruachan, in a part of the glen still intensively cultivated. On one side of her lives a son and his wife and some of his children – the older ones are away. On the other lives a grandson and his wife and two small children. Another son, with wife and children, live with her. That is how she expresses it. 'They live with me.' She is the matriarchal queen of this little hamlet, still a working member of it.

Outside, in the yard formed by the steading, a young woman in a bright red headscarf was chasing a little boy of about three.

"I was chust listening," she apologised with a quick smile, "for young Alison talking to Jamie – that's my little great-grandson – to make sure she speaks to him in the Gaelic. She sometimes forgets, ye see? And I insist that the very first words the little ones understand iss in the Gaelic. What were ye saying then?"

"Why did they do it?"

"It iss hard to understand. I chust cannot believe that God wants good living and God fearing families to be split. I suppose they thought after the last war that people were losing the feeling of *belonging* to the particular church. Still, I myself cannot judge them. Maybe they were right, because even after the First War there *was* some slipping away, especially after the Island folk came in here and made difficulties for us."

"How did they do that?"

"It iss hard for ye to see that maybe. This iss how it was. First of all most of them were Free Kirk. We were used tae the ways of oor *ain* Free Kirk folk. But these Island folk were strange tae us – they were rough, hard, wild. Another thing was, when they came intae the glen many of them spoke *no* English! No English at all! They were always bothering us tae speak for them, or help them with official papers and so on. And all the time we had in oor minds the sadness – well we took it from our older folk, but some of *us* could remember – aboot oor ain men lost in the Great War. And what were we doing helping these people tae come in and take their places? Aye, that time was full of bitterness for us."

She pulled a grey shawl closely about her and leaned forward to prod the logs in the deep hearth. The strong westerly wind sent cool draughts swirling about the room. Then she straightened up and her pale blue eyes had clouded.

"But it wasna' only that. It was the way they went aboot things – riding rough-shod over the way *we* felt aboot the right ways to go aboot life! Och here's an instance that might help ye tae understand that. For a long time after they came, they lived in *huts* – aye huts! Chust one room if you could call them that. They lived like – well – I will say it like this – it was nae better conditions than we had for oor beasts. And they reared six, eight, ten children like that. Ye'll see in a minute why I say that. One family – please do not mind if I do not say the name! But it wasna' the only one I could speak of! Anyway, it was a shameful, an extraordinary thing. They came tae oor hoose and asked us for the loan of a room for a Free Kirk missionary tae baptise their child. Och my mother didna' think. And she said 'Yes'. And the day came, and everything was got ready in oor hoose. And then when the missionary came, we could see that he was a bit put oot – because it wasna' chust the *child* tae be baptised but the *father* as well! Aye – well there ye are then – they didna' understand how we folk felt about it. That was the kind of upset they brought upon us."

She talked about the 'back-sliders' and the occasional conversion in recent years. "Sometimes they stay solid after that. Sometimes, I'm sorry to say, they do not."

I thought of Agnes Mackinnon, a young woman of twenty-five, the only local girl who, after training as a nurse, returned and settled in the glen. She is blonde and bouncy, but with a certain sadness in her eyes. She is a compulsive talker, and has a religious obsession that made me think before I knew *she* was one, of the recent converts. They cling to the life raft long after they have reached dry land.

One day I was waiting to go into the mobile bank, a large van that stops near the old jetty once a week. She came up to me. "I think yer steps were guided here. Is that not true? I believe that is why ye came to the glen."

That, after all, is a way of putting it.

I said, "I suppose you could say that."

"There ye are!" she said eagerly. "Now wouldn't that be wonderful if ye heard the word of God here? I heard that ye are coming to oor church next Sunday! There was a wonderful conversion there a few weeks ago – a woman cried out! Oh, it would be wonderful, wouldn't it? I was converted, ye know? Oh, I was a rascal before that!"

"What do you mean, a rascal?"

She blushed. "Oh, a rascal! That's all! And then I heard the word."

"But a *rascal*? I *am* surprised."

"Oh well, I was interested too much in, ye know, worldly things!"

'Worldly things' was obviously a borrowed expression.

She would go no further. At that moment, my turn came to go up the two steps into the bank van. I could not resist a parting sally. "Well, when a young woman says she was a rascal, it usually means only one thing."

She convulsed in rosy laughter, and in the same moment stretched out a hand towards me, the forefinger and little finger pointing – the ancient sign against the evil eye. Rocking in a new, heightened excitement, she gasped, "Oh ye'es!"

"Agnes Mackinnon stopped me on the road today," I said, "and told me that *she* had been a rascal – her very word – before her conversion."

The old lady spoke out vehemently: "Och no! That one! Och she didna' tell ye, did she?"

"Tell me what?"

"I *know* she did not! She was a rascal all right! It iss a shameful thing that she goes about talking like that. *I* know what she did! I have known her since she was a child. She iss one of the Island folk ye know. All I can tell you iss that she would have broken my heart if she had been my daughter. Not a single night but she – no I must not say . . ." She turned her face away, and blew her nose forcibly. Turning back, she demanded, "And what else did she tell ye?"

"She mentioned that there had been a conversion a few weeks ago, that a woman had cried out in the Free Church. That my steps were being guided . . ."

"Oh, it iss wicked! That woman doesna' learn any sense at all. And she a grown woman with children of her own."

She sat looking into the fire, then sighed. "Aye – well I mustna' talk aboot her. But as for the woman she spoke of that iss, we must hope, something different. I will tell you aboot it. It iss a relative, Jean Macvoe, a distant relative. Well not that distant, no one of uss iss distant! Anyway that family has had a lot o' sorrow. Their men were all tae do with the sea. In the Great War, her grandfather and *his* two brothers were torpedoed and drowned. And in the last war her father and *his* three brothers were lost as well. In a way they are still tae do with the sea, because her husband Hamish does the maintenance for the big lighthouse. Well one night, chust as they were going tae bed, she looked out and saw that the light was oot. So Hamish must go oot tae the light and switch it over tae emergency power. Now ye know that the light, at the end o' that line o' rocks, when the tide's oot, the only way tae get tae that far rock is by boat. Aye, well it happened that Hamish had hurt his foot, and he wouldna' be able tae bear down on it tae haul the boat doon intae the water by himself. He should have got his cousin Ian oot tae help him, but that iss a distance away, and it being so late, Jean said she'd help him. So she took the child in her arms and off they went. Och they got the boat intae the water right enough and she got in with him, and he started rowin' oot. Well, now the boat had been laid up a' winter under cover. Ye can guess what was wrong?"

"The timbers had dried out and the boat was letting in water?"

"That iss right. And lettin' in a fair amount o' water! Well Hamish decided tae carry on. So Jean put the child doon on the stern seat and held him tight with her back while she baled and baled as hard as she could. The sea was calm at the time. Now they had got to the last but one of the line of rocks and had about another couple of hundred yards to go when the wind started tae come up – as it can do very suddenly on this coast – and Hamish decided tae put Jean and the child off on that rock, and go on himself. And the night got black and cold. And Hamish was having tae stop rowing every so often tae bale and then row again and so on. It was so dark now, and he wasna' carrying a light – he should have done – and she lost sight of him; and she was frightened, for with the wind freshening and the noise of the waves that were coming up now, she couldna' hear his oars. At last she saw his torch go on and knew he had got tae the rock. And then she saw the great beams o' the light swing oot over the sea and she knew he'd done it, and she was happy for her man."

There was an answering pride in the old lady's eyes.

"Wait!" she said to me, pushing her lips up, "Aye, there's more! Jean saw his torch light go on again, and knew that he was making his way doon the rock from the light. But suddenly the torch light seemed tae fall and then go oot. She knew he could not be all the way doon the rock yet. And the torch didna' go on again! And there she was, alone on the rock with the child! Anyway, what had happened was this. Because of his bad foot, he slipped and fell on the wet rock, the torch fell away intae the sea. His ankle twisted under him and he was in terrible pain. He couldna' stand up. So he crawled on his hands and knees down tae the boat and managed tae get in and pushed off. Well . . ."

She wiped her eyes with a lace-edged handkerchief. "Ach – everything! Well the sea was running high by then and the waves broke over the boat, sending in a deal o' water; the tide was on the ebb, and there's a strong current oot there as ye know? Whenever he stopped rowing tae bale, he lost way and the current took him. She couldna' see him, except when the lighthouse beam swung over and she got a glimpse o' the boat. In one o' these flashes she saw the reflection of the light in the water *inside* the boat!"

She looked at me with a strange expression on her lined face – pride, stiff irony, fatalism.

"Aye – Jean thought that was the end. The boat was filling up faster than he could bale and he wasna' makin' enough way! Now I suppose ye know that in many families to do with the sea the men never learn tae swim? If something happens it only makes the suffering last longer. Aye – that iss what they say. So Hamish canna' swim. But Jean iss a very good swimmer. She used tae win silver cups for swimming at school. But what was she tae do? Was she tae stay with the child and let her husband drown? But if she swam tae his assistance the rising sea could wash the child off the rock! She put the sleeping child down on the rock and went down on her knees and prayed for guidance. And suddenly she felt a strong hand grip her shoulder very hard. And then she knew what tae do. She threw her clothes off and went intae the sea naked. She doesna' remember about gettin' tae the boat. When she got there it was so full of water she dared not try tae climb in. So she hangs on wi' one hand, took the baling can, and baled and baled, with the sea running high and washing over her head. Anyway, somehow they got tae the rock where the child was. He was still asleep! At last they did get home – it was two o'clock in the morning. And the minute they got intae the hoose she began trembling all over and couldna' stop. She couldna' hold a cup in her hand. She couldna' hold the child. She couldna' sleep. And this went on for days and days. Doctor Boddie couldna' help her. She wouldna' swallow any pills tae calm her doon. So it went on. And one night she got up and went straight oot o' the hoose and doon tae the shore. Hamish rushed after her with the child in his arms, afeared for her. At the very water's edge she stopped, for she heard a voice say, very slowly in her ear – a great deep voice,

'Go thou up to the hill tae my green pastures'

And she turned straight round and walked past Hamish and went intae the hoose and intae bed and slept peacefully! Next day was the Sunday. She had stopped the trembling. She went up tae the Free Kirk. The church has a green door. Inside, she took the Holy Book and it fell open at Psalm 23, and when she read Verse 2:

He maketh me to lie down in green pastures:
He leadeth me beside the still waters

she cried out aloud tae God."

Mrs. Macvoe's features had taken on an aspect of awe and suspense, as if Jean Macvoe's perilous journey still continued. No one dare say to the traveller, 'Fare well.' You must hold your breath and be still.

"There's all the difference between that," she spoke as if pronouncing sentence, "and the way that rascal of a woman came to *her* conversion. Still, I mustna' say anything! The minister says that it doesna' matter *how* a body comes tae God."

She put her hands on her knees to lever herself up out of her chair and went through into her kitchen. She called out, "Ye'll take a cup of tea?"

Later she said, "They say conversions are happening all over the district! Now that this has happened to *us*, I admit I am worried. And I think Hamish is worried too. Ye see, Jean is expecting!"

She had lost me. I said with care, "She was pregnant at the time?"

"Of course she was!" She looked at me in a puzzled way.

"I am sorry, I did not . . ."

"Och, don't ye see? Hamish iss Church of Scotland!"

I saw. "You mean he won't go to the Free Church to hold his child for baptism?"

With great firmness, she said, "How could he?"

Seven

Fingalian voices

In June summer deserted the glen. The heat and drought of May left the lower slopes of the mountains clothed in autumnal brown. While June advanced great rains came, first of all with a brief, violent overture. And then, a week or so later, there began a long, wet, misty, harsh twilight. The gods of spring, given too short a time earlier in the year to bring the earth out of winter, have seized power again, and re-imposed the grey ferocity of March.

The drought broke with a heavy mist in the early morning that blanketed out the high pass and brought thin rain. We woke to a world from which the mountains had been erased. The dark curtain of cloud hung down almost to the roadway. Out of its bottom shreds a lamb would emerge and stand still, as if in wonder at rediscovering the spread out world.

And then a great west wind gathered itself up and roared through the gorges from the sea, reverberating between the high buttresses of Beinn à Shellach and Beinn Dhu. Sheep stood and stared into the wind affronted, then turned round forlornly, their wool flung up in tatters. Lambs tried to run against it and fell over, then wandered on unsteady feet to shelter with the rest in the lee of the dry stone dyke.

That afternoon, with the wind increased to a full gale, I was returning over the great pass and had just driven over one of Wade's narrow granite bridges when my heavy vehicle was shaken by a tremendous crash, followed by the heavy groan and crack of a tree breaking. I drew into a passing place a few yards further on. I glanced back to see that a fir tree had fallen on the bridge.

I walked back. It had been a near thing for me, a matter of a second or two. The tree had come down slantwise, virtually demolishing the broad parapet of grey granite blocks all along one side, and dislodging a number on the other. Smooth, square cut, disturbed from two hundred and fifty years of solid placement, they lay tumbled with the fallen timber, forming with the massive trunk and lengths of splintered limbs and branches – not only of the fallen tree but torn from neighbouring ones – a total barrier.

129

A length of lower trunk lay jammed between two blocks that remained more or less in their original position but prised apart; and virtually the whole of that side of the bridge was now open to the drop of two hundred feet to the boulders in the burn.

Little of the roadway was visible through the piled-up material. If the main structure had suffered, the glen's road link was cut!

In meditative mood I walked back to the Land-Rover, started up, and concentrated on the tortuous downward passage into the glen. From that point, the nearest house is about three miles away, John Connal's in fact. I must get word to Malcolm quickly. Apart from anything else, now that the summer ferry service has begun from the old slipway in the bay, a steady stream of holidaymakers comes over the bealach these days, and in a little while there would be a line of trapped vehicles up there behind that bridge. If a lorry were among them it would not be able to turn and would block everyone else. And in any case not many vehicles would attempt to turn on that narrowest of single track roads. As for trying to reverse, you need skill and good nerves even to travel forward on some parts of that road. Even now, having driven over it countless times I should not like to try reversing along it for any distance. On the far side of that bridge, it is about a mile to the nearest place – where a forestry track joins this road – for a large vehicle like a lorry or camper to try to turn round. Again, this is the season for towed caravans, not easily manoeuvrable even in ideal conditions. If one of these were caught up there, the average driver would give up and wait for help.

Several of these bridges, up there on the heights, bear signs of tree falls. At one, the parapet still has part of the trunk of a crashed fir embedded in it; a number of its roots, wrenched out of the side of the gully, seem to writhe in the air like the serpent tresses of Medusa; the remainder being still fixed in the steep slope. The trunk had been sawn through flush with the stonework to clear the roadway, and the cut, now weathered brown, stares at you with the hurt of a raw wound.

John Connal was at home.

"Och come on in!" he shouted from the porch. He looked at me narrowly as I came towards him. "H'm – ye'd better have a dram! Sit ye doon then."

He pointed to the big chair beside the red telephone, shuffled noisily into the house and reappeared holding a bottle of Carrdhu. "Ye look a bit peaked and no wonder! Here ye are then. Drink that doon."

I had not been aware of feeling shaken. Some reflex, controlled till now, was released by his words. I shivered, and gratefully took a gulp of the honey-coloured malt.

"Go on then," he commanded, "drink a bit more before ye spill it!"

I said, "I ought to ring up Malcolm about it?"

"Aye – that you had. I saw him a while ago doon by Duncan Macpherson's. Try his number."

Jemima answered, "Och yes! Malcolm's chust gone to get Jamie's tractor with the power grabs on it."

"How on earth did he get to know so quickly? I have only just come down from there! And no one else could have come through after me!"

She laughed in a kindly way. "Och Robert Wallace was on the look-out with his binoculars from doon below. Some other trees blew doon, ye know? At that minute he was watching your yellow Land-Rover coming doon from the bealach. When he saw that one fall on tae the bridge just behind ye he went into Maggie Macvoe's house and got on the phone and tracked Malcolm tae here."

John Connal sat down near me. He leaned forward and studied me. Reassured he sat back, reached for the Carrdhu and poured himself a small dram. "One o' these days," he said, smacking his lips, "a bridge on the bealach is going tae give up the ghost for good an' all! And then the folk here are goin' tae be in a gey pitiful state, with nae other proper road in – ye canna' count the wee estate roads that wind away in an' oot up by the auld drove road. An' I doot very much if the Council would bother tae repair it if that happened! Most likely they'd scrap it and put in a new one. Och and that's goin' tae take them a fine long time! Could be even a year. And how would the folk here manage – with the bealach closed for all that time? They canna' bring in supplies by sea – at least not in any decent quantity without a jetty! And if it's the visitor season how are visitors goin' tae get in an' oot? Aye – sea transport's goin' tae have tae come back intae its ane again here. An' folk are goin' tae learn they're better off when they're linked tae the sea as we used tae be! They'll wonder how they ever came tae let all that go! Aye – and anyway that sea transport's cheaper. *And* it brings business back tae the glen – *and* the trades tae feed the business an' make it grow! And what's more – that they can do with both – the road as well."

On he went, with the infectious zeal of the born dealer. He was selling *me* something.

And he was feeding me with my own arguments!

"It's a strange coincidence," I said. "Did you hear Radio Highland this morning? The Garroch Bridge is pronounced unsafe! Any moment now, officials say, it could collapse under somebody's car and drop it into the loch! If that bridge went – or rather *when* it does – they talk of a detour of 150 miles for people coming up from the south to get on to the big ferry at Insh. And now that this has been put out over the national radio – that the bridge is dangerous – you can see what's going to happen. A lot of tourists are going to be put off coming to this part of Scotland. The summer trade of the whole district is going to be badly hit."

"Och that bridge? They've been saying it's unsafe for years!"

He spoke absently.

My thoughts, still entangled with the crash on the bridge, swung away too.

The gale shook the house. Dark clouds seemed to touch the eaves as they passed powerfully by, pressing the earth below. Fingalian weather, heroic, portentous – a day to see Fionn and his band pass with giant strides along the ridge of Beinn Dhu and vault across to the Island on their hunting spears.

In all this noise of might and fury, the hidden mountains radiating their mystery, gods and demons shrieking on the racing wind, the solid world a-tremble, who can question that this is a place of wonders? A place where legends choose to be born?

The Fingalians leave their foot marks, the toes deeply imprinted, diurnally renewed as they pass over the mountain above Cruachan.

The heroes ride the storm. They do not bend to it. They face nature as equals, partaking of her power, her magic. They enlarge our spirit. They whisper in our hearts the wonders to strain for. In them our courage is renewed, and we see our fulfilment march in glory across the sky.

Here, where the mountains lean close, the heroic powers are particularly present. In the unending twilight of a summer night, their shadows mingle with ours. In the movement of trees in the wind they whisper to us. When the elements are loose their voices are raised too, for they parley with the gods as familiars. We must hearken as best we can.

Yesterday, Duncan Macpherson went over to the Island in a motor launch. "Ye know, it was really bad! The waves were high and the wind nearly stopped us once or twice."

"But it was a calm day yesterday. There was no wind at all here!"

"Aye, I know. We could see that. We were only half-a-mile away at one time." Then his bland expression changed. A soft breeze had that moment stiffened, perhaps in augury of the coming gale. In his fisherman's pullover, patterned in geometrical black and grey, his muscular neck weathered like a tree, he stood very still, listening to the wind's altered voice as if caught by an overheard conversation.

"Sometimes," he said, still drawn away, "the wind follows a single boat. There must be a reason. Aye, but we mustna' pry too far into things like that. Maybe – och maybe it was the wrong day for us tae take that boat over there?"

The heroes also tell us, quietly, firmly but with the gentleness of the strong, where we truly stand – at the feet of nature, her acolytes.

I said to Connal, "In this gale it's going to take Malcolm a good while to clear the bridge?"

"Aye," he nodded thoughtfully, "and what about after that? The

132

county engineers have to come and test it for structural damage and so on before they'll let folk use it again."

"I can see," I said in the light tone that often creeps into our talks, "that you have been doing some hard thinking since we talked a while ago – about replacing the jetty, the kind of business that could move across it, and the other things that could be started here and so on." Then I added, venturing to tease, "A minute ago I was thinking of the Fingalians. Who knows, maybe *you* could be a latter day hero of the glen."

His eyes gleamed. "Aye, and well ye might think of Fionn! Ye'd have need of him and all his band to blow their hunting horns on every doorstep and sheiling, to make these folk get up on their hind legs and take heed for themselves!"

His face softened, and he chuckled at a secret thought.

Then he resumed his alert, quizzing expression – the hunter picking up the scent again. "Ye'll have heard the latest aboot the Corpach paper works? And the Government's final word?" he made the thumbs down sign.

"Yes. I was sure that would give you food for thought."

"Aye – well. I might be thinking of doing something, an' I might not!" He waved a hand as if dismissing the matter. "Och well – yes, maybe I have – ye're right. And I'm thinking," he pursed his lips, "I'm thinking I might even get *you* to come in with me! And what would ye say to that?"

That was a surprise. And yet it was not.

I saw how logical it could be – for him. He would get my professional expertise. He would get access to my study of business possibilities here. And, his buccaneering mind doubtless convinced that I do have business aims in the glen, he would expect to 'get in on the ground floor' there too.

I was aware of other, disturbing motives.

He could be aiming, perhaps half-consciously, at an exquisite revenge. Reversing the verdict of long ago, he would compel the locals to acknowledge him. *He* would control the destiny of the glen. *He* would raise them up a bit. *He* would throw them a few crumbs of opportunity. And not, plainly, for their benefit! He would do it to render tribute to his own memories. He would raise monuments to his bitter-sweet success.

And I would be a cat's-paw. In a business alliance with him, I who have flaunted my impartiality, my lack of business interest, my benevolence, would be 'unmasked' as a self-seeker after all! Just like any other. Like John Connal himself!

That would be important not for my own feelings, but for the effect on movement in the glen. The locals have only just convinced themselves that, against all the odds, I seek no personal benefit. And that may have helped – who knows? – in the new stirring of purpose. Having found one person with faith, they can trust *themselves* once again?

133

If that person's image were shown to be false, would their fragile self-confidence also break down? Would they retreat once again, seeing their inertia as justified after all?

He interrupted my thoughts. "If you hadna' come in just now, I was going tae get on tae you for a wee talk aboot business."

I waited for him to continue.

He sat and studied me, biding his time.

The noise of the storm increased. The rain battered the windows. In the meadow and on the hillside the colours dulled. The mist turned the world grey.

At last he gave a characteristic urchin grin, pleased with our game and with his own thoughts.

"I'm going tae try something on you and you can bless me if it's no' tae your liking."

He reached down beside his chair and put a smart document case of heavy hide with brass fittings on his knee. He took out a folder, closed the case and laid the folder on top of it.

"Folk have called me many things – a 'good for nothing' once upon a time. Aye, and an old scoundrel! Well, it all depends where yer bowl of porridge is sitting! Anyway, one thing I'm telling ye is this. Anyone who comes in with me keeps his heid tight shut about my business. An' I needna' tell *you* that there are ways and means of seeing tae that!" His eyes ranged over my face with sudden coldness. "Well, anyway, that's enough o' that for the now. What I want tae say tae ye is this. I wouldnae mind having yer advice now and again."

He threw out the words with the casualness of the skilled bargainer.

"What I've done," he continued, " – now ye can say 'No' if you want when ye've heard this – I got my solicitors tae get a subsidiary company registered. All the directors' documents and so on are ready." He tapped the folder. "I'm asking you tae come in with me as a director, with a nominal holding of one hundred shares at one pound each. Now wait a minute!" He held his hand up. "Ye don't have tae put yer hand in yer pocket. I'm doing that."

He showed his teeth in that villainous grin of his, and leaned back, watching.

I said, "Give me a few days to think about it."

He continued as if I had not spoken, "I'll talk in detail when ye've made up your mind tae come in."

He was tilting the balance now towards himself. *He* was calling the tune.

"As I say I have decided you can be useful tae me. And don't forget that *I'm* taking the risks, because the investment capital – well, I'll look after raising that!"

134

The dreich world outside chimed in with my thoughts. I ought to feel some sense of victory, but I did not.

Will life never answer truly? Will people never act for the right reasons?

I have walked the glen through the turning year, in the storm and snow and the frozen silences, in the gleam and quiver of spring, in the uncertain opening out of summer – and I have spoken to the wind.

And now the wind brings an answer. But it comes with a crooked smile.

John Connal, driven by pride and by the past, aims a blow at fate, far out of time.

Why should his motives worry me? He brought *an* answer!

Yes, John Connal will put in a new jetty. He will run some boat trade – tourists, local passengers, goods. He will reorganise the timber trade, and start local processing and some ancillary businesses. In doing all this, he will replace the Forestry Commission as the principal provider of employment to supplement the crofting. And the pernicious dependence on a single large employer will continue.

I had hoped for a growth of dispersed enterprise, truly local, small businesses run with mainly family labour – like some of the jobbing building firms in the region – a balancing force against the dominance of one single source of venture capital and, worse, economic power.

If I were to join him, how could I still work for that balance? I might even have to *oppose* the spread of small business! For it is the instinct of a monopolist – as Calum Johnson showed in opposing the bakery project – to thwart new entries into areas of business where he *can* be a monopolist.

And John Connal's instinct, too, will be to oppose small business growth – for instance in road haulage or timber, or in coastal trade, or even some of the ancillary trades like maintenance, joinery, metal working – that could threaten the company's monopoly power, present or future. Harnessed to his chariot, how could I encourage such threats?

My questions are to some extent beside the point. He has made his business decisions. He will go ahead whether I join him or not.

John Connal is surely better than nothing?

And the balancing force? Is that hope gone for ever?

Malcolm's dream of 'the old Highland ways' is a cry of defiance, the single spirit to be sovereign once more. And what is life worth, after all, if it negates that?

I stand on my doorstep late one night – about three in the morning – and look up at a gibbous moon that hangs above Beinn Dhu between great banks of black cloud. In the hard cold light the rushing river gleams like bubbling mercury. Shadows are etched on the little ledges, multiplied along the glen's winding length, where once lived five thousand souls.

Five thousand!

In 1846, in a single day, six hundred people went down to that shore to take ship for America.

In what currency do you price the sadness of the heart?

For what sum can you redeem it?

I thought of Maggie Macvoe and the people living in huts. No one lives in huts now. There is no poverty. No child now walks to school, as they all did when Maggie was a child; she herself used to walk seven miles to school. Where, then, is the urgency to act?

No wonder Duncan Macpherson and Robert Wallace and the others, for all their talk, hold back.

And Malcolm – valiant dreamer sending out your call! When will you break ranks and fight?

The moon leans over the ridge and stares down at me with a light that is equivocal, hard, cold, indifferent: the single, sightless eye of the Cyclops.

The river, full fed by the storm, mutters to itself in the gorge below me.

The wind moans in the eaves above my head, grumbling and keening. The Eumenides whisper, "There are no 'answers'! We know only the laws that begat us – long ago. *We* conform! Man must conform too. If not – nothing, nothing, nothing . . ."

But how do we know when we *are* conforming?

The cloud banks swing across the moon, and the nocturnal twilight darkens, then lightens again as the moon shines through. Far away, high up on the bealach, pinpoints of light appear. Headlights dance in the trees in the high plantation. The car weaves down the long approach. Another follows. A little later, a few more. They return from a dance at Garroch. As they come near, the wind brings to my ears, above the drone of engines, a confusion of drunken song.

Maggie Macvoe says, "Aye – I say this – live for the day. Tomorrow will tell ye what God chooses to give us!"

At seventy-eight a policy of *carpe diem* is perhaps understandable.

I turn and follow the waving headlights. From the wide sweep of the road above Cruachan comes the splintering echo of a crash. The following car stops. There is some shouting and the grating sound of metal on stone. The leading car has driven into the roadside wall. They drag it back onto the road and continue. The drunken song roars out with exultation into the tremulous night.

For some days a sizeable sheet of metal, ripped loose above a wheel on Robert Wallace's car, will make a noise of cymbals as he drives along. Finding the music disturbing to his beasts, he will bind up the break with broad bands of red adhesive tape.

No, there is no lack of *carpe diem* in the glen.

Maggie said, despairingly, "In my young days the young folk never took the dr-rink like that! It iss the dr-rink that makes them ruin themselves! When I went tae the dances as a girl there was no such thing. Och no – anyone coming in with dr-rink in him was put oot!"

"Who would do the putting out?"

She looked surprised. "They couldna' say 'No' – the M.C. would say they had tae go out. That was all."

Her sprightly blue-grey eyes must have been captivating as a girl. They are engaging even now. At this moment they shone with inner light as she looked back down the years. "When I was aboot seventeen, I used tae walk six-and-a-half miles tae the dances at the village hall, and in my bare feet ye know! Took me two hours. I used to walk tae the village for the messages and walk back with two full baskets, one in each hand. Och – that was my dream – tae get tae go for the messages! I used tae get all the work done – the milking, and the potatoes peeled for the dinner, the floor scrubbed and the doorstep pipe-clayed – all in double quick time – so as tae get tae go! It was a rough track right enough but my feet were hard. Ye can do that when ye're young!"

She grinned with mischief. "Aye, the dances. I used tae go on intae the night and start walking home about four in the morning. Get home about six! And never go tae bed that next day either! Och it iss all right when ye're young! An' I would do all the work again – and that night I would go tae bed and not know that my head touched the pillow! Wake up the next morning and wish and wish tae get tae go for the messages again."

"Why the messages?"

"Och ye got tae see the folk in the village that way. Oor house was by itself – far away from anyone. Aye – the messages and the dances! I didna' think of the thirteen miles."

Then she added, "I couldn't do it now though!"

Late yesterday the bridge was cleared for traffic. A helicopter brought the county engineers. They gave it a provisional bill of health for loads of up to five tons pending a fuller survey. The local traffic – except the timber lorries – and the tourists could use the road for the time being. The timber, in smaller lorries, would have to use one of the old private estate roads that wind through the plantations on the southern flanks of Beinn Dhu.

This last was an irony. The government's decision not to continue to support the Corpach project meant that the timber lorries would shortly stop too. They might never thunder through the glen again. Tree fellers would be laid off; or if they were put on to other forestry work, would earn less than the felling piece work rates. Lorry and other equipment contractors would lay men off, temporarily till they found alternative contracts, perhaps permanently. Other jobs, in servicing, maintenance, supply, would wind down too. And so also would demand. Already there were hints of this in the local businesses; not only Calum Johnson, but the shopkeepers at Insh, are saying that the locals are spending less.

When Corpach had been threatened, then reprieved, a few years ago, some of the forestry workers had read the signs in the sky and found other work. Many commuted a hundred miles to the oil platform base at Kishorn. Others, like Norman Innes, set up a motor repair workshop at Insh. He is one of the lucky ones. But if the Garroch bridge collapsed, or were to be closed for safety, and traffic to Insh diverted, his business might not survive. Again the glen folk are only too well aware that the Kishorn employment, proceeding contract by contract, offers no security. Demand for oil platforms, depending on the changing nature of oil exploration and technique, may fall away. Kishorn could become obsolete. And then the accommodation ships, the great derricks and the complex equipment, the offices, could fade away and leave behind only a vast emptiness of concrete.

On the near side of the bridge, news of the tree fall having spread quickly in the glen, only a handful of vehicles had come up towards it unawares. The fates had decreed that there were no towed caravans or lorries or large vans among them. And gradually, using the wider passing places, they managed to turn and go back, leaving the approach clear for Malcolm and his equipment.

On the far side, had it been a fine day, many more cars would have been stranded. The early start of the storm thinned out the numbers coming this far. Even so there were some fifty vehicles, including a dozen caravans and campers. By the time Malcolm had finished, and the engineers decided to let them through, some had been up there on the bealach for five hours.

The people with the caravans and campers were in the main luckier, being stocked with food and equipped for cooking, producing hot drinks and so on. Those in cars and vans were not; and this led to a near riot. A few of the camper and caravan people shared cups of tea and refreshment with their near neighbours in the long stranded line – a welcome kindness, for up there in the fierce wind many felt the cold. However, some would not share. One man, having appealed in vain to the occupants of a nearby camper for some refreshment to give his children, gathered a few supporters and in his anxiety and fury was about to attack the vehicle, when the appearance of the helicopter hovering low to land in a clearing close by, stopped them.

Food supplies did arrive a few minutes later. When the news about the bridge filtered down into the glen, Bill Walsh had been inspired to load up a little van with boxes of sandwiches, urns of tea and coffee, soft drinks, and even hot milk for the children. With Willie Davies helping him, he went across the bridge – somewhat against the better judgment of Malcolm and the engineers still working on it. Besieged by hungry, cold, anxious travellers they sold out in minutes.

Maggie Macvoe expressed the disapproval of the older generation at this mercenary approach to people in distress.

"In the old days we would have thought it a shame on oor hoose tae take money for helping folk in trouble. We would have done what we could. It chust goes to show what has happened tae oor world here."

She had stopped her little cart near the War Memorial. As I walked up she was sitting there, erect on the wrought iron seat fixed to the cross-bench, reins looped over her left arm, gazing at the great inscribed plate beneath the dark figures silhouetted against sea and sky, still but in motion.

Her face was set hard.

"The trouble is," she turned to me, "the young folk chust will not take it intae their heids that ye have tae haud on tae what ye believe, and haud tight! Or ye lose everything!"

She shook her head and the tears were running on her wind-reddened face. She held a handkerchief to her eyes, then slowly, almost reluctantly, dried her cheeks.

"Aye," she said at last, "the young folk walk past these names up there without a thought of what they mean. And mean for them! Even now! Aye, and the visitors come and gape – chust as they gape at *us*. And nobody really wants tae see!"

She blew her nose furiously, releasing violence. Then she carefully folded the lace handkerchief and tucked it away in a pocket of her long tweed coat.

The wind, even after several days of gale, still had a bite to it; and the sea, running high, broke with a roar and a sharp rattle of spray over the line of great jagged lumps of stone and concrete that had been the jetty.

"Aye, I can see ye understand a bit why I sit here sometimes. I go back tae the world I could understand. Och no, that's not right! I didna' understand it! Only God does that! No, a world I knew, and lived by as best I could. Now, I will tell ye in a minute about something that happened to me once – when I was away in service – that will show ye a bit more how it was. But wait now – whit was I going tae say? Aye, it is this. Nowadays the youngsters think that folk were stupid tae suffer and die like that. They say: 'Whit was the use of it – look whit happened afterwards?' Och but they don't see – *won't* is the truth! – ye canna take life and add up the bits – like a piece of arithmetic at the school! Life doesna' *let* ye stand back like that! Och no! Ye have tae put yer faith in God an' keep tae the right ways of livin' that those who went before ye learnt to trust – aye and die for if need be! Ye have tae suffer even when ye canna' see *why*, but ye know in yer heart that God has put the responsibility on tae ye. These young folk think that nothing is worth *anything*! An' if ye think *that*, then ye canna' have any respect for *anybody*! An' if they go around like that –

och well naebody's goin' tae have any respect for *them!* God forgive me, but I am sometimes glad I'm an auld woman!"

We were silent. She seemed far away. There was a slight movement from side to side, as in a keening. Then she shifted a little and stared hard, longingly but with jaw set tight, at the naked woman kneeling at the feet of the winged figure – archangel, messenger of fate.

I thought of Mary Menzies and *her* affinity with that figure – though from the outside.

So, between the generations, could some of the links hold?

Here, standing in the crisp breeze, my eyes are held by the proud ribbon held taut in the air, tied to the laurel wreath.

I look at the fallen jetty, symbolic of the glen's collapse. Is that ribbon, flying bravely above it, simply the tattered flag of a forlorn hope?

Is it, then, madness to go on believing – with Maggie, with Malcolm and the few other remnants of the defeated force?

And Mary Menzies, hungry to 'belong'. Is she a deluded visionary, chasing a mirage?

And the wind answers,

If some believe, there is something left to sustain the spirit!
If none believe, there is nothing left but bitterness –
And bitterness destroys everything!

The links that remain are seen diversely now. Maggie sees that woman as representing real things, real events, sacrifice, belief, hope – hope against hope – real emotions still repeating their signals in the mind and in the heart and holding life in one piece, as the great dry stones of the old 'black house' of her forbears, still standing below the shieling, hold it erect by their weight and by their close-fitting pressure.

And Mary Menzies, at the other extreme, sees the bronze woman as a symbol of what she too wants to believe, but vicariously: emotion without underpinning in the past, a talisman in the mind, strengthening her dream of belonging.

So the generations shout across the barrier of time and memory.

'The words are the same but the meaning is different . . .'

Is Mary's stance 'wrong'? Or of lesser value? Or is it simply better than nothing?

Belief that strives to come close, with honesty and humility, *must* be better than nothing! Sometimes the new convert destroys by overstatement – lacking the finesse, the flexibility, of firm grounding in the tradition. If Mary Menzies stays and holds fast, and places herself with Malcolm and the others in a new certainty, that affirmation will itself sustain her. It is the best that she, or anyone, can hope for.

140

Maggie stirred, and adjusted the woollen shawl. Quietly, deferring to my reverie as she drew me away from it, she said:

"Here comes young Morag. Chust to show you, I will ask her what *she* thinks about taking money from the folk stranded on the bealach."

In her even temper and generosity Morag is cherished among the locals as if she were part of them all. Maggie, perhaps seeing in Morag a vision of herself long ago, treats her with special affection.

Some incomers, alas, misunderstand Morag's naturally serious mien for coolness, and are inclined to be tart in return – and even more so when she remains unmoved.

She sauntered up to the cart and gave us her soft smile of greeting. After the usual exchange of family enquiries, she listened gravely.

She rested her hand on the rail of the cart in a movement that subtly conveyed respect, and said in her faraway voice, "Och I can well see what ye mean, but it was different all that while ago – the way folk felt then." She blushed. "I mean . . ." She seemed to cast about for a gentler way of presenting the difference in time and view. "Aye – nowadays folk don't expect ye tae do things like that for nothing! And anyway them folk up there on the bealach I think were glad enough tae see the food at any price! It's no' as if they didna' *have* the money."

She was on her way to meet her father at the doctor's surgery. She moved away in her erect, floating gait, along the winding shore road. We saw her pause near the lifeboat station to talk to Mary Menzies then move on, wave to Flora Burke at the boat yard, and pass on her confident way.

This world is hers – all of it. She acknowledges it and keeps pace with it, perhaps not understanding it but, like Pippa, sees it as she wants it to be, and gives it her blessing as she passes.

Where else could she find this dominion?

In the past year she has changed from an angular slip of a girl into a smooth, lithe, beautiful young woman. When I saw her in the Free Church, in tight-waisted grey suit, high-necked white blouse with lace ruff, and a wide-brimmed white hat, I had to look twice to be sure it was she.

Even in her workaday dress of jeans and shirt she shows a poise, a collected air, that is new. There in her Sunday glory, high cheek bones apple red, a shimmering light in her blue eyes, she burns like a flower in full bloom. The only flower.

A few days ago she remarked to me, "Och I've decided I'm no' going tae Glasgow tae take that hairdressing job. I'll wait a bit longer. My father's no' too well, ye know?" She said it calmly, in a mature way, with none of that twitch of impatience, of longing and deprivation, I remember from last year.

Maggie Macvoe thinks she'll never leave the glen. "That iss a good girl!

She iss a good home girl. And she would never leave her father anyway. No – no! She'll stay."

Jemima Macpherson scoffs at this view. "Och I think she'll surely go! Where is she going tae find a man here? There's no young marriageable men here any more!"

She stretched high to reach the clothes-line. The wind blew her long wrap-over apron tight round her body; she is young enough to understand the impatience of youth. She stuck a clothes-peg between her teeth and went on talking with a rush. "Och this isna' a place for a woman! If I was a girl again I believe I would go. When your children are getting old enough tae go away tae school, there's not much for a woman tae *do*! You're stuck aboot the house a' the time! Duncan doesna' like me tae talk like this, I know. But then he's always oot and aboot. It's not the same for him."

"Will you say this to your girl when she's older?"

She finished hanging up the washing in silence. Then she stood, hands on hips, and looked down the glen towards the lighthouse, on whose rock great sheets of white spray leapt up high as the steel-grey waves rushed upon it. "Aye, ye're right," she said, biting her lip. "It is hard for a mother. A year ago, or maybe longer, I would have answered you, 'Yes!' Now, well," she shook her head, "it is hard to say it. Maybe, I'm not sure."

For Jemima and the middle generation, work is less total than in her mother's day; and for most of them there are no immediate neighbours, no extended family close at hand as in Maggie's little hamlet. Contacts are fewer, and commitment is weaker – and doubt grows.

Perhaps we need responsibilities for ever knocking at our door to keep faith alive?

The horse began to kick the ground with the edge of his shoe. Maggie roused herself. "Will ye walk with me for a bit then?"

I fell into step beside the cart.

"Aye, well, ye see that? Even young Morag, one of the best of the youngsters. It iss like talking a different language! They do not accept, as I did when I was her age, that ye have tae have faith and trust in things chust because that iss how they have been handed on tae ye!"

We went on in silence.

"Let me tell ye," she said, "something I've kept in mind for sixty years nearly. When I was a girl, well, a young woman ye would say, I was in service in the Free Church manse over at Insh. Well – ye see – they were very str-rict aboot the Sabbath, although not any more str-rict than we were at home! Now I always had my own Sunday paper delivered and I would keep it over and read it on the Monday, after I had finished my work. Aye, well the paper boy used tae put it on the doorstep when he went by on his bicycle on the Sunday forenoon – usually after the minister had gone tae the church. Aye, that was all right. But ill fortune came one Sunday. The boy came early. And the minister came oot on tae the doorstep and saw that paper lying there – it had my name written on it – and he shouted, 'Oh – wicked woman!' and he went back in, came out with the fire tongs, picked up my paper and threw it away intae the street. Och I was upset! It wasna' chust the paper. It was everything. I couldna' bear the minister thinking I was a bad woman. I was a good living girl. I *never* once read my paper on the Sabbath."

I said, "Didn't you explain it to him?"

"I did not get the chance."

"You don't mean you got the sack – for that?"

She turned to me, astonished, and shocked. "Good Heavens, no, I went on working there – I think about a year, and then I came back home and got married. Aye, it iss not easy for you tae understand how it was. In those days a girl in service did not chust go up and talk tae the master! She had tae wait till she was spoken tae! Aye, well on that day the minister came back in after throwing my paper intae the street, went tae his room and called for hot water tae wash his hands, and then went off tae take the service at the church. And when he came home he never went out of his way tae speak tae me. And it was not my place tae go up tae him. So I never got a chance tae explain, and I never have read the paper on the Sabbath tae this day! And none of my family will either. And all these years I have minded that I was condemned as a wicked woman! And for something I never did!"

I said, "Why do you think the minister didn't speak to you about it?"

She thought for a long time.

"I suppose," she said at last, "that in his mind there was no need! He knew the home I came from. He knew that *I* knew what was right! And in doing what he did – in throwing my paper into the street and calling out, for everyone in the world to hear, 'Oh – wicked woman!' he had said all he needed tae say!"

She tried, this late in the day, to balance the value of 'certainty' – of rule and discipline – against the dangers of freedom. The minister's certainty might result in accidental harshness but it made life predictable.

After another silence she added, "Maybe it was my own fault for having the paper delivered on the Sabbath?"

When I attended the Free Church for the first time the following Sunday I felt I could understand Maggie's inner world, and Agnes Mackinnon's and Malcolm's – and their 'certainty' – rather better.

Well before six o'clock cars began to assemble on the grass verges along the road. Some eighty people, with about twenty children, stamped their feet and hunched their shoulders in the cold wind. The gale had kept up the bombardment for nearly a week, and only now, reluctantly, was slackening off.

The austere appearance of the building was confirmed within. Rows of benches of thick, brown-painted wood, a high and stark pulpit, walls in shiny white paint. An aseptic world. No symbol, or sign, no word to take the mind away from total commitment. All or nothing.

Voices hushed as we entered.

In the tiny vestibule, on a small thin-legged table covered in oil-cloth, were a few copies of the Metrical Psalms.

Malcolm whispered, "Here's the Psalms for ye." And crushed my hand in welcome.

He seemed to want to say something more, but in that one instant, while others shuffled behind me in the narrow space, he could not find the right few words.

He said softly, "I'm pleased ye've come."

I sat down at the back behind Maggie Macvoe. At the other end of the long bench were Duncan Macpherson and Jemima. Others I recognised only after a moment's thought – in their Sunday best. The men's cheeks shone in the glazed pink of the freshly shaved; their hair combed flat. The younger women wore demure hats, girl-guide pattern, with broad brims and wide ribbons, in cream or beige, white, pale blue. The older ones wore brighter versions of the familiar close-fitting knitted caps of thick rope-like wool.

Duncan and a couple of other men wore the kilt, with shirt and tie. The rest were in sober suits.

Except for the children, naturally restless, attention was concentrated, full of interior expectancy; but there was also a sense of being connected, like the detached familiarity between members of a large family reunion.

Old Jamie marched down, his boots thundering on the floorboards, and took a seat in the great railed pew beneath the pulpit – the precentor.

Promptly on the dot of six, Mudie strode in, head bowed, mounted the pulpit and sat down, disappearing behind the high reading desk.

There was a crash of the main door being shut. Malcolm tiptoed in.

In front of me on the ledge lay a dog-eared Bible. It was printed in parallel columns of Gaelic and English. Another one beside it with even more signs of use, was totally in Gaelic.

Maggie Macvoe had warned me of the length of the prayer. "Och I do not know why this minister makes it so long! Last Sunday he went on for twenty minutes! I had tae sit doon halfway." She shook her head, "Even some of the younger folk have tae shift aboot from one foot to the other. You will see!"

"And the sermon?" I asked. "What was that about?"

"Och that went on and on as well. Yess it did!"

"I mean, what was it about?"

"Och it was – well . . ."

She looked at me, and blinked, at a loss. I was sorry I had asked.

I was, I suppose, totally unprepared for the sermon – or the preaching as Mudie steadfastly corrects me. With an effort I can force my mind back to how it began – somewhere in Acts 25 or was it 26? But in essence it was a succession of sustained trumpet blasts that quickened the air, stirred the pulse, took the mind away far beyond thought, or logic, or time, or the perceptible world. This was sounding brass of stupendous force. It commanded the blood. It raised you up and carried you on great wings far away to a universe of simplicity, of certainty, where there are no words but only meaning, where truth and action are fused together.

Then the trumpet was silent.

He announced the Psalm to conclude. I glanced at the engrossed faces. They too had returned from that world. They looked at each other and sighed in silence, accepting the common life again.

Outside, among the dripping trees, in that freshness after rain when all scents are newborn, I understood why Maggie Macvoe could not answer my question about the sermon.

I saw its irrelevance.

Perhaps that question always is?

They walk dreamily about for some minutes. Their desultory talk rings thinly in the air – random sounds – echoes of lost thoughts – signals to make contact once again. The words of sleep-walkers slowly returning.

Morag links her arm attentively in her father's. Had the 'certainty' been the same for her as for Maggie? For Malcolm? For Jemima?

While the brass trumpets stirred their blood and the great wings upheld them it *was* the same. And then, as the common world took them in its grip once again, in their separate ways they move away from it – not trusting it.

The high season is beginning; the common world comes upon them with special urgency and force, bringing discordant themes. The 'mainland' comes in, the visitors from the South, essentially unfriendly, to be used but excluded.

Though the gods still play at dice with the seasons it *is* summer. And the visitors come – with money.

"But not as many as last year," said Calum Johnson sombrely.

"Och it iss early days yet," said his wife Morven. "I think most of the holiday houses are let. Aye, and the manse as well – the old Church of Scotland one on the glebe, I mean. So, maybe it won't be so bad?"

Morven is a rounded, nimble little woman, completely white-haired though still in her early forties. She scurries rather than walks, yet speaks with a slow deliberation – a dramatic contrast with Calum's mercurial quality.

Calum, slightly put out, muttered, "Och it's the petrol prices! That stops a lot o' folk from doon South."

I said, "You really think it does – the petrol alone?"

"Och aye it does," he said with some force. He paused, thinking about something, and rushed on, "An' when they get here it costs even more!"

I felt he had intended to work round to this.

"I don't mind tellin' ye," he continued earnestly, "if I had any spare ground here – but I havena' got any as ye see, this auld hoose is hemmed in – I wouldna' mind puttin' in some pumps and a wee workshop, and undercutting the other folk hereabouts."

In many parts of this region, each petrol station and vehicle repair business is miles away from competition. Calum Johnson, a monopolist in his existing business, instinctively sharpens his sword.

I thought of John Connal. Obviously he would plan a vehicle repair workshop and petrol pumps, both to support the new enterprises he had in mind and as businesses in their own right. The cream to be skimmed off these local monopolies would not have escaped his notice either.

Surprisingly, Morven spoke out with some anxiety. "Och no Calum! When would ye get the time? We've both got oor work cut out as it is with the shop, and me at the post office as well!"

She nodded, as she spoke, towards the railed off space – some five feet square – next to the vegetable rack and the toiletries, where she reigns as postmistress.

She went on, "And then ye've got yer deliveries, and collecting goods over at Insh. Ye canna *do* any more! Ye'll have a breakdown – and then where would we be?"

Calum was absorbed in stamping prices on packets of tea and stacking them on one of the open shelves standing in the middle of the little room. I caught a sideways glance at me, speculative, slightly shame-faced.

I thought I knew what was coming.

It is some months now since we talked of new ventures, when I had recklessly mentioned the bakery project.

Partly answering Morven, but seemingly thinking aloud for my benefit, he said, "Aye – maybe it's up tae folk like us tae give a lead? Maybe we could make a wee job for somebody – if we –" he searched for a word – perhaps one that would not sound too mercenary – and gave up, "if we were tae expand our business interests?"

And then, directly to me: "Ye know we've got *your* subject on the agenda for next Community Council meeting?"

"*My* subject! What's that?"

"Och *you* should know. *You've* been goin' around talkin' tae everybody

146

aboot gettin' things goin' in the glen! Aboot creatin' jobs tae keep the young folk in! And dinna' be pawky wi' us – that's oor privilege!"

He grinned as he said it. It was the nearest thing to a friendly pat on the shoulder. I was being admitted – just a little. In telling me, in that tone, not to be pawky, I was being *allowed* to be – just so far.

I matched his tone. "But it's *your* subject – I mean the local folk's – not mine! I don't belong here. Remember?"

He smiled quickly and, bending to his task again, said with assumed gruffness, "Och well – ye've been among us a gey long time now. Ye're gettin' tae know us a bit, aren't ye?"

"And you've got to know me?"

"Aye, maybe we have a bit."

About a week ago he said to me, clearly weighing the matter with care, "Are ye goin' back up past Hamish's? Ye see I couldna' get his papers up tae him this mornin' – an' he hasna' been by yet."

He pointed to *The Press and Journal* and *The Oban Times* lying on the rack of Calor gas cylinders.

"Certainly – I'll be glad to drop them in. I'm going past his house."

Many locals pass Hamish's house. There was no need to choose me. It was a further sign.

Earlier in my stay, when they were still circling warily, this would not have happened; it would have been considered something of an affront to the recipient, forcing him, too, into a premature familiarity. I, the stranger, would have been seen as an inappropriate link, wrongly inserted in the emotional chain.

It would also have placed *me* in an embarrassing position, and the traditional code would not permit that either.

But now their long observation of me had produced a provisional confidence. 'We know enough of you to start to fit you in just a little – into the chain.'

Enough? How far is that?

Cautiously he said now, "Aye – I was goin' tae mention this tae ye anyway. We'd appreciate it if ye could come tae the Community Council meeting. Ye could help us tae see what could be done."

In the early spring – years ago it seemed – *I* had asked *him* if I might attend!

I must have hesitated longer than I thought. He broke in on me, "Aye – here's yer chance! Ye've been on at us for long enough, haven't ye? Ye've said, off and on, that ye'd help with advice if any of us thought of starting up a business. Well we've decided tae take ye at yer word. Och ye're no' going' tae . . ."

He broke off, pretending that something had gone amiss with his price-stamping machine.

The uncompleted statement was plain enough. 'Och yer no' goin' tae back oot, are ye?'

Part of him, I felt, would be perversely satisfied if I did back out.

'There ye are then,' he could say to the others, 'fine words – that's all it was! Aye – when it comes tae the bit, what does the likes of him care what happens tae us here?'

Thinking of his interests, my presence could cramp his style, if I helped the weak by showing them the likely effects of action by the strong – himself perhaps?

John Connal was a complication yet to be revealed to him.

No hint had leaked out. The new economic overlord was keeping his counsel well.

Only a few hours before, I had given John Connal my answer.

He had listened to my thoughts. He knew.

He studied me for a long time. There was a moment when he seemed about to say something, to argue further. Then he got up, took the Carrdhu from the cupboard and banged it down on the table:

"Aye – ye're a hard man all right! I'll say that for ye! I took a chance," he tapped the folder of company documents, "it didna' come off – this time. But let's drink tae the company anyway."

We touched glasses.

"To the company's success," I said, "in helping the glen back on to its feet!"

"Aye, I'll drink tae all of that!"

He put the glass down noisily, and showed his teeth in that fighter's grin. "I respect ye for it – don't think I don't! So ye're going tae stay on the sidelines – 'impartial' like ye always said ye'd be! But I'll tell ye this," he tapped the folder again, "one o' these days I'm goin' tae persuade ye tae change yer mind about this! I think ye could do more good this way – with me! An' I'm makin' ye a promise! The offer remains open – whenever ye like tae come in!"

I said, "I didn't find it easy to say 'No'."

"Aye – well," he nodded, "for everybody's sake, I hope ye don't stay outside too long.

"Anyway," he said, "I've been meanin' tae say this tae ye but I bided my time. Aye, ye wear yer heart on yer sleeve some o' the time. Och it does ye credit, dinna' mistake my meaning! An' I've learnt tae judge folk in my time. Just as I learnt tae judge beasts! But after all – ye've done what ye could! It isna' *your* fault if ye've talked yer heid off – an' these puir wee folk canna' see the nose in front o' their faces!"

"They're frightened too."

"Och – frightened are they?" he shook his head in mock despair for them. "Will ye tell me, pray – who isna' frightened in this life? It's no' oor fault, is it? When it comes tae the bit ye've got tae chance yer arm, haven't ye?"

I sipped my dram. Of course he was right.

He was still fighting them. Yet when he spoke against them he hurt himself too. And the more his self-justification demanded that, the more it hurt. Oh yes, he knew!

We sat in silence for some minutes. He nursed his glass between his two broad hands.

"D'ye think," he spoke with an ominous quietness, "I wasna' frightened? I could've stayed on here as a shepherd – worked the skin off ma' back an' fared nae better an' nae worse than them. But I would've had tae say 'yes' tae the price they put on me as a man. No – I couldna' do that. I'll tell ye this much. When I went tae sell ma' first stirk I didna' have a single copper coin in ma' pocket! I'd borrowed money tae buy the beast. An' if I had lost money on that deal I wouldna' have had the heart tae face my puir mither sittin' there waitin' for me. Och what's the use of talkin' aboot it all? I'm not doin' it for them, ye know?"

"I know that," I said as gently as I could.

He gave me a sharp glance.

In a grumbling tone, he continued, "Well, maybe I *am*, in a way!" And then the arrogant chuckle flashed again: "But that's *my* business." He slapped his knee, underlining the thought. "Anyway I'm not sure I would have bothered with all this if ye hadna' kept on about 'the glen this' and 'the glen that'! So ye've done yer bit for the glen! Ye don't have tae bother yer heid aboot *them* any more!"

I felt sad, seeing enacted on his face what I had sensed in him from the first. He cared. He has cared all his life.

It was I who had shown him, unwittingly, this settlement with his past. And now he was bound to it.

And I was not!

Why should I be allowed to spur people on from the side-lines?

That, in its way, hurt too. In their various ways they all felt that.

I had no answer to that one.

I said to Calum, "Thank you for asking me. I'll come to your meeting. I will help in any way I can."

Eight

The heart in the onion

"It hasna' been a good visitor season at a'," said Ushan Macilroy at the Garroch petrol pumps. "This year we've only sold about a third of the petrol we did last year up to this time."

"You're speaking as if the season's over already! Or maybe you want it to be over?"

I must have caught an impatience in his voice that I had sensed in many of the folk, almost since the visitor season had begun.

With a grimy finger he rubbed his nose where a little scar halfway down was the only sign of his injuries in the great fight at the Inn.

He seemed to speak from far away. "Och it's funny – now ye mention it – there's a feelin' it's hard tae explain! It's no' that we dinna' *want* them here! Och no! It's interesting seeing new folk right enough – but in the visitor season we havena' any time tae oorselves at a' – nae time for a *ceilidh* or a dance – things like that."

Ushan put it in his own way – a *ceilidh*, a dance; time to find yourself, time to understand that knowledge, to express it, share it.

Private things. The visitors' presence contaminates them.

We stood on the road beyond the bealach which skirts the far side of the mountain chain that encloses the glen, *its* fortress walls. From here, looking up at the grim cliffs that drop sheer to the tree line, seams of quartzite gleaming sullenly, narrow gullies cold and forbidding, the defences seem impregnable. It is not hard to see why the life of the glen behind them, failing though it is, remains stronger than in many other parts of the Highlands.

The heart in the onion!

I thought of old Murdo's warning about my quest for it – so long ago now. Did he understand, what Peter Gynt discovered too late, that the heart in the onion is the onion itself! Each layer, each 'skin', is an essential part of it; if you remove one, you destroy part of the heart; if you cut one, you cut part of the heart also! Yes, I think Murdo knows. Malcolm knows. Old Jamie and Maggie know. A few of the younger folk – George, Matthew, Morag, for instance. Knowing and yet not knowing.

150

A slender force.

Here at Garroch you look through a gap in the mountains, as through a gateway, out towards the Atlantic beyond the Islands. Seeing all that open sky, the narrow defile of the glen proper – with its discipline on the mind and spirit – seems another world. That is an illusion. Apart from this 'window' the same atmosphere of *enclosure*, of man's minute stature in the greatness of things, is ever present. At every other point of the compass the mountains are piled closely one on another, peak after peak crowded together like the heads of giants peering over each other's broad shoulders.

In all these hamlets, as in the glen itself, folk long to draw their known world tightly around them.

Ushan underlined this in contrary fashion. In complaining of the poor visitor harvest he seemed to say, 'We go tae a' this trouble tae open ourselves up tae the world – which we'd sooner not do anyway – and look at the poor returns we get for oor pains!'

They want the visitors and yet they would rather not have to! With part of their minds they live wishfully in the future, when the visitors will have gone, and they will experience the in-folding of life that comes with the darker days.

Looking back to the early part of the year I realise that they went about the preparations for the visitor season in a mood of pretence, not admitting their purpose. Nothing specific seemed to be done. Here and there in the capricious spring days someone painted the window frames of his house, mended a broken window, re-hung a garden gate – the common run of household tasks. Uncommitted.

'This is not really for the visitors coming,' they seemed to say. 'We are doing it anyway for oorselves. After all it is oor ain hoose!'

And then one day, as when the crocuses steal out and take you by surprise, you go along the glen, and there – on wicket fence and paling, on wooden rails nailed to roadside trees – the Bed and Breakfast signs are up.

They are committed.

You notice changes in demeanour. Reluctant actors, they force themselves onto the stage.

Delicate sensibilities are at work. Deep down a myth is cherished – akin to the feelings Maggie Macvoe expressed when she condemned Bill Walsh for taking payment for feeding the stranded people on the bealach – an old Highland pride. 'You do not take money from the stranger for giving him shelter under your roof!'

The myth enshrines enough of antique truth to be worthy of respect – and to produce guilt.

To have strangers sleeping under your roof and breaking bread with you for payment is to do violence to it. To entertain *friends* on some 'understanding' is perhaps tolerable – only just. Therefore a compromise is to attach to your bed and breakfast business an aura of friendliness, of 'hospitality'.

But you cannot *feel* friendly to strangers – any strangers – you would rather not bring into your house at all! Yet not only do you bring them in – you go to some trouble to attract them!

You project the resentment on to the visitors. *They* are forcing you into this knot of stress.

Tolerate them. Take their money and wish them gone.

Yet conflict will not subside. Something, some bitter twist of vision, insists that a revelation will come too.

'Maybe, this visitor season will change something?'

It is after all the time of closest contact with the outside world. Surely this next one will shed a new and final light on our perplexity? These visitors with their freedom, their luxury, their seeming status above us, *must* possess a secret. Surely, this time, we shall find it and take it from them?

Here is a painful irony. The visitors cherish a similar illusion.

Both are locked in a tantalising relationship. Each dreams of a fuller life to which the other possesses the key, and longs to seize it.

There is a further twist. For each side, awareness of the other's envy revives an unbearable doubt. When you have convinced yourself that your pilgrimage is nearly over, that one more step will bring you to the secret, only to find that others see it in *you* – that is frightening.

The glen folk cannot believe that the visitors see a higher essence in the life they find here and long to possess it. Instead they feel the visitors are simply patronising them and hiding the fact in hypocritical talk and burlesque behaviour. And they hate them for it.

The visitors' emotional demands must tax their patience. Some crave a special recognition; they want their admiration of the way of life here, even their envy, to be received as homage, deserving an immediate welcome, an overflow of warmth – ardent pilgrims. Being met, instead, by what they see as a wary coolness, they are hurt.

Another visitor, perhaps in a minority so far, looks for none of this. He is a customer, nothing else. If he thinks of the locals at all he sees himself as doing them a favour. To him, totally detached, they are no more than service equipment, animate unfortunately, but existing for no other purpose than to supply his needs of the moment. They should 'jump to it' when he beckons.

And while the 'ardent pilgrim' will tolerate some inefficiency, laxity, even the occasional resistance in the form of the deaf ear, the detached visitor will not.

I stood talking to Mudie at his gate when a large car approached; a woman wound down the passenger window and shouted something.

As the car stopped alongside, I said, "I beg your pardon?"

"The ferry!" she yelled as if determined to make someone hear on the far side of the glen. Large and florid, of a certain age, her face became tomato red as she shouted again, "The ferry! The ferry!"

Perhaps I was especially slow that day, but I admit I was nettled. I must have hesitated too long. She turned away angrily and barked something to the man at the wheel. The car moved on some yards and turned aside into a passing place and stopped. She made to clamber out. The driver's door opened, and a burly man in a smart suit and shiny brogues, with sleek grey hair and gold half-moon spectacles, ran round and seemed to push her back, closing the door on her.

He turned and walked towards me, face very set.

"I really ought to apologise!" he shook his head deprecatingly. "I see you're not one of these locals! Our mistake. We really have been having a bad time with them. They seem to take some satisfaction from making you repeat every damn thing you say! It seems to us, sometimes, that they do it to needle you. Though what on earth they think they're up to beats me! They want our money – well they can bloody well jump to it and take a bit of notice! Oh I'm sorry, minister." He nodded to Mudie, who looked his most severe. "Excuse the language. Afraid we've been sorely tried. No offence, I hope?"

Mudie's expression did not change. He was offended, plainly, by something more serious than the language.

The man turned to me again, affable now. "There it is! Anyhow, if you do happen to know the way to the ferry I'd be very grateful."

When they had gone, Mudie said sombrely, "Did ye notice that they smelt of str-rong dr-rink?

"And a *woman* in dr-rink!" he added. "Och that iss wur-rse than in a man! Aye, the whole car reeked with the whisky. It iss a cur-rse – a cur-rse!"

Drink – an old concern of the clergy here. In the Kirk Session Records of the 1830s it is laid down that not more than two glasses of whisky might be drunk before 'lifting' the corpse at funerals and not more than three after it had been buried.

I once mentioned this to Mudie, who made a wry face. "Aye, it all depends on the size o' them glasses!"

In recent years, under the pressure of affluence, of 'modernism' and of indifference, attitudes have shifted. Not long ago a leading divine was publicly criticised for trying, with the object of limiting drinking, to curtail wedding festivities.

Mudie would not agree with such critics. In his own inspired fashion he fights on. And he does win a few victories.

Amazingly, big Donald has stopped going to the Inn.

And he was sober, it seems, at the recent 'club clippings'. At these, some six to ten crofters, with their sons if old enough, come together to do a combined shearing at each croft in their group. This, the high peak of the pastoral year, is a working 'party' in the fullest sense, the sheep man's harvest home, properly celebrated. The cluster of cars and Land-Rovers at the steading, and the long table with its shining white cloth set out ready in the barn, announce that this is the proud day for that croft. And the hard work is helped along with liberal drams.

And Donald, who naturally participated in all the club clippings in his group, did not touch a single drop.

I met him on the road near his croft, a few hundred yards down from John Connal's, the day after the last clipping. "Donald, you look miles better than I've seen you for ages."

A grin spread slowly over his broad face: "Aye, well, it's that new minister of ours! I wish we'd had him here years ago. Aye, he's a fine man."

He stood thinking about it.

The sun, a stranger it seemed for months, shone fitfully through a high ceiling of thin cloud, producing a diffusion of bright light. Now and then a few drops of rain wetted the air, and the tall fronds of swaying bracken were suddenly encrusted with thousands of diamonds.

He wrinkled his eyes against the sky's dazzle. "Ye know there's been some conversions recently?" He shook his head, "Och I wish I could understand the changes going on!"

"You sound a bit disturbed."

"Och I am – an' then again I'm not." Then he added quickly, "Och I don't mean about the conversions! It's – och it's a *feelin'* that's goin' aboot. The younger folk are lookin' at the world in a different way. Ye see *we* were brought up tae have these great ideas aboot goin' oot intae the world an' climbin' up high! Ye never thought o' stayin' on here. Ye had tae fix yer mind on getting a grand education so as tae go oot there an' thrive an' turn yer back on the hard life here. Aye, well it's no' goin' tae be like that any more. A lot o' the young folk are sayin' 'No' tae a' that. Take young Morag for instance. An' my ain children! They say *they're* goin' tae stay! What are we goin' tae *do* with them? What are *they* goin' tae do? If *they* are turnin' their backs on the mainland like that we'll *all* of us have tae look at life differently! One thing is sure. We'll all have tae make do with less."

"You mean the old problem – not enough local jobs?"

"Aye, mainly that. An' then there's hooses! But forbye a' that – what's the use o' their fine education if they're goin' tae stay back here an' work on the crofts? Och they canna' be crofters any more. I mean no' just crofters an' nothing else! Them days are gone. You an' I have talked on aboot a' that often enough? Och I know you've said it's a' in the mind, and not what ye can buy in the shop. Aye, an' that's what the minister says as well –"

The thought stopped him. He studied my face as if for the first time, then sighed. "Aye, maybe, after all, that's right? But it's goin' against everything we ever thought – everything we used tae hear the older folk sayin' when we were children, sittin' by the fireside a' them long winter evenings! It's worryin' a' right."

He heaved his great chest out and sighed again.

I had never seen him so deeply concerned. Perhaps, abstaining, he sees the world with a new clarity? Or is the perspective itself changed?

"Och well," he said, "maybe a' those thoughts really are in the past! Aye, but what is there for them here? What *could* there be? If only they'd rebuild the old jetty, that could start some trade moving through here like it used tae? An' then if new businesses came in there could be something tae turn their hands tae – maybe as mechanics or doing maintenance work, or shiftin' cargo? Maybe a wee local factory if, God willing, some of these schemes ever get started here?"

Had some whisper on the wind come to him?

A gulf has opened up between his generation and the young. Many of the middle and older generation – Donald himself, Malcolm and others – have scourged themselves over the years because, for family reasons or because time somehow slipped past them, they failed to get away. And now the young, with a disquietingly unsentimental vision – and the unthinking cruelty of their years – are driving home a painful verdict, that the years of mortification were wasted. The dream was worthless.

It belongs to the past, the great days of Britain's economic dominance, when people still spoke of 'Britain – the workshop of the world', when you could go to any British ship and call down to the engine room: 'Mac', and a Scots voice, or more than one, would answer; and when Glasgow and Clydeside hummed and hammered and beckoned the Highlander. And other cities beckoned him too, or seemed to.

For Morag and her generation that old vision has lost any meaning, let alone validity, that it ever had. The city beckons – yes – but not with the promise of old: opportunity, status. If *seems* to offer escape and gratification, but for many of them the reality has broken through – that these are neither certain nor lasting. Their vision unobscured by the old dream, they look about them with what their elders must feel is a prosaic detachment.

Faced with the increasingly uniform and constraining metropolitan world, their logic is simpler. The word opportunity has lost its romantic aura. The dead ends are only too apparent.

How *can* the older folk still go on talking about 'opportunity'? They are evidently confused, out of touch with reality.

To stay close to the known and the trusted seems a mature choice.

In the glen there is cheaper living under the parental roof, emotional warmth, the comfort of the familiar in this small world, the support of its clear relationships.

I thought of Matthew Maclellan. Huge, languid, keen-eyed, in his early twenties, he moves with the poise and sure-footedness of a man of the hills, more at home setting snares than working at the boatyard. All year he has grumbled about there being 'nothing to do' in the glen. "Och I think I'll go off South an' get a job. I canna' stick it here."

"Can you get one that easily?"

He would become thoughtful. "Aye – well, there ye are! I've been South more than once – but I always come back. In a way, it's not too bad here – a bit o' shootin', an' fishin' an' that!"

One morning, a few days ago, I saw him outside his home. He had thick bandages on his left hand.

"What have you done to your hand?"

"Och I put it too near a power saw!" he laughed. "If I hadna' been wearing thick plastic gloves I wouldna' have had much of a hand left! Och it's no' too bad. The doctor's just given me a line for another week off."

Three other young men came up, moving with the soft, long-limbed loping gait they might maintain for hours if need be; guns at the port. He reached into the doorway for his gun and game bag. A silent greeting passed, and they moved off together. He half-turned and waved his bandaged hand. "Och it's no' too bad if I can get off like this!"

He leaves many things unsaid.

They stride away together, aiming for a copse on the old drove road above Cruachan.

Close to companions of his childhood and adolescence, whose every mood he knows and who know every one of his, where thought and sensibility can flow directly, there is an immediacy and freedom, an amplitude of life he knows he cannot find in the city.

For the time being, perhaps for always, he has made the fine balance.

The truth is not that the life of the glen has risen intrinsically in their estimation; but that with the old dream out of the way, the city is seen in a truer light – and the glen gains from the comparison.

Donald said softly, "Were we all daft tae think like that? What's happened? Och maybe it's just these times we're livin' through?"

He wanted to go on believing.

He mused on, "Aye – maybe that's all it is, makin' the young folk turn their backs on the mainland? Aye that, an' the minister's talk?"

"What does *he* say then?"

He looked at me as Maggie Macvoe had done when I asked her what the sermon had been about.

"Och it's no' what he *says*! It's – och it's hard to put it intae words . . ."

"You mean," I ventured, "he feels that the answers are within yourselves?"

He looked startled. "Aye – now ye put it that way – yes."

He studied me. "Och it chust struck me," he said wonderingly, "that iss, in a way, what you've been saying!"

I said to Mudie, "Donald seems depressed about the younger people."

"You mean because they're choosing to stay?"

"It's the reasons that upset him more. They no longer believe in the old myth of 'going out into the great world of opportunity' – and that hurts."

"Aye, I know it hurts well enough."

He hugged his arms round his chest, a hand on each shoulder, and looked past me towards the sea – and far into time. "Aye – I used tae believe in it myself! It took me ten years, with the help of God, tae see that it iss the temptation o' the devil. An' if the older folk are sad, at least they can be thankful that the young folk are seein' the truth at last!"

A line of vehicles came past – cars towing caravans, two with half-decked boats on trailers. The heavy beat of pop music boomed out on the still air. The sheep fled high up the hillside. A large camper went by, festooned with kitchen utensils and plastic bags. Hanging at the back of it, a broken rubbish bin leaked a trail of refuse on the road behind.

He stirred from his reverie. "Aye – ye see the fight is never-ending! The devil compels them to spread their corruption wherever they go."

He seemed to turn to another aspect of the fight. "I am giving some attention to Sabbath desecration, for instance in the matter of receiving visitors in the bed and breakfast houses on the Sabbath. Aye – and catering for them on the Sabbath. I must admit that things are better here than in some other places on this coast."

He smiled shyly. "Nevertheless, with God's help I am hoping to improve the situation."

I could see what Donald meant. Mudie, dour and dogged fighter, is strengthening the old defences, building on what firmness remains; especially where they are most vulnerable to the freewheeling world.

"There remains," he added, "the difficult matter of the licensed premises. Serving meals on the Sabbath iss bad enough. But str-rong dr-rink as well! That iss a bad example, especially to the young!"

"That's a hard one!" I said. "You really *will* be going against the mainstream then. Nearly everyone's been attacking the sabbatarianism of the Highland folk for years – business, the media, even governmental bodies – arguing that it's against their best interests, damaging the tourist trade, bad for local employment and so on!"

He straightened severely and ran his fingers through the long beard, reminding me of Michelangelo's Moses – great determined eyes and the hand bulging through the flowing strands.

"Of course things are difficult! Life itself iss difficult. Ye have tae decide – with God's guidance – what iss important. That iss the heart of the matter. After that ye make your own choice. That iss always a personal matter. Once you *force* yourself to look for alternatives, who knows? There might be other ways, other enterprises, other material goals! After all, the word of God comforted folk here long before the visitors started coming! And *since* they came the folk *are* no better off in the things that are at the heart of life. Alas that iss only too clear. We as a Presbytery take this view – we welcome employment for the folk but not at the expense of Sabbath desecration."

A great black cloud, that had been hovering over Beinn à Shellach, sank down heavily on its flanks, and the pelting rain came down again.

He was wearing a short-sleeved shirt. As the first heavy drops chilled the air, he grinned. "Come on in for a cup of tea! Aye – ye might say that that," he glanced up at the cloud, "iss maybe as good a comment as any! There has tae be more tae these folk's life than a few weeks of being at the beck and call of the visitors."

Mrs. Mudie had the tea trolley ready. She stood by it while he said a long Grace.

When we were settled over cups of strong tea, he went on, "Aye, if the Highland folk havena' any other hope than tae exist as servants o' the visitors an' destroy their spiritual basis in order to win the visitors' custom – then they are lost indeed! Just as the word of God tells us tae respect the life of others, so these others must respect ours. If not, then folk canna' have any *self*-respect at a'."

"Identity first – business afterwards?"

He looked at me narrowly.

"I'm sorry," I said quickly, "I didn't mean to be cynical."

"You really agree?" he said. "Don't you?"

"We follow different roads and yet we coincide! That is the remarkable thing!"

"There iss only one road – the wur-rd of God. I feel that folk here have only just begun to face a profound truth – that they canna' continue tae look outwards tae the secular world for deliverance. They must look inwards."

Sometimes the glen folk do appear to be totally absorbed in self-examination, the things of the spirit dominant. On those days one could easily believe that Mudie's concentration upon the eternal verities has spread to them all.

Perhaps it is because we are in the late summer lull? Nothing new can now be expected from the visitor season. No revelation has come! It will not come now.

The hay has been got in and fenced – spread out on the fences to get a better chance of drying from the intermittent rain. There is little to do, between now and the season's end in a few weeks, but to 'sit the visitors out' as stoically as possible. And so the deep questions come crowding back.

It is a temporary state. They will eagerly seize upon a reason for turning away. The one that came surprised me. I had not expected it so soon; nor to appear with such drama. It brought a telling glimpse of what in my mind I had begun to call 'John Connal's way'.

Suddenly the moist air is a-quiver. Folk hail one another on the road to shout out the news. It seems that at every gate a group is assembled to thrash out the implications.

There is wonder, envy, doubt, hope.

The visitors are ignored as if they had been spirited away.

First of all, word went about that Bill Walsh's development plans have run into trouble. Fish-breeding rafts, under a government sponsored scheme, are to be brought into the bay, more or less in the middle of the sea approach to his proposed marina. Apart from this, powerful interests, planning to rejuvenate the depleted fisheries, are opposing his scheme on grounds of increased pollution.

And then the great news leaked out.

Malcolm, attuned as always, called out to me as I passed him working on a pot-hole near the old port, "The jetty! Did ye hear about it? It's tae be rebuilt. I mean there's goin' tae be a new one! An' ye'll never guess who's goin' tae do it! Johnnie Connal! Who'd have thought it? Och ye can bet yer boots he's got other money-makin' schemes to go wi' it! Aye – there's more tae it than just the jetty!"

The jetty. They say the word caressingly as if speaking of a loved one, given up for lost, now to return.

Connal has done some clever homework; and he has managed his intervention with skill and panache. Prompted by memory, he got his lawyers to delve into official records. Many years ago, they confirmed, the government had authorised the building of a new jetty, for use primarily by the navy. That authority, never withdrawn, pre-empted subsequent applications for *any* type of construction on the shore, or in the sea approaches to it, for a considerable distance to the north and south of the old jetty. Invoking this still valid authorisation, he presented his plan, devised precisely to fit it, for implementation, with the result that Walsh's scheme was automatically set aside. Before Walsh could decide upon a riposte, Connal's contractors began operations to the north of him, virtually on the site of the old port.

How long, I wonder, has Connal been turning over in his mind some such development? A few years ago he had acquired a considerable acreage fronting on the shore, using it for fattening store beasts. It is this land, providentially, that he is using for the shore-end jetty structure, the quayside facilities, and the approach road.

Perhaps, with the instinct of the speculative dealer, he bought the land when an opportunity offered, and bided his time till he found a good use for it, or a good price, later on?

Some locals, especially those owning shore-line land, express a sense of having been cheated. Maggie Macvoe, one of whose daughters-in-law had inherited a small parcel of land on the shore not far away, was bitter. "Fancy him knowin' all those years ago – an' buyin' up the land in readiness! How iss it that *they* can do it an' wee folk like us can't? Och it must be the auld story! Ye have tae have the right friends."

It is nearly the end of August. July blew itself out with gale force winds. Now there is an enfolding softness in the air. Grass and foliage are luxuriant. The foxglove is high and gleaming. Yet here and there the verdure has a tenderness that belongs to spring. Still, has the high summer come at last? No. Even now, the year turning again, not yet. The hints are mixed, enigmatic. There is still a springtime tremor of uncertainty, the flash and shimmer of new light on the high tops, coolness at night and a crisp world in the morning. Behind the high cloud the thin brightness of the sun sharpens the air and the senses, and fills the mind with innocence and hope – belonging to the earlier season.

And is Connal, they wonder, a hint of a new spring?

Only light breezes ruffle the sea now. The land is drying out. Ideal construction weather. Some of them mutter enviously, 'Johnnie Connal scooping the luck again'.

In these first days nearly everyone seemed to be drawn hypnotically to the construction site, suddenly become a forum.

A little group, constantly changing in composition as people stop their vehicles and others move on, stolidly watches – excitement under control – as if in all that roar and movement, the very world was shifting before their eyes.

Earth moving machines grind back and forth, levelling the ground for the quayside. Lorries move in, are quickly unloaded and depart to make room for others. Stacks of material grow up – pre-cast units, girders, sub-assemblies, motors, cable. A group of men are putting together a huge mechanism, already higher than a house, probably a pile-driver. In a newly erected cabin, from which telephone wires stretch to a roadside junction box high on a new pole, two men bend over plans spread on sloping tables, and a girl works at a typewriter.

John Connal's style. Make up your mind, then hell for leather and devil take the hindmost.

Duncan Macpherson scratched his upstanding hair, eyes bright, trying to be balanced. "Och he's takin' a big chance right enough but it might work – the jetty, I mean. He's a canny man is Johnnie Connal! He must know what he's doin'. Och I hope he does, for a' oor sakes. The main thing is – will other businesses come?"

Old Jamie looked at the busy scene stonily, standing away. He caught my eye. Plainly he did not want to join in the general excitement and talk. He wanted to say what he felt, but to someone apart. "Och Johnnie Connal's bringin' back some things we'd sooner forget – some of us! Aye, but it's a' too late anyway!" He shook his head slowly, upper lip curling. "Is he just puttin' up a monument tae himself?"

He sounded more than usually bitter. John Connal has awakened too much.

I said carefully, "You don't think this will help?"

He put his mind to it reluctantly; and the deeply incised lines on the wind-red face grew hard. "Aye – well." He would not look at me. " – If ye put me tae it I'd say there's maybe an ootside chance! That's a'." He grimaced, pushing it away, then added, "Och but only if he's got some other business ideas tae go wi' it. I mean, tae bring business acoss that jetty! Or maybe, who knows, once it's *there*, other folk may wake up their ideas and do something tae put business across it?"

Some other thought caught his sardonic fancy and he gave me a sideways grin. "Maybe the Garroch bridge'll go at last! An' then the jetty here'll come in handy! The traffic for the Insh ferry could come through here then?"

He glowered again. "Och it's a shame really! Johnnie's no' a youngster as ye know? He's aboot ten years younger than me. God forgive me saying it, but who knows – it's a bit late in the day for him tae be startin' on somethin' really big like this? An' who knows whether them sons o' his'll take an interest.

Morag sees the gleam of a quickened future.

"Och this is what you've been dreaming about! Just think! This is joining us up wi' the world again – in the old way! Like the old folk say it used tae be! We could grow intae a busy place on our own again. Och it's exciting!"

'On our own . . .' In our own right!

Guided by intuition and by faith, she could take up the train of sentiment from the past direct, with hope. Borne up by her emotions she insisted on carrying aloft the light from the past like a brave torch. Everything was possible.

Robert Wallace said, "Ye remember ye called me the Wolf of Cruachan's latter-day successor? Aye, I know ye were joking! I don't mean that. But it's no' the wee folk like me – it's folk like him! Och I know he's a local man right enough. But in a way it doesna' matter who it is!

There's always a Wolf – whatever we do we canna' get free of him!"

The tone, the attitude behind the words, saddened me.

I said, "Robert, forgive me saying something I've said before. If you and the other locals fought harder, you could do *something*! Even if it is something small, you wouldn't be leaving him a clear field, or someone like him?"

He set his jaw. "Once folk like him get started they take away the chances for the wee folk like us."

I said, "You mean they're too pushy."

Oh that word 'pushy'. How insistently they had repeated it like a protective charm. 'We are not to blame. It is the world.'

The temptation to throw it back had been too strong.

He managed a shame-faced smile. "Aye, I know," he said sadly, "ye think I'm evading the issue again? Well, it seems as though the whole lot, the official people out there," he gestures at the world beyond the bealach, "and even folk like him – knowing his way about and keeping himself tae himself – are too strong for us."

Many feelings come together.

There is envy. They feel in their bones that he will succeed where they would fail. There is guilt and remorse among some of the older folk for having looked down on him long ago. And a certain anger and frustration; having broken away from their ranks, he has risen far above them and shamed them. True, they have long known of his success, but the signs were far away in the mainland. He has not flaunted it in their faces – until now. 'He's gettin his ain back. He's goin' tae lord it over us!'

Meditating on all this, I walk on the road in the upper glen where the forest comes down close. A car comes purring up behind me. Automatically I step to the grass verge to let it pass, and forget about it.

A raucous helicopter engine sounds overhead. I look up and see that the machine is fitted with spray booms. It flies on low, at about a hundred and fifty feet, and winds its way in and out of the tight bends of the glen between the jutting spurs of the mountains. The pilot is surveying the bracken growth. Soon he will come through again to spray it down. Long ago when I used to come here, they burned the bracken. I can still see in my mind's eye the stretches of sullen blue smoke on the slopes. And the low-hanging drift of burning, woody and somewhat acid in the nostrils, hangs in the memory too – every mountain sending up its solemn sacrifice to the powers of earth and sky.

Beside me there sounded a gentle motor horn. John Connal grinned at me from the driver's seat of the purring car, a new-looking Rolls – a silvery blue Corniche. I have never seen him in anything but his battered Range Rover.

In a flamboyant gesture he banged the steering wheel with the flat of his hand. "Aye, an' what aboot this new toy o' mine, eh? I thought if I'm goin' tae be the wicked local warlord, as ye kindly put it, I might as well look the part!"

His grin faded. "Don't take me the wrong way. This is Johnnie Connal's last throw!" he grimaced. "Let the puir wee folk gape! Let them go green. Aye, let them!"

I said, "I didn't expect you to come into the open quite so soon."

His eyes narrowed: "Och I had tae move fast. I had tae have my workmen on the site immediately tae stymie Walsh. With the construction work started – well!" He rubbed his chin. "It'd cost him a fortune tae shift me! Aye, it's a hard world as ye well know!"

In the first week of September came the meeting of the Community Council that Calum Johnson had invited me to attend, when they would discuss, under the heading of Employment Creation, prospects for new local enterprise. The July and August meetings had been cancelled because Council members were busy with the visitors.

The Village Hall, built in the spartan style of many wartime buildings, has minimal refinements. The glen's only public toilets are in the little lobby just inside the main door. The evening being warm and oppressive, both inner and outer doors stood open. So the Council's deliberations were punctuated by the comings and goings at the Ladies' and Gents', the flushing of cisterns, whispers and giggles. Outside, a row of majestic oaks spread a rich green shadow. A little way beyond, the quiet sea moved in a long slow swell and flashed like brass in the declining sun. The Council sat at a long trestle table, the bare pine imprinted with beer stains and pitted with cigarette burns.

I sat in a corner next to the old upright piano, the only member of the public present.

They moved slowly through a long agenda: sewage disposal, goal posts for the football pitch, street lighting proposals – again turned down, protection of the lifebelts from vandalism by visitors, control of campers, beach pollution, distribution of a Home Office booklet on nuclear fallout, the mobile library. When they came to the item: 'Employment Creation', Calum Johnson forestalled discussion with the proposal that the Regional Council be asked to send an official to address them on procedure.

Before 'Connal's way' had obtruded, they might have entered into such a discussion with some freedom. But now the balance of economic power has shifted. Calum is no longer the chief commercial influence. With John Connal's buccaneering style sending its wind and power through the glen, doubtless a deliberate effect, they do not know how to fix new bearings. Where else will he strike? How will it change things?

This is surely a time to keep one's own counsel and sit tight?

163

They look for signs. They try to read the future in the shadows.

The school holidays are over. And there are more children at the school – fifty per cent more than last year. They seize upon this as an augury.

"How many of these new children," I asked George Macfarlane, "are from local families?"

He tugged at the spade beard. "H'm, well, about one-third. Aye, I see what ye're gettin' at!"

As it happened, the re-opening of the school for the autumn session had not impinged upon me; somehow my path had not crossed that of the teachers. One afternoon, passing the school, I met Jessie Thoms coming away, looking unusually smart – not in her old working rig of slacks and blouse, but floating along in a pretty dress of crisp cream linen.

"Och it seems years ago, doesn't it?" she greeted me gaily. "It always does after the summer holidays!"

She looked at me closely and then down at her dress. "Och I might as well say it for you!" she went on in her impatient, downright way. "You're surprised to see me looking so respectable? Och well, the school holidays do something to me! I was back at home, doing a lot of thinking! D'you know, if I could have got a job there I would have tried to stay? Anyway I did decide something very important. I've gone back into the Church. I bet *that* surprises you?"

I said, "I felt you were in the balance. You had to move much further away – or closer in!"

She gave a quick shrug, "Maybe. I don't know." She paused, then rushed on, with a kind of appeal, "Aye, and I've given up smoking as well! Och I suppose folk'll think me old-fashioned? I don't care."

She swung the hair away from her eyes and tapped a foot on the loose cobbles. "Still, I'd sooner be here than in the city. Here at least you've got the chance tae think things out for yourself. In the city – I had a job in Glasgow for a bit – folk always want tae drag you along with *their* new ideas about life, and you never know where that might lead you? Here, and back on the Island, folk don't go that fast. They take time tae understand . . ."

Later in the conversation, I said jokingly, "And Mudie. Have you made your peace?"

The freckles showed bright. "Och no! It never was like that – really! Och ye didna' mention it tae him!"

"Of course not. I'm teasing you! Still, knowing this place I imagine your views got back to him! Especially if others felt as you did about his 'modernity'."

She was pensive. "Aye, well, I suppose I *was* running away."

It had been Isobel's hunger for rationality and order that had brought her to reject the city, Jessie longs for an absolute emotional simplicity. Young and still testing herself, the wildly swinging compass needle of the

164

city had frightened her. And instinct had made her flee here, seeking something akin to the fixed bearings she had grown up with.

Mudie's message to the young, that you *can* reach out for a degree of modernity, carefully chosen, without a total sacrifice of faith and the old codes, has helped her. And now she may rest here.

So, in subtle fashion, 'Mudie's way' is at work. But who can say how far it influenced Matthew's decision to opt for the countryman's life here? Or Morag's in cleaving to the emotional comfort of the relationships around her? Or George's in embarking on his new venture?

The only local initiative, of the modest family type I had hoped for, has come from George. With two cousins he has started a small building firm: jobbing building, extensions and conversions, general maintenance and repairs.

Since existing houses come on the market so rarely, there is a demand, small but growing, for new ones – mainly from incomers, and from exiles coming back to the glen to retire.

"At the minute," George said, "the prospects are quite good. Ye see, there's a limit tae the amount o' replacement plumbing I can do here. An' then again, once I've gone over an auld hoose an' put in new plumbing – well, with this modern stuff it's goin' tae be in there for a guid long time. I could see that sooner or later I was goin' tae run oot o' that type o' work. That is if I wanted tae stay in the glen at a'! I'd have tae branch oot intae something else."

He smiled to himself. "Aye, these new 'kit' hooses are givin' oor business a lift!"

This is a new type of structure for the glen. It reaches the site more or less in pre-fabricated units. George and his partners are building one; erecting and installing might be more accurate. A few weeks ago they started work on a plot by the road near the great pool of the Allt à Shellach. They levelled the ground, put in the septic tank and laid water pipes to the mains. About a week later the concrete platform for the house was in place. Then came a pause. The partners went off on other jobs until the 'kit' of units should arrive. Last week as I drove out over the bealach I met a lorry coming in loaded with timber sections. That must be the house! A week later they had put together what appeared to be a complete timber house. In fact it was the inside of the house. Soon, with the plumbing and the electrical equipment connected, an outside cladding of brick put on and the roof fitted with asbestos composition 'slates', the key will be ready in the front door!

"Aye, it's funny!" He clicked his teeth, "In the auld days when ye built a hoose, ye started frae the ootside! First the foundations and the ootside walls and the roof, and then the floor – and *then* ye put on the inside walls, plaster on board or battens and so on. This is the opposite. Ye build it from the inside oot! Och it's logical enough – and easy forbye – but it somehow doesna' seem real!

"Mind you," he added quickly, "they're fine hooses. Och aye! An' guid value for money too – these days!"

He nodded solemnly.

In my talks with Connal about converting the timber locally, I had mentioned the production of composition panelling suitable, among other things, for such building units. I felt sure his plans would include that. Here would be a chance for George's little firm – a supply of materials close at hand.

I said, "What about thinking of making the units yourselves? The techniques are simple enough. You could scale them down for small batch work for the district here?"

He smiled slowly, kindly, "Ye talked aboot that when ye first came intae the glen more than a year ago now, a year last Easter!"

"I'm sorry, I'd forgotten. I shouldn't repeat myself!"

"Och ye mustna' think we forget what ye say! It doesna' go in the wan ear an' oot the ither! No, I've been thinkin' aboot that. Och give us time. Who knows?"

"An' then again," he said, "there's a bit of a demand for what *we* call the traditional hoose. Aye, well it's no' the real old one – what we call the 'black hoose'!" He laughed self-consciously. He knew that I knew. "Och no, it's the one with the two stone gable ends with chimneys in them, an' then front and back walls of corrugated on a timber frame. Aye, the demand's mainly frae some o' the incomers. They think it's very – what's the word – och aye, ethnic! That's it." He shrugged, and though he spoke lightly he was not amused, "Och well if they want tae *look* ethnic, that's up tae them."

"You mean like big Donald's old house up on the hillside? Before he moved into his stone house?"

He sighed. "Aye, ye see that's the way we always seem tae go! The local folk tryin' tae move oot o' the traditional hooses as soon as they can an' there ye have the incomers thinking it's very romantic tae live in them! We're always goin' in opposite directions! Aye, in this and in nearly everything else!"

"Still," I said, "if you do build one of these traditional houses it's not like that! It's the appearance they're after. You make them a bit bigger, put in modern facilities and so forth. They won't really be the houses the glen folk want to move out of."

But that, I knew, was beside the point. The other, deeper, question – whose standards? – remained.

"Aye, well I suppose you're right. We do that right enough. An' then again I suppose one attraction is that they're a bit cheaper tae build.

Anyway we've got a couple of orders in hand, one frae a doctor an' his wife, retiring from Glasgow an' another frae an American artist and his wife."

He smiled as he added, "Och that work's more interesting right enough!"

I said, "It would be fine if you could put up enough of these traditional houses to replace all these caravans!"

Already the lower slopes and the glen bottom are bespattered with a motley deposit of fixed caravans and their lean-to sheds – green, dirty white, rusty red. Many of them poorly maintained and long past their healthy life; they are the nuclei of shanty villages.

New workers recruited to the forestry, or wandering incomers such as Willie Davis, for instance, or even newly married sons or young relatives of locals, often bring them in 'for the time being'; a term that may mean years. If they move on out of the glen, or into solid houses here, these shanties remain. They may be used for other incomers, or for letting in the summer.

He said carefully, "Aye, ye're right really. But what are the wee folk tae do? They canna' afford tae get a new hoose built! Och we've talked on aboot this often enough? It's only when a body *dies* that an auld hoose comes on tae the market! An' then what happens? The incomers bid up the price an' that leaves the local man nowhere! Aye, the balance is shiftin' right enough. We need more young people! It's a vicious circle!"

"But now, with the unemployment in the cities, fewer young people are going to leave the glen?"

"Och so they say," he shook his head, a little angrily. "But I wonder sometimes." He looked round carefully. But the rattle and crash from the construction work guarded against being overheard. "I suppose I should-na' say it but," he nodded significantly, "a fair few of our lads could go and get a job in, say, Glasgow, just like that!" He snapped his fingers.

"How?"

"Simple. Just by takin' less pay!"

"That must make them pretty unpopular?"

"Aye, well." A savage note entered his voice. "The Highlander's never been very popular down South!"

"Even so, some of the young folk are saying that they want to stay here?"

"Aye, maybe! And that gets us back tae the vicious circle again, jobs and hooses, hooses and jobs!"

Within the true nucleus there are too many people of middle age and upwards. The locals talk optimistically of 'more young people coming up', but they forget that they are referring to the other end of the age range, the numbers at the primary school! The critical shortage is of people between

eighteen and forty. Without them the sinews of identity, loyalty, inter-
dependence – the heart of a true community – cannot grow strong again.

The *local* population has shrunk so far that it could not supply, *in time*,
the labour and enterprise for an adequate blood transfusion. By 'in time' I
mean within the next ten years. After that, the anaemia will have gone too
far.

A workable compromise would be a new graft, as when the Island folk
came in, of people close enough in tradition and aims in life to put down
emotional roots – far down towards the ancient source – and build for the
future in every sense.

Some of this recruitment might even bring exiles back from the city; a
far healthier policy than to *keep* them there, and even to attract more, by
putting new investment into the city under the modishly emotive slogan of
'urban renewal'.

It was urban growth that took so many young men and women away
from the glens in the last hundred years. Most of the social evils are at their
worst in the cities. Let the cities shrink! And regenerate instead the small
communities whose closer internal links provide better defences.

If only I could see more economic growth 'from the bottom' – small-
scale, drawing on local skills and talent! If only that were to happen, local
folk could bring in people they *knew*, kinsfolk and friends of kin or natives
of the district. They would then be choosing new additions to the glen
with affinity in view. The culture would not be over-diluted, the graft
more likely to take.

Growth from above, necessarily on a fairly large scale as in the John
Connal pattern, does not usually follow this careful, selective, seemingly
leisurely route.

Alas, it looks as though the odds are on that side.

That is, if at all! As old Jamie said, who knows how long John Connal's
impetus will last – one way or another?

With the earth turning again, the last visitors depart. The holiday houses
are shut up one by one.

In the window of the shop the first *ceilidh* of the winter season is
announced for next Friday, the first in October. And on the following
Saturday there will be a Bring and Buy Sale for the local hospital.

The new jetty takes shape, but the steady activity on the site no longer
draws attention or comment. Folk hurry past it now, heads down, as if
they dare not speculate any longer on what it portends. Destiny will show
its hand soon enough.

But one surprising movement has come about, they say, partly by that
route. Rumour has it that Matthew and Morag are courting. John Connal
has taken Matthew on for maintenance work on the new quayside machin-

ery shortly to be installed; and he will in due course have a little cottage near the quay.

The day I heard that news I met Mary Macduff, back home on leave from her first year's nursing training at Inverness. She stood alone on the edge of the construction site, hair tossed by the wind, and gazed in wonder at the transformation. The cluster of huts and sheds, great machines and trucks looked like a thriving new township.

She spoke of Morag with hardly concealed envy. "Aye, she's lucky in a way! Och I don't mean I'm sorry I went away for the training! It's very interesting right enough – and being away, meeting new folk an' that, but oh it's – " she looked away, "it's no' the same – I don't know how tae put it – there's something missing! Aye, that's it – something solid isn't there! You feel everything's moving too fast! Aye – and" . . . she lowered her voice as if speaking to herself, ". . . and nothing people say means much!"

"You sound as though you wish you were back here?"

"Och no! It's a grand opportunity I've got! Och but if I'd known . . ." she bit her lip. ". . . Och I don't know? How could I have known things were going tae change like this? Still, I'm happy for Morag. I really am!"

I walk through the great arching avenue of chestnuts by the old Church of Scotland manse, where, years ago it seemed, I had once seen old Jamie walk away in a halo of evening sunlight, bent under his thoughts, the earth blooming round him.

Now the leaves are falling, and their dry rustle round my feet sounds clear and sharp in the still air.

The glen returns to its own silences.

I passed the schoolhouse just as Isobel came round the corner of it from her vegetable patch. She waved and came over to the gate, flushed from stooping, pulling off her gardening gloves. "Oh dear!" she said, "I've had so little time for the garden since I came back. There's been such a lot to do, especially with all these new children to be absorbed into the school. But what about these changes in the glen? I didn't expect all that so soon!"

"Still, there's been no big 'wind of unreason'! Remember?"

She looked away thoughtfully towards the football pitch down the road where an evening game was on, against the Garroch team. The long narrow road was packed with vehicles. Some of the Garroch supporters had brought cans of beer and bottles of whisky. Angry cries, curses, the confused hubbub of a clash, floated to us on the wind. A police car and an ambulance came fast down the road from the bealach.

"We'll have to see," she murmured, absorbed. "Look what's happened to Jessie. Looking back, it's easy to say, 'Och it was bound to happen, with her kind of upbringing!' – but still" – she shook her head. Then she laughed shortly, pushing other thoughts away – "It's the silly things that strike one! It'll be hard to get used to there being no cigarette ends in the staff room! And to remember not to offer her a drink when she comes round!"

She tossed her head, "Och come in for a cup of tea. I'm thirsty after all this gardening.

"Anyway," she said over her shoulder, leading the way, "who knows? Maybe I was trying to frighten myself! And still – look what's happened? It's like a different world. Would you believe – I sensed something different the moment I came over the bealach the first time after the holidays! I had a sense of everyone being *shaken*! – looking over their shoulders wondering what on earth was going to happen next! And I have that feeling still. And here *you* are – the one unchanged person!"

Had she, I asked myself again, secretly wished for an upheaval to force her away from these moorings?

The glen is still a man's world. The woman of education and intellect is not given particular recognition unless, like Annie Dalyrymple, she forces her way to dominance in her chosen field. And if she is single she has a further disadvantage; other women, resenting her – and possibly envying her too – maintain an ultimate barrier.

Yet Isobel's position gives her a ready-made realm over which to reign. The school house is of a manse-like dignity – a manse of the great old world. In it she lives in a style far beyond the reach of most other women in the glen, certainly among the locals. Gentility is still respected. Here, before her, other genteel women lived lives of worth and position. Here she can still feel a sense of influence – though from a distance; and of respect.

Yet always isolated.

Inside the house, it seemed incongruous to sit in front of a log fire at this season. But the fire was necessary. She had been away during the recent storms, and the old building, with its thick stone walls, had remained closed and unheated. A residue of chill mustiness hung in the air.

But that was the only difference. Here, sitting on either side of the great tea tray, with its spring-loaded legs that transformed it into a handsome table, in these surroundings of dark oak within and brooding mountains without, rain clouds darkening the sky, it seemed as though there had been no interruption. Looking out through the deep-set windows in their shadowed embrasures, the colours beyond already more sombre, some trees beginning to let the further hillsides show through their thinning foliage, others turning yellow and russet and brown, there was reassurance too. The spirit of the glen moved on true to itself in the turning world, welcoming the dark days.

Nine

Lodestone

This morning the air was sharp, the hills outlined hard against a cloudless sky, hints of a coming storm. The road showed streaks of frost, quickly dispersing now. On the high tops the first snow has come. The old silence has returned.

The ferry is closed for the winter, so there is no through traffic. In the chill darkness of early morning, well before six, a few cars grind past my window, commuters off to work at Kishorn. A little later, in the damp twilight, another group of vehicles passes, the forestry workers going up to the plantations. They come down again about four in the afternoon. The Kishorn men return in the evening. During the rest of the day an occasional car takes someone over the bealach for substantial shopping at Insh, or down to the village shop, and the echoes of its engine vibrate in the stillness long after it has gone out of sight. The road may remain empty for an hour and more. The sheep wander on it in peaceful communion.

Here among the upper hamlets the stillness presses on the mind. People speak little. They greet one another minimally. Their inner absorption recalls the time when I came here last year as Ne'erday approached; all joined in retreat, sombre figures casting about in a darkened landscape.

They brood on the year that has all but gone. They turn away from the outer world and contemplate what remains of their own. I have a vision of warriors returning from yet another battle and raising the drawbridge behind them, grimly counting their numbers again, reading faces, questioning the present, turning away from the future – thankful for the lull.

The mountain-sides are clad in dim greens and browns. The withered bracken droops. The close-cropped verdure glistens with the surface water held there. And as the water from the heights forces its way down, there is an all-pervasive murmur. The earth seems in movement. Far below, the Allt à Shellach, swollen within its steep banks, hurls along the mass of brownish water with a throaty rattle that becomes a deep roar in the gorges further down.

I pause, as I have done so many times as the year has run its course, at the curve where the road traverses high on the lip of the gorge opposite

171

Cruachan. I look down into the great pool, turbulent now. Above it the grey keep radiates stillness and strength, maintaining its mystery – watching and waiting.

Before the main gate stands a rusted harrow, its wheels deep in the rough grass where once the Wolf had penned his booty.

Some six weeks ago, in the last days of September, that sloping meadow had heard a great clamour, reverberating between the narrow mountain walls, a high excitement and tumult of people and of beasts.

A cattle sale, with people from as far away as the Borders attending. A few days before it old Jamie stopped me in the long avenue of oaks near the old Church of Scotland manse. The leaves, gold and red and brown, were blowing down, and rustled about one's feet like old dry paper.

He said, "Have ye heard aboot the cattle sale we're having on Thursday?"

A smile, compounded of dry humour and sadness, hung in the lines about his mouth. Beneath it was an unusual excitement, grimly battened down.

He went on, "Aye, that's a surprise tae ye. An' I'm tellin' ye, we havena' had one for over fifty years!"

At a livestock sale the husbandman 'shows' not only his beasts but himself and his life. From what depths, far away in the rear of their being, had they summoned up this reassertion of identity?

I thought of Mudie's coming, after an even longer interval.

"Why so long?" I asked. "And how do you come to start again – now?"

"Och tae tell ye the truth I don't know." Restless as always he scanned the far grazings, and kicked the leaves to the side. "An' I'm no' sure it'll dae any good the now."

He turned back again, and the deep-set grey eyes softened a little. "Ye see, this place was always famous for fattening beasts. Aye – famous. Folk here prided themselves on that. Aye – well . . ." He shrugged. "Maybe there's some o' that old pride showin' itself again, who knows? Och but it's a' too late! Still, that's whit's happening."

He added firmly, almost brisk. "Aye, you go along on Thursday! See whit ye make of it."

The day of the sale was blustery, with cumulus scudding fast. The glen folk stood in little groups round the railed enclosures in the muddy field. A few wives were there with their little ones too young for school – some of them held up on high to sit on the topmost rail to watch, their scarlet faces glistening.

From all this buzz and noise, at this moment when life and work were arrayed for judgment and price, there arose an affirmation: "Our world is still here and whole. It bears our imprint and we belong to it!"

But it was fleeting. I saw why old Jamie had been torn. I saw what he had tried to tell me, and why he had wanted me to be here.

The sale had started at ten in the morning. Soon after midday the loading enclosures were being emptied and the long cattle trucks were manoeuvring up the steep track onto the road, engines roaring and the imprisoned animals lowing mournfully. The field emptied of people more slowly. They looked around them hesitantly as the gathering split up into fragments and ceased to be a unity, holding them to it no longer. And then in a few more minutes the long line of vehicles that had lined the grass verges melted away.

On the slope below, the trampled mud littered with cigarette packets, a gate on one of the empty enclosures swung and creaked in the strong gusts. A ghostly noise of beasts and people hung in the air.

Perhaps old Jamie was right, and nothing would remain.

Duncan Macpherson, face flushed, greeted me on his way to his Land-Rover. "Aye, the prices were no' bad – quite guid in fact!"

He turned and looked down at the empty field. The cigarette packets were drifting in the wind like dead leaves.

Frowning, he added, "Och but no' guid enough! It doesna' pay tae rear beasts any more here! No' like it used tae be. The government's tryin' tae drive us crofters off the land!"

His first satisfaction had been genuine, but it had to be overlaid by the traditional complaint of the countryman, for ever railing against fortune. But there was more. Emerging from the spell of this gathering of glen folk, the only one of such strength he and his contemporaries had seen in their lifetime – perhaps would ever see again – he seemed to echo old Jamie's words, but without the older man's matured sadness.

In Jamie's long years of stoic meditation he has faced the truth – that the old solidity of life here, the steady heart of things, has all but slipped away. For Duncan and his generation that truth is only now breaking through, taking them by surprise, tripping them up, provoking defiance.

"Then why," I asked, "go on fattening beasts?"

It was not even a rhetorical question. He knew it. We played out ordained parts.

He gave a little toss of the head, turning to sniff the wind. "Och it's what folk have always done here! I don't think we'd feel we were the same folk if we didna' rear beasts any more."

It was more than rearing beasts.

We must know who we are and keep that as our lodestone.

I leaned over the roadside wall and looked down into the great pool of the river. The dun-coloured surface reflected little. I thought of the children at the cattle sale, perched on high, effervescent, impassioned by the older folk's excitement. Did they, with the acuteness of their years, sense the underlying doubt? Will they look back, when grown up, and understand it at last?

And when that day comes, will they still be living in the glen?

From far away, down by the old port, there came a faint hum and rattle of machines. John Connal's way is taking shape, though still skeletal. Even during the recent equinoctial gales the pace did not slacken. Much of the site, after levelling, was gravelled or concreted; so the wet weather has not hampered the movement of vehicles or machines. Connal intends to be in business early in the new year.

Of one thing the glen folk are certain. Connal's way will compel an important shift, as yet unimaginable, in their lives and in their view of themselves. And they fear it.

Meanwhile as the nights draw in and enclose them, and Ne'erday approaches fast, they turn to it in welcome. They have begun their descent to it, weary travellers, hungry for the time when the world will be halted. And when destiny, perhaps, may hold its hand.

The fish-farming venture is also going ahead, and the first three rafts are moored out in the bay opposite the remains of the old jetty.

I reached the War Memorial and stood contemplating the rafts; Robert Wallace drove up. "Ye see!" he said in a tone of challenge. "*There's* one of yer new enterprises! Aye – an' all *we* get is more incomers arriving tae take the new job!

"Och I'm sorry," he added quickly befoe I could say anything, "I didna' mean it in a personal way."

And so Jamie, Duncan, and now Robert, each in his own style, voiced the complex mood of the glen, recessive, waving the flag of a forlorn hope, wanting to be left in peace.

Do they see the future truly?

Connal's way and George Macfarlane's way are in some ways complementary – or they could be. In others they are opposed. Connal needs quick fruition of his considerable investments, and that usually means bringing in people chosen primarily for their skills, leaving affinity a long way behind. George's way, careful growth from below, grafting on new people who are sympathetically linked to local tradition and outlook, may be too slow – unless many more follow his example soon – to provide the strong infusion of young blood the glen needs.

And George's way is not likely to be energetically taken up by governmental bodies like the Highland Board and the Development Authority; bureaucracies are ill-fitted for the sensitive approach, for they are driven to think only of projects, not people.

Connal's way could yet turn out to be a golden compromise. He will not ride too hard over local sensibilities. His business sense will see to that.

His group of ventures centring on the jetty – transport, timber processing and conversion, wool, other small-scale manufacture using adjusted high technology – could bring a powerful economic boost. And unlike tourism it would not be seasonal.

As for the new people he needs, in giving Matthew Maclellan a job and a house and encouraging him to settle at last, he is demonstrating sensitivity, telling the glen that he will try to choose new faces that seem likely to fit.

Provided old Jamie's doubt is confounded and Connal does live long enough . . .

The voices on the wind do not speak clearly.

Here on the promontory under the War Memorial, the air strikes cold. The slow sea, gleaming like undulating glass, glides softly in, whispering on the shingle. At its edge some gulls strut in promenade. Then they too stop and stare out to sea, and seem to wait.

Once again I look up at the dark figures on the Memorial. There, time has stood still, the voices are unequivocal.

The world whose certainties they sought to sustain lives on only in the hearts of old Jamie and the other survivors for whom, long ago, the new world that followed was not worth sustaining. And then, too late, they saw that what came after was worse still. That is what Jamie means – 'It's a' too late!'

Our perennial dilemma: to compromise and save what remains of old certainties, or to destroy and start afresh?

'To make, then break, the spring time fancy.'

Destruction and emptiness, of earth and spirit, have spread fast across the world. And the wonder is that the glen has kept the roots of its certainties alive and flowing when so many places have given up, grown spiritually empty and, in essence, dead.

And it has done so in spite of all the demonstrations of defeat and desertion.

In that persistence, can we discern a Sign?

Will the glen take courage from it?

And the rest of us too?

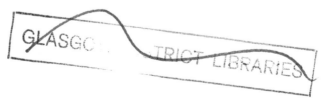

LITTLE AILLSE

ISLE
of
AILLSE

Light

Sound
of
Aillse

Loch Aillse

Old Port

Free Church

Col.
Marriott

Manse

Foot
Bridge

Great
Pool

Barracks

Hall

Cruachan
Castle

Allt à Shella

School

Basin
Spit

Inn

Graveyard

Lighthouse

Church of
Scotland

Old Jetty & Memorial

Coast
guard

Life boat

0   1   2

Miles